Guru Granth Sahib
The Sikh Scripture

Guru Granth Sahib
The Sikh Scripture

Editor
Dr. Jaspal Singh

K. K. PUBLICATIONS
NEW DELHI

Guru Granth Sahib : The Sikh Scripture
Dr. Jaspal Singh (Editor)

Published by

K.K. Publications
4806/24, Bharat Ram Road, Daryaganj, New Delhi - 110 002.
Ph.: 011-47340207, 23285167
e-Mail: kkpdevinder@vsnl.net | info@kkpublications.com
Website: www.kkpublications.com

I.S.B.N.: 978-81-7844-080-4 (HB)
First Edition, 2018
Price: ₹ 595.00

Paper & Size: *80 gsm; 5.6875 x 8.625in (Demy)*
Pages: *244pp*
Typeset & cover design by: *Kumar Computers, Jahangir Puri, Delhi -110 033*
Printed by: *R.K. Printers, Shahadara, Delhi - 110 032.*

To my father
Giani Tirath Singh Ji
and my mother
Sardarni Pritam Kaur Ji

Foreword

Guru Arjan Dev, the fifth Sikh Guru accomplished many such noble deeds in his days of Guruship as would be remembered till eternity. But the greatest of all such great deeds, which shall be remembered throughout the ages, was the compilation and editing of Sri Guru Granth Sahib. On the one hand, this great accomplishment gave a new direction to entire humankind, on the other, it made the Sikhs the followers of the Word, the *Shabad Guru*. There is a general belief that the devotees of a faith must have with them the written word – the Scripture – to maintain unity of thought among them and to keep alive this unity for ever. In the context of the Sikh tradition also, this belief is reflected in several historical writings. It is mentioned at one place in *Mahima Prakash* that Guru Arjan Dev felt that the number of Guru Nanak's followers had increased manifolds and it was necessary that all Divine Utterances (*Bani*) be compiled as a holy scripture:

Yah man upjī pragatio jag panth
Tih kāran kīje ab granth.

How the compilation and editing of the Holy Granth was undertaken, needs to be looked into in depth and some detail. History tells us that towards the end of thc final round of his preaching of Sikhism, Guru Arjan Dev remained for a year in Gurdaspur region and returned to Amritsar in 1601. After reaching Amritsar, he devoted his entire attention to the compilation of Guru Granth Sahib.

In fact, all the Gurus before Guru Arjan Dev had been making stupendous efforts during their time to collect hymns alongside composing their own. This process had been consciously started as early as during the time of Guru Nanak. The annals of history indicate that Guru Nanak always kept with him a note-book in which he noted down the Divine Word as it was revealed to him by the Almighty as also the compositions of Saints and Bhaktas.

Such evidence is also available which reveals that Guru Nanak himself collected the hymns of the various Bhaktas and Saints. It is also mentioned in historical writings that while enthroning their successors, the Gurus passed on to them their own compositions, as also those they had received from the previous Gurus and in this way all the hymns reached the fifth Guru, Guru Arjan Dev. Some scholars are of the view that some of the writings were available with Baba Mohan also, which had also been procured by Guru Arjan Dev.

The next problem was of writing and arranging the hymns in proper order. After deep thought, it was decided to entrust the responsibility of writing the hymns, in the desired order, to Bhai Gurdas, who according to the scheme started compiling the hymns edited by the Guru. There is no doubt that the compilation and arrangement of verses was not an easy task. It required spiritual vision of the highest order. Also accomplishing the task required not only the transcendent vision, a very thoughtful analytical approach to practical aspects of life was also needed. The facts bear out that the Guru selected the verses after very careful analysis and then got them arranged in proper order with great skill.

Positioning the hymns composed by the Bhaktas on equal status with those of the Gurus is a unique feature of Sri Guru Granth Sahib. From this angle, two things need special attention. The first is including the hymns of the Saints alongwith those of the Gurus; and the second is deciding not to include the hymns of some other saints. It is clear that both these decisions had the underpinnings of sound doctrinal thought and ideological commitment. The Guru had permitted to include the works of only those saints who subscribed to the same principles, theories and way of life as were propounded by the Gurus themselves. If we look at the whole idea more closely, we will come to know that by including the hymns of Bhaktas belonging to different castes and faiths, Guru Sahib tried to eradicate the caste system and inculcate the spirit of tolerance among the people. In fact, no other scripture of the world contains the compositions of holy people of other faiths and of the people who are treated as outcastes. This particular uniqueness of Guru Granth makes it different from other scriptures.

In brief, it can be said that Guru Arjan Dev had with him the collection of all the hymns in writing and he had edited it in a sequential order under his own supervision which was penned down by Bhai Gurdas. This stupendous task went on for three years and in the year 1604 AD, the compiled and edited Granth was installed in the sanctum sanctorum of Sri Harmandar Sahib. It is worthy of mention here that Baba Buddha was entrusted the responsibility of proper upkeep of the Holy Scripture. He was appointed as the first *Granthi*. What the great scholar Bhai Kahan Singh Nabha has written about the compilation, editing and first installation of Guru Granth Sahib is noteworthy:

> *The Master of all the religious texts, the most Holy Granth of the Sikh Faith – Guru Arjan Devji collected the hymns of the first four Gurus and had Bhai Gurdas begin the compilation and editing in the year 1603 AD on the bank of Ramsar (Amritsar). It was completed in 1604 AD by including his own hymns and those of other saints and in the same year in Bhadon Shudi, it was installed in Harmandar Sahib for propagation of the Faith and Baba Buddha was made the Granthi.*

Such proofs are also found in the history that after the first installation, as a mark of reverence for the Holy Granth, Guru Arjan Dev took lower seat for himself than the Granth and this tradition continued in the times of the Gurus who succeeded him. When the tenth Guru, Guru Gobind Singh assumed the Guruship, he initiated special programmes to complete the process of establishing the Order of the Khalsa. The Guru had also resolved that after him, the Guruship shall vest in Guru Granth Sahib. That is the reason why in the Holy Granth, compiled and edited by Guru Arjan Dev, the first installation of which was done in Sri Harmandar Sahib, the hymns and verses of Guru Tegh Bahadur were included, and Guru Gobind Singh himself got the Holy Granth written under his own supervision at Damdama Sahib. This very *Damdami Bir* was then installed on the Guru's Throne in 1708 AD. Bhai Kahan Singh has described this installation of Guru Granth Sahib as Guru in these words: "The prefix Guru was added to Granth Sahib in 1708 AD, when Guruship of the Sikh Faith was vested in Sri Guru Granth Sahib at Abchal Nagar."

Some references in this regard merit greater attention. *Gurubilas Patshahi 10* is a very important traditional historical source, in which mention is made of conferring Guruship on Sri Guru Granth Sahib:

Tab puni āp uthai sab sangā.
Paise pānch nariel su angā
Lai ke tāhi arap ki bandan.
Pardakhan karte man rangan.
Kaha joi bach kīna chāhe.
Pāth karai Gur ko sukh pāe.
Yā sam aur koī guru nāhī.
Binā kān sachu bāk bhunāhī.

Then Guruji stood up with others
Had five paise and a coconut to offer
And he placed before the Holy Granth

With reverence a round he took.
And said any one desirous of talking to Guru
Should feel happy reading through.
None is equal to the Holy of the holiest
Without any hesitation,
The Guru has revealed the truth.

Kesar Singh Chhiber writes in the *Bañsāvalīnāmā* that when the question of leading the Sikh masses rose before the Guru, he replied that Guru Ganth shall be the Guru:

Gharīb nivāj, Sikh sangat Hai terī Isdā ki habāl?
Bachan kītā tab Granth hai guru laṛ pakṛo akāl.

What shall thy followers do O our lord, helper of the poor?
Quoth he, Granth is Guru now whose Word be obeyed by all.

There are other references also in the *Baūsāvalīnāmā* with regard to bestowal of Guruship on Granth Sahib:

(a) *Age guriyāī dā tikkā Granth Sahib nu de gae*
Pūjā asthān Sri Amritsar ji bhae.

The mark of Guruship thus was Given to Sri Guru Granth Sahib and Amritsar became the Hallowed place of worship.

(b) *Dasvān pātshāh gaddi guriāī dī*
Granth Sahib nu de hai gaiā.
Aj pratakh Guru asādā Granth Sahib hai
Soī gaiā jo Granthon gaiā.

The Tenth Master has conferred the Guruship
On the Holy Granth.
Granth is today our Guru incarnate
Those ignoring this shall all be deviants of Guru's holy path.

These lines of Panth Prakash by Giani Gian Singh are recited daily after the prayer in all Gurudwaras:

(c) *Agiā bhaī akāl kī tabhī chalāyo panth.*
Sabhi sikhan ko hukam hai guru mānīo Granth.
Guru Granth jū manio pragat gurān ki deh.
Jo prabh ko milbo chahai khoj shabad main leh.

The Order of the Khalsa was established
As was the command of God
This is now the commandment for all the Sikhs
Accept the Granth as the Guru.
Know Guru Granth Ji as the visible body of the Gurus
He who hath a properly trained mind
Shall find confirmation thereof
In the contents of the Granth itself.

An analysis of the history of Guru Granth Sahib shows that two volumes of the Holy Book were compiled. The first was the one compiled and edited by Bhai Gurdas under the guidance of Guru Arjan Dev. This is referred to as Bhai Gurdas's *Bir* also. The second *Bir* is the one which was got compiled by Guru Gobind Singh at Damdama Sahib. It is known as *Damdami Bir*. There is a third compilation also, which is often talked about and is referred to as Bhai Banno's *Bir*. This is an unapproved copy of the first volume in which some additional hymns were interpolated by the copier. The Guruship was bestowed upon *Damdami Bir* at Nanded in 1708 when the tenth Master abolished the tradition of human succession to the Guruship and declared the Granth as the Guru Eternal.

From the point of view of its structure, the *Damdami Bir*, as compiled by Bhai Mani Singh under the supervision of Guru Gobind Singh, contains the hymns of six Gurus – Guru Nanak Dev, Guru Angad Dev, Guru Amar Das, Guru Ram Das, Guru Arjan Dev and Guru Tegh Bahadur. However, Bhai Kahan Singh Nabha holds a different view in this regard. According to him, the *Damdami Bir* contains a single *sloka* of Guru Gobind Singh also and thus the hymns of seven Gurus are contained in the Granth. According to Prof. Sahib Singh, the hymns of six

Gurus are included in the Granth Sahib. Prof. Gurbachan Singh Talib also supports the view that Guru Granth Sahib contains the hymns of six Gurus only. Besides the hymns of the Gurus, the verses of fifteen saints – Kabir, Farid, Namdev, Ravidas, Ramanand, Jai Dev, Trilochan, Dhanna, Sain, Pipa, Bhikhan, Sadhna, Sur Das, Parmanand and Beni are also included in the Holy Granth. In addition, the Ramkali Sad of Baba Sunder, the verses in *Rag Bihagra* with reference to Bhai Mardana, Vār of Satta and Balwand, and compositions of the *Bhatt* poets have also been included in Guru Granth Sahib. Except for a small portion, the entire *Bani* is composed in different Ragas, which are thirty one in number. In fact, the whole compilation of Guru Granth Sahib can be divided into three parts: (1) Compositions for daily recitation (pages 1-13); (2) Hymns in different ragas (pages 14-1352); and (3) Verses free from Ragas (pages 1353-1430).

From the angle of the language, Guru Granth Sahib has been composed in the language of common parlance. The composers of the hymns aimed at communicating the Divine Word to the common man and therefore, they made use of the language spoken by the masses. According to C.H. Loehlin, six languages have been used in the Granth Sahib, the dialects are countless. A special noteworthy feature of the Holy Granth is that though different languages and dialects have been used to compose the *Bani*, these different languages have been written in the common script, Gurmukhi. In this way the diversity of the Indian languages is moulded into the unity of one script. Writing the verses composed in different languages in single Gurmukhi mould symbolizes the universal and liberal nature of the path of Sikhism shown by the Gurus.

One more point may also be highlighted here. Undoubtedly, the main thrust of the *Bani* enshrined in the Granth Sahib is on spiritual quest and adherence to the Divine Will. But it does not mean that the essence of the message contained in it is limited merely to spirituality. We find that the verses show complete awareness of this-worldly matters too. The Word is conscious of the contemporary social and political realities also and has a definitive stance towards them.

I have gone through the details of compilation and message of Guru Granth Sahib because the concern of the articles contained in the book are related to these basic contexts and themes. I think the topics covered in the book, in fact, have wider relevance and are of immense importance as far as perception of various aspects of the holy text of Guru Granth Sahib is concerned.

In the first article of the book, Dr Prithipal Singh Kapoor, signifying *Guru Granth Sahib as a Scripture with a Difference,* enunciates that it outrightly rejects the ideas of asceticism, celibacy, austerity, ritualism and formalism. Although its major concern remains spiritual, the Sikh Gurus have delved deeply into doctrinal matters visualizing a world of absolute monotheism. Dr Kirpal Singh, treating Guru Granth Sahib as *A Vision for Universal Religion,* opines that of all the Holy Scriptures, it is only the Adi Granth which recognises that all religious dispensations were capable of elevating the human soul. Dr Sutinder Singh Noor, while highlighting the idea of *Global Consciousness and Guru Granth Sahib*, underlines the thought that the multi-cultural concept, the ideological, social and dalit consciousness makes this text most relevant for the contemporary age, both in the epistemological and the experiential context, having established the paradigmatic signifier to be realised in the future more forcefully.

Dr Jodh Singh, while referring to the *Concept of Interfaith Dialogue in Guru Granth Sahib*, calls attention to the fact that in Guru Granth Sahib, dialogue was the wholesome process of knowing, saying and understanding each other earnestly. He focuses upon the internal and introspective dialogue before establishing a meaningful external dialogue. Elaborating the *Transpoetic View of the Concept of Sahaj in Guru Granth Sahib*, Dr Gurbhagat Singh explains that sehaj can be rendered as cosmic equilibrium, spontaneity or the normal state of a human being when he can hear the unstruck melody or the creative sound of the total and integrative cosmic life.

Dr Darshan Singh touches upon the significance of *Ethical Concepts of Sikhism* in their totality for building a healthy and wholesome society, as the ultimate concern of Gurubani was the wellbeing of every individual and all the peoples of the world without discrimination and deprivation. While discussing the pluralistic model of Guru Granth Sahib in his paper, *Guru Granth Sahib and Religious Pluralism*, Dr Dharam Singh says that the Granth recognises the value and validity of multiple religions, acceptance of cultural and religious plurality in human social existence and advocates the integration of the world and worldly life with the idea of divinity.

Considering Guru Granth Sahib as a *Repository of Universal Values*, Prof. Riyaz Punjabi underscores the unity of different religions to bring forth the indivisibility of diverse spiritual experiences. Dr Rattan Singh Jaggi stresses upon understanding the then prevailing conditions and the prior compilations before making an effort to understand the mode of *Compilation of Sri Guru Granth Sahib*. Dr Gurnek Singh, while tracing the history of *Formation of Guru Granth Sahib*, focuses on the embalming and perennial effect of its poetry and music that sublimates and leads the soul towards union with God. While talking about *The Poetics of Guru Granth Sahib*, Indra Nath Chowdhuri pronounces that the most revealing aspect of the text of Guru Granth Sahib is that it is not arranged subject-wise but according to the musical measure in which a hymn is meant to be sung. It builds a world of spirituality and establishes ever-new rhythmic relationship of notes, which reveals to us the universal mystery of the Divine.

Dr Maheep Singh, while verbalizing the significance of celestial and divine poetry of mystic saints, makes a special mention of Baba Sheikh Farid, Namdev, Kabir, Ravidas and Dhanna as *Saint Poets in Guru Granth Sahib*, who share the common element of oneness of God in their writings. Referring to Gurbani as the outpouring of the divinely inspired spirits, Dr Wazir Singh underscores the status of *Bhatt Bani in Sri Guru Granth Sahib*. Bhatt Bani, he says, has ideological affinity with Gurbani as well as Bhagat Bani and its uniqueness lies in the panegyrics, glorifying the Sikh Gurus. Dr Mohinder Kaur Gill emphasizes that Guru Granth Sahib is the largest collection of spiritual hymns in the medieval period, and that no other language has the honour of having such a prestigious collection in this period. In her article, *Editorial Techniques in Guru Granth Sahib*, she opines that it is not only an ideal collection of divine compositions but it also contains a very important message of spiritual welfare of mankind.

Dr Mohinder Singh shows his concern towards the important aspect of making attempts at *Conserving Guru Granth Sahib Manuscripts* after locating, cataloging and digitizing the invaluable spiritual treasure that it constitutes. Dr Satnam Kaur, while articulating the *Concept of Faith in Guru Granth Sahib,* illustrates that of the seven different words used in Sikh religion in the context of the life of faith viz. *oat*, *tek*, *bharosa* (or *bharvasa*), *adhar*, *as*, *asara*, *sardha* (or *sraddha*) the right word is *sardha*, a variant of *sraddha*. *Oat*, *tek*, *adhar* and *asara* my be said to stand for the objective side of the relation as experienced, indicating how God appears to us as a shelter and as an anchor or support, or as the foundational reality, and *bharosa* and *as* may be said to characterize what or how it feels to have faith in God, she concludes. Depicting Guru Granth Sahib as a great *Source of Sikh Values,* Dr Harbans Kaur says that the historicity, authenticity, universality or catholicity of this Holy Scripture gives it a unique place amongst the world religions. As our life is a part of the society we live in, therefore, religion provides the moral and ethical values, which binds a man with the society and the world at large. These values are not only reflected in the Bani of Guru Granth Sahib, but more than that these are reflected in the lives of the Gurus themselves. Anurag Singh, while making a comparative analysis of ancient and medieval Indian religious traditions, illustrates the *Perennial Oriental Wisdom of Guru Granth Sahib* as it deals with the epithets of Indian religious literature with amended and extended connotations, thereby giving them new content, meaning and continuity.

Expressing Communion as the supreme form of communication and as a *Cardinal Message of Guru Granth Sahib,* Dr Gurmeet Singh Maan describes *sehaj* (equipoise) as the highest state of consciousness to achieve the Ultimate. It amounts to reaching a state of effortless effort or *let go* through Communion, when the idea of *doing* stops and the reality that *everything happens just like that only* dawns.

I am grateful to all the scholars who have contributed their articles for the preparation of this book and I am sure this volume will help the readers to understand the eternal message of Sri Guru Granth Sahib.

Dr. Jaspal Singh

Contents

Guru Granth Sahib: A Scripture with a Difference

Prithipal Singh Kapur

Guru Granth Sahib is well known as the holy book or scripture of the Sikhism. It is a voluminous anthology of the sacred verses by six of the ten Sikh Gurus and hymns of some fifteen Hindu and Muslim Bhaktas, Sufis or holymen. Its compilation in 1604 AD by Guru Arjan, the fifth Guru, made the year a landmark in the development and growth of Sikh religion. By that time, the Sikhs had an authoritative line of the Gurus, a sacred script (Gurmukhi), an organised religious community and a religious capital at Amritsar with its central shrine.[1] The primary feature that lends distinction to Guru Granth Sahib is authenticity of its contents and the variety of its contributors, who came from different socio-religious backgrounds — high and low, Muslim and Hindu. Some of them are represented by only a verse or two and some voluminously like Kabir with over a thousand verses.[2] This peculiar feature of the Guru Granth Sahib led Macauliffe to describe the Guru Granth "probably the most difficult work, sacred or profane and hence the general ignorance of its contents." Another exclusivity that Guru Granth Sahib can rightly claim is that it defies the definition of high place that is usually lent to religious scriptures, that is, "Scriptures are meant to be quoted, not to be questioned or doubted[3]". Guru Granth Sahib is treated by the followers of Sikh faith as the revealed Word, the embodiment and presence manifest of spirit of the ten Sikh Gurus. Guru Granth Sahib commands the reverence that was shown to the living Gurus. It remains at the centre of all Sikh usage and ceremony.[4] The Sikhs had been told to revere the bani or the 'revealed word' right from the times of Guru Nanak who himself said:

Vahu Vahu Bani Nirankar hai
Tis jevad avar na koe

Hail hail the word of the Guru
which is the Lord formless himself.
There is none other, nothing else
to be reckoned equal to it

(*Guru Granth Sahib, p. 515*)

Guru Ram Das, the fourth Guru says:
The bani is the Guru
and the Guru is the bani

(*Guru Granth Sahib, p. 982*)

The finality of the Guru Granth Sahib is a fact rich in religious and social implications of Sikh system. It remains the acknowledged medium of the revelation descended through the Sikh Gurus. For the Sikhs, it is the perpetual authority, spiritual as well as historical.

The Sikh scripture does not contain historical narrative (except a few cryptic references to contemporary events in some of the hymns of the Gurus or Swa-yyas of Bhatts) or prose teachings as are found in the New Testament. The main thrust of the bani of Guru Granth Sahib is the spiritual key. It is the poetry or hymns of pure devotion. The doctrine that is enshrined in these hymns is uncompromising monotheism and is enunciated right in the beginning in the Mool Mantra, which explains all that God is and all that God is not! Japji, the daily prayer of a Sikh which he/she is also expected to memorize; has been composed by Guru Nanak in rhymed verse but is not in accordance with the tune of a raga (musical meter) as is the case with the rest of the Guru Granth Sahib. Nanak's monotheism presents God as indivisible and with a fully universalized complexion. This is more apparent in his rejection of the doctrine of incarnation in totality:

Shiva, Brahma, Devis
all land thee
shining in splendour
given by thee
Indira on his throne
along with deities
sing praise at thy doors.

(Japji, Pauri 27)

The teachings enshrined in Guru Granth Sahib systematically proceed to explain that monotheism does not mean deification of God that will lead the individual to resort to such practices with a view to attain the favour of God/gods/goddesses in a manner that would mean the negation of the established order of the universe which in the words of Guru Angad is the dwelling place of God Himself[5]. In this way, the unity of God implies the sanctification of all relative existence[6]. This is how the teachings enshrined in the Guru Granth Sahib reject asceticism, celibacy, austerity, ritualism and formalism in totality. There is no palpable heaven or hell according to the Sikh belief. The idea of liberation in Sikhism differs distinctly from the idea of *mukti* as found in the traditional Hindu belief. Compared to this, *Jiwan-Mukt* is the ideal of life upheld by the Sikh Gurus in Gurbani. This is not liberation after death. Such liberation is achieved through a life piously lived and dedicated to devotion.

Liberated is one who by love
of God is inspired
whose senses are under restraint
and who abides by discipline

and whoever on the Master's word meditates
Such devotion to the Lord is pleasing

(Guru Granth Sahib, 122, Rag Majh Ashtpadi 20, Mahila III)

For those practising Yoga and severe austerities, Guru Nanak uses strong words to bring out the futility of such practices vis-a-vis the attainment of liberation:

Yoga lies not in the patched quilt
nor in carrying a staff;
Yoga lies not either in rubbing
ashes over the limbs (of body).
Yoga lies not in earrings,
nor in close cropping the head
nor in blowing the horn
to abide undefiled amid
Maya defilement, is the true
way to attain success in
Yoga praxis.

(Guru Granth Sahib, p. 730, Suhi Mahila I)

In the Sikh scheme of religion, as outlined and explained in Guru Granth Sahib, the seeker yearns to be bestowed with the grace of the Almighty Lord. He/she does not pray or meditate for the sake of material benefits. On the other hand, it is a game of complete surrender with a yearning to be endowed with such a grace as to enable him/her to tread the righteous path within the orbit of His *Hukam* or *Raza*. This is complete surrender before the Will of the Lord which remains key to what can be termed as path of salvation in the Sikh religious scheme.

We draw heavily from Bani of the Gurus while trying to decipher and understand the teachings of Sikhism. But we have to remember that the whole corpus of the Bani of the Bhaktas and Muslim Sufi holymen is equally relevant in this context. Guru Nanak's pronouncement: "There is no Hindu, no

Musalman" is well illustrated in *Kabir Bani* too. One can safely conclude that Kabir defies all attempts of being labelled as either a Hindu or a Muslim[7]. Such is the powerful dissent discernible in the insightful hymns contained in his Bani that legends or myths/rumours were floated by Brahminical people that he was born of a Brahmin widow to show as to all his wisdom belonged to the Brahmans. Even doubts have been cast about the marriage and parentage of Kabir. It is equally interesting that the Qazi was reticent to pronounce the word from the Quràn which was to give name Kabir to the child of a poor weaver because it meant 'most exalted' in the Arabic language[8]. Likewise, Ravi Das, the cobbler saint, dared the Brahmins by addressing God:

> *When I am thou and Thou art me*
> *then where is the difference?*

The following words of Guru Arjan have to be read alongside the above assertion of Ravi Das to understand the theory of submersion within God:

> *Beloved! Those thirsting after you,*
> *no distance from you feel*
>
> *(Malhar M. 5, Guru Granth Sahib, p. 1269)*
> *(Trans. G.S. Talib)*

Interestingly, four Shabdas and 112 slokas of Farid, the founder of the famous Chishti Sufi order in India find place in Guru Granth Sahib. He is well known to be a devout preacher of Islam. This fact did not deter Guru Arjan to include the bani of Farid in Guru Granth Sahib. In fact, the motive seems to have been to initiate a spiritual dialogue that could usher in an era of co-existence, tolerance, equality and give fillip to the idea of universal concept of religious living. Farid is known to have written in a vein that represents *vairagya* in the Indian and Sufi terminologies. Guru Arjan appended a hymn of Guru Nanak alongside the hymn of Shaikh Farid in the Suhi raga as a corrective because Farid's hymn appeared to view the future of human soul in a pessimistic light. Similarly, we come across a saloka by Guru Amar Das serving as a corrective to another averment of Farid[9].

Although major concerns of Guru Granth Sahib remain spiritual, the contributors have expressed equal concern for quality of life in its totality. The social, economic or even political matters have not escaped the scrutiny of the Gurus as well as the Bhaktas. The Gurus delve deep into the doctrinal matters and visualise a world wherein equality and monotheism are absolute so as to obliterate social strife and religious fundamentalist tendencies that surface because of emphasis on formalism, ritualism, priestly hegemony and caste hierarchy. The Bhaktas in Guru Granth Sahib carry on their forceful tirade against Bhrahminism in a practical way but in no way ignoring the spiritual concerns.

It will be unfair to miss an important postulate of the teachings of Guru Granth Sahib, i.e. the significance of the Guru, the spiritual guide or the holy preceptor. In Gurmat, as the teachings of the Granth are referred to in the Sikh terminology, the Guru is no ordinary mortal being like any of the professed heads of the so-called numerous religious denominations. The Guru is an inspired being, completely attuned to the Supreme Being. That is why the Guru has been called Sat Guru as well. This has not to be misconstrued as man-worship. As in case of identification of Guru Bani or Shabda with God, the Guru has to be reverenced for his divinely experience[10]. The designation of the Granth — the repository of divine knowledge — as Guru in the Sikh system is to be seen in this perspective.

A distinction of the gospel enshrined in Guru Granth Sahib has also to be made with regard to the fusion of the temporal and the spiritual and presentation of God as transcendent as well as immanent in relation to the mundane, thereby providing an opportunity to all human beings for self-realization in order to attain union with God[11].

Guru Granth Sahib lends authenticity to the doctrines of Sikhism as they stand out in a different position from other religious systems. Most of the great religious teachers of the world are not known to have left a word of their composition. All that we know about their teachings comes to us through tradition or some other kind of second hand information which is written or compiled by the adherents. The Sikh Gurus made it a point to preserve their own compositions, making available to us their teachings and principles of Sikhism, as pronounced by themselves. Since the Gurus employed the vehicle of verse, their authenticity could not be challenged and interpolations, if any, could easily be deciphered because of the distinct style of the contributors of the Guru Granth Sahib. It has also to be noted that Guru Arjan, while compiling the Granth took care to vigorously examine the authenticity of writings of the Bhaktas and Sufi saints whose compositions were included therein.

Guru Granth Sahib, unlike scriptures of other faiths, contains neither history nor mythology nor any collection of incantations. The spiritual poetry, called the Divine Word, as enshrined in the Granth presents the vision of the cosmic order and exhortation to higher life. In that respect, it is a scripture with a difference among the source books of religion. It remains a collection of communications of the Divine Word in a spirit of deep humility and compassion for mankind — a repository of Divine knowledge. The followers of the Sikh faith look upon the Granth not as a scripture but an embodiment of the light and soul of the ten Gurus to which the principle of transfiguration extends. This fact is emphasized in the daily prayer — *Ardas* of the Sikhs. In the Sikh religious assemblies, the holy Granth is the presiding presence as a sacred person. All bow before it and make offerings. All the decisions taken in the presence of the Granth remain binding on the individual followers of the faith as well as the body of the Khalsa Panth[12].

We do not come across any tradition of writing critical commentaries on Guru Granth Sahib like the ones we find on

Gita, Bible, Quran or scriptures of other faiths. Perhaps, this is because of the special position of the scripture in the Sikh religious scheme. On the other hand, there are quite a few traditions of the exegesis of Gurbani, enshrined in the Granth. Exegesis has been defined as a creative exercise, which aims at unfolding the underlying meaning and significance of an empirical writing of a high order[13]. The process of exegesis of the Shabda started with Guru Nanak himself during his discourses with the sidhas, jogis, sufis and such professed divines of other faiths during his long odysseys and thereafter in his orations before the *Sangat* (congregations) that converged at Kartarpur — now in Pakistan. There is no doubt that the understanding and interpretation of the holy Granth is manifestly difficult. It is not because of the language used, as Trump would like us to believe; but more because of the vocabulary and terminology; which remains outside the range of the experience of common man, besides it being philosophical and mystical. It has to be understood by a special effort of learning. Moreover, the symbolical and metaphysical language used in the Granth can be understood only by initiating the mind into this process. There are also difficulties of interpretation of various terms and the context of the usage of mythical references, drawn largely from Hindu and Muslim literature as also from the Jaina, Buddhist and Jewish traditions[14].

The tradition of the exegesis of Gurbani was carried forward by the successors of Guru Nanak themselves and also by the pioneers of the Sikh missionary orders. Here, two factors warrant special attention viz. (a) the principal contributors of the Granth, the Sikh Gurus present a school of exegesis within their own bani-compositions[15] and (b) schools of exegesis developed by the missionary orders. A distinct tradition of oral exegesis of the Shabda, contained in the Granth was started by Bhai Gurdas at the behest of Guru Arjan himself. This developed into a powerful medium of the propagation of Sikh faith. This was virtually the dissemination of the doctrine of Shabd-Guru and presentation of life stories or history of the Sikh Gurus strictly in accordance with dictates of Gurbani. It is in the light of this that we should be able to assess the significance of the Vars of Bhai Gur Das (also described as key to the understanding of Gurbani) and the writings of Professor Sahib Singh and Sohan Singh Sital.

The Udasis (the sect of celibate mendicants, followers of Sri Chand, the elder son of Guru Nanak, who chose to become the missionaries for the preachings of the doctrine of Guru Nanak) and the Nirmalas (a sect that originated after Guru Gobind Singh sent five of his Sikhs to Banaras (Principal Hindu seat of learning to dispel the erroneous belief that only the high castes could receive knowledge in higher learning through the medium of Sanskrit, considered to be the language of gods) developed their own traditions of exegesis of the Gurbani which remained inclined towards such interpretations or the exegesis of Gurbani that were closer to Hindu philosophy or Vedanta. All the averments about Sikhism, being a schism or sect of Hinduism, or its being a syncretism of Hinduism and Islam, trace their origin from such exegesis, interpretations or commentaries on Gurbani, enshrined in the Granth. A close study of the concepts of Sikhism in the light of the contents of the Guru Granth Sahib shall make it amply clear that Sikhism "bears the character of an India born religion". At the same time, a deeper study shall also make it amply clear that Sikhism differs from other religious systems in its basic postulates. "The postulates of both Hindu and Muslim creeds are that the world is suffering and the highest end of life is to secure release from its snares". The release, it is said can be affected only through self-culture and abandonment of desire. Seen in the light of the theory of Karma, 'the total emphasis is to salvage an individual rather than a corporate society'. On the other hand, the semitic religions like Christianity believe that "life is born out of sin and that through sin, it can be redeemed." But

Sikhism says that life is of Divine Origin. God is the sole creator. Impurities gather around it only on account of delusion. Therefore, Guru Amar Das exhorts the individual to know the divine source:

> *My self! in aspect art thou image of Divine Light:*
> *Thy own exalted origin realize!*
> *My self! The Lord is ever by Thee;*
> *Listen to the holy Master's teaching and live in bliss.*
> *He that realizes his origin shall realize too the Lord,*
> *And gain insight into the mystery of life and death.*
> *As by the Master's grace he realizes the Sole Creator,*
> *Disappears attachment to duality.*
> *As the mind finds rest, the fanfare of joy arises, and the self with the Creator finds acceptance.*
> *Saith Nanak: My self! in aspect art thou image of Divine Light —*
> *Thy own exalted origin realize! (5)*
>
> *(Asa Mahila 5, Chhant III, Sri Guru Granth Sahib, p. 441.Trans Gurbachan Singh Talib, Vol. II, page 934)*

The entire Sikh philosophy and history flows from this premise and asceticism becomes a taboo. It is a whole life philosophy and religious system where societal concerns always remain in focus. That is where the character of the study of the Divine as found in Guru Granth Sahib becomes universal and exclusive in its approach, character and expanse. This makes the Sikh scripture conspicuously distinct from the other religious scriptures. The hymns contained in the Granth are neither addressed to the followers of Sikhism, nor invoke the favour of the Akal (Almighty God) for the Sikhs only; nor they present a code of conduct for them. On the other hand, we find numerous verses that invoke the favour and mercy of God for the entire humanity:

> *The entire universe is His reflection who has neither father nor mother.*
>
> *(Maru Mahila I, Guru Granth Sahib, p. 1038)*

O' Lord save the universe
whichever way it can be redeemed, redeem it
The true Guru shows the path
of solace and comfort.
With the understanding of Shabda
Without the Almighty Lord
Nanak sees no other pardoner

(Slok Mahila 3, Var Bilawal,
Guru Granth Sahib, p. 853)

Much stress has been laid on the role of the Guru in Sikh scheme of spiritual elevation. The Guru has been described as the sole guide in man's quest for spiritual enlightenment. "Through him God's word, Shabad, enters into human history. The guidance of the Guru is essential. No spiritual gain can accrue without the guidance of the Guru." This has been repeatedly reiterated in Guru Granth Sahib:

Were there to rise a hundred
moons and a thousand suns
besides, without the Guru
it will still be pitch darkness
(Var Asa, Mahila II, Guru Granth Sahib, p. 463)

The transfiguration of the Guru is a special and an essential feature of the Sikh theology. The Guruship passes from one Guru to another as one candle lights another. In this scheme, the real Guru remains the God, as source of all light. But Guru Nanak clearly states in his bani that He is revealed through the Shabad. The word Shabad and Guru are juxtaposed. Often they are mentioned as one word; *Shabad Guru*. Guru Ram Das clearly states Shabad and Guru are the same:

The Shabad Guru is the profound teacher;
without the Shabad the world remains in perplexity.

Guru Nanak also testifies that *Gurbani* is the Divine Word:

As I receive the word from the
Lord, so do I deliver it

(Tilang Mahila I, Guru Granth Sahib, p. 722)

In the Sikh terminology, the word Guru is used only for the ten pontiffs, and thereafter the *Shabad Guru* in the form of sacred scripture was apotheosized as Guru Granth Sahib by Guru Gobind Singh in 1708, when he invested the scripture as the Guru. Guru Granth Sahib was proclaimed as the Guru in the presence of the Khalsa fraternity and finality of this pronouncement has remained a cherished truth with the Sikhs since then. Hence, Guru Granth Sahib itself is an important constituent of the Sikh theology which distinguishes it from other religious scriptures.

References

1. Lachlin C.H., *The Sikhs and their Scriptures*, 29, Lucknow Publishing House, Lucknow, 1953.
2. Kulandai Swamy, V.C., *The Immortal Kurl*, 4, Sahitya Akademy, New Delhi, 1994.
3. Harbans Singh (Ed.) *Encyclopaedia of Sikhism*, Vol. IV, 239 (Punjabi University, Patiala).

   "ਇਹੁ ਜਗੁ ਸਚੈ ਕੀ ਹੈ ਕੋਠੜੀ
   ਸਚੇ ਕਾ ਵਿੱਚ ਵਾਸੁ"

   "This world is the Holy Lord's Chamber,
   in it is his abode"

   (Guru Granth Sahib, 463, Asa Mahila II)
4. Shashi Bala, *The Concept of Monotheism, A Comparative Study of Major Religious Scriptures*, 62, ABS Publications, Jalandhar, 1993.
5. Sethi, V.K., Kabir: *The Weaver of God's Name*, 6-8, Radha Soami Satsang, Beas, 1984.
6. For details see Giani Gurdit Singh, *Itihas Sri Guru Granth Sahib*, 340-356, Sikh Sahit Sansthan, Chandigarh, 1990.
7. *Sri Guru Granth Sahib* (English Translation), G.S. Talib, Introduction, XCV, Punjabi University, Patiala, 1984.
8. Shashi Bala, op.cit. 189.

9. Macauliff, Max Arthur — *The Sikh Religion*, Vol. I (Introduction, ii-iv and xii-xiv).
10. Gurbachan Singh Talib, *Sri Guru Granth Sahib*, English Translation, Vol. I (Introduction, xxi), Punjabi University, Patiala, 1984.
11. Taran Singh, *Gurbani Dian Viakhia Parnalian* (Punjabi), Introduction Page I, Punjabi University, Patiala
12. Bhai Gurdas, *Var 5 Pauri 13* (edited by Bhai Vir Singh, Page 92, Khalsa Samachar, Amritsar, 1984).
13. Harbans Singh (Ed.) *Encyclopaedia of Sikhism*, Vol. III, 236-37 (Punjabi University, Patiala, 1997).
14. Gopal Singh, *Sri Guru Granth Sahib* (English Translation), Vol. I, page XXVI.
15. Harbans Singh (Ed.) op.cit. Vol. II, page 200-202.

The Adi Guru Granth: A Vision for Universal Religion

Dr. Kirpal Singh

We are fortunate that we are celebrating the quadricentennial celebration of installation of the Adi Guru Granth. It was completed in 1604 AD at Ramsar and was installed in Darbar Sahib, now called Golden Temple. The Adi Guru Granth, has thirty six contributors including six Sikh Gurus. Its contributors belonged to different strata of society. They belonged to different religious traditions and different parts of India. Long before the dawn of modern civilization based on science and technology, the Sikh scripture taught the lessons of co-existence and tolerance which are so essential not only in the religious sphere but also the strife-torn national and international spheres.

Bhai Gurdas has rightly stated that Guru Nanak Dev saw the world aflame. The world was burning with egoism, fanaticism and religious antagonism. During medieval times, the christians considered non-Christians as pagans. Portugese destroyed one biggest Hindu temple in Ceylone at Trincomalee because of religious antagonism. Sir William Jones, the founder of Asiatic Society wrote, "It would have remained for the present day a venerable relic, had not the misguided religious zeal of the portugese razed it to ground in 1622 AD". As Bhai Gurdas has stated (in First Vaar, Pauri 20), Muslims were divided into seventy two sects and all were antagonistic to each other. There was sharp rivalry between Shias and Sunnis. Mohammed Ismail, a Shia ruler of Baghdad was burning the mosques of Sunnis in early sixteenth century. In England, Queen Mary of Scotland burned alive some missionaries calling them heretics. In India, the situation was no better. The muslim rulers were destroying the Hindu ancient temples. At Mathura, Sikandar Lodhi (1488-1554 AD) who was contemporary of Guru Nanak, had destroyed the Keshwa temple at Mathura and also other temples in various places. In his days Baudhan Pandit was persecuted and killed by Qazi's Fatwa and his only fault was that he said, 'Hinduism as true as Islam'.

Despite all round religious antagonism, the Adi Guru Granth has got universal appeal. The Sikh scripture was for the unification of Indian people, who needed a scripture which should synthesise their beliefs and cultures. Dr Radha Krishnan has stated, "a remarkable feature of the Adi Granth is that it contains writings of the religious teachers of Hinduism and Islam[1]". The Adi Guru Granth made unique contribution in bringing the people of different cultures in the mainstream of national life. Arnold Toynbee has rightly stated, "The Indian and Judaic religions are not notoriously different in spirit. Their principal meeting ground has been India, where Islam impinged on Hinduism violently. On the whole, the story of relations between these two great religions on Indian ground has been unhappy tale of mutual misunderstanding and hostility. To have discovered and embraced the deep harmony underlying the historic Hindu-Muslim discord has been noble spiritual triumph[2]".

Long before the dawn of modern civilization and centuries before the establishment of United Nations Organization, Sikh Gurus had the vision to have universal religion for the entire humanity. For this purpose Guru Arjan, the fifth Guru of the Sikhs took practical steps. Guru Arjan ushered in a new era in the history of religion when he declared that true religion consisted of two things only-Love of God's name and purity of conduct. The Guru dispensed with all formalities in favour of these two things which were never contradicted by the saints. They may be differing from the Gurus in their method of worship but did not differ in their aim. Guru Arjan Writes:

ਸਰਬ ਧਰਮ ਮਹਿ ਸ੍ਰੇਸਟ ਧਰਮੁ ॥ ਹਰਿ ਕੋ ਨਾਮੁ ਜਪਿ ਨਿਰਮਲ ਕਰਮੁ ॥
ਸਗਲ ਕ੍ਰਿਆ ਮਹਿ ਊਤਮ ਕਿਰਿਆ ॥ ਸਾਧਸੰਗਿ ਦੁਰਮਤਿ ਮਲੁ ਹਿਰਿਆ ॥
ਸਗਲ ਉਦਮ ਮਹਿ ਉਦਮੁ ਭਲਾ ॥ ਹਰਿ ਕਾ ਨਾਮੁ ਜਾਪਹੁ ਜੀਅ ਸਦਾ ॥
ਸਗਲ ਬਾਨੀ ਮਹਿ ਅੰਮ੍ਰਿਤ ਬਾਨੀ ॥ ਹਰਿ ਕੋ ਜਸੁ ਸੁਨਿ ਰਸਨ ਬਖਾਨੀ ॥
ਸਗਲ ਥਾਨ ਤੇ ਓਹੁ ਊਤਮ ਥਾਨੁ ॥ ਨਾਨਕ ਜਿਹ ਘਟਿ ਵਸੈ ਹਰਿ ਨਾਮੁ ॥

Of all religions the best is the practice of Name with purity of conduct
Of all rites the best is to purge one's heart of filth and evil tendencies by association with those who have disciplined themselves.
Of all devotional practices, the best is the constant application of the heart to the Name
Of all sacred texts, the most sacred is that by which one hears the praise of beloved, utters it to others.
Of all holy places, the holiest is where one feels the stir of the Name in one's heart.

In the atmosphere of all round religious antagonism the Sikh scripture exhorted interfaith dialogue and declared 'One God is father we all human beings are his children.'

ਏਕੁ ਪਿਤਾ ਏਕਸ ਕੇ ਹਮ ਬਾਰਿਕ ਤੂ ਮੇਰਾ ਗੁਰ ਹਾਈ ॥

One of the fundamentals of interfaith understanding is the recognition of efficacy of other faiths in dealing with the ills of society. Usually, no religion considers other religious equal to itself. It is only the Adi Guru Granth which recognizes that all religious dispensations are capable of elevating the human soul. Guru Amardas, the third Sikh Guru has stated in a hymn:

The world is burning, save it O God
Out of Thy mercy

Save it through whichever dispensation
ਜਗਤੁ ਜਲੰਦਾ ਰਖਿ ਲੈ ਆਪਣੀ ਕਿਰਪਾ ਧਾਰਿ ॥
ਜਿਤੁ ਦੁਆਰੈ ਉਬਰੈ ਤਿਤੈ ਲੈਹੁ ਉਬਾਰਿ ॥

The Adi Granth has accepted the separate identity of the Hindus and Muslims with their diverse customs and ceremonies. Guru Arjun has stated in a verse

One man invoked Ram another Khuda
One man worshipped Gosain another Allah
Some speak of the causes of causes
other of the Benevolent
Some talk of the extended of mercy
others of the merciful
Some bathe in Hindu sacred places
others visit Makka
Some perform Hindu worship, and others bow
their heads in the Muhammadan fashion
Some read Vedas other the Mussalman books
some wear white others blue
One calls himself Muslim and one calls himself Hindu
One desires the paradise of Muslims and the
other heaven of Hindus
Says Nanak, he who realizes God's Will know
the secret of Lord Master.

The Gurus were strictly monotheistic and had no truck with Avtar worship or faith in theory of incarnation. Some of the medieval Bhagti saints whose verses had been included in the Adi Granth rarely rose above the belief in Rama and Krishna or incarnation of God. They are not averse to idol worship. Farid, a Muslim curses himself for not going to mosque five times for offering namaz and refers to souls in grave, waiting for the day of resurrection[3] which clearly cuts across the Gurus' belief of transmigration of souls. The saints may be different from the Gurus in the method of worship but did not differ in their aim, which was to love God and to do good. The various streams that merge in the statements of Sikh

Gurus transcend all barriers and boundaries to symbolize a universal human vision.

The Adi Guru Granth gives a lot of information about the prevailing religions and various formalities embedded in them. Guru Nanak had described the religious practices of the Vaishna-vites as follows:

> *Nanak the formless one is without fear. Now many stories there are of Krishna; How many Veds and religious compositions. How many beggars dance as mendicants wheel round and wheel in rhythmic trend. Those mercenary people come and stage their performance in the market place. Kings and queens sing their parts and utter all sorts of chatter. They wear ear-rings and necklaces worth hundreds of thousands of rupees. They bathe in holy streams, perform idol worship and adoration, use sopious incense of sandal. The Jogis meditate on God the creator, who they call unseen.*

Guru Nanak has also exposed the hypocritic manners of the Hindus. When the Hindus could not resist the compelling force of Islam, they secretly tried to be true to their Hindu ceremonies and customs. Outwardly, they conformed to the Muslim practices to please the rulers.

> *On their fore-heads are sacrificial marks;*
> *On their waists redish dhotis and in their hands knives, they are the world's butchers.*
> *Putting on blue clothes, they are acceptable in the Muhammadan court and while taking bread from the Malechhas, worship the Puranas.*
> *They eat-he-goats killed with unspeakable words, and allow no one to enter their cooking squares. Having smeared a space they draw line around it, and sit within false that they are.*

Kabir (1399-1518 AD) was the inhabitant of Kashi, which has had been the sacred place of Hindus. So he had described the dress of so-called religious heads of the time:

They wear loin-clothes three and a half yards long
And sacrificial threads of three strands.
They carry rosaries on their necks and
glittering brass utensils in their hands;
They should not be called saints of God
but cheats of Benaras.

Before undertaking his long missionary tours, Guru Nanak categorically said that 'There is no Hindu and there is no Musalman'. It created a stir among the Muslim officials of the town who argued that Musalmans were there and they were ruling over the country. On their enquiry Guru Nanak said:

ਮੁਸਲਮਾਣੁ ਕਹਾਵਣੁ ਮੁਸਕਲੁ ਜਾ ਹੋਇ ਤਾਂ ਮੁਸਲਮਾਨ ਕਹਾਵੈ ॥
ਅਵਲਿ ਅਉਲਿ ਦੀਨੁ ਕਰ ਮਿਠਾ ਮਸਕਲ ਮਾਨਾ ਮਾਲੁ ਮੁਸਾਵੈ ॥
ਹੋਇ ਮੁਸਲਿਮੁ ਦੀਨ ਮੁਹਾਣੈ ਮਰਣ ਜੀਵਣ ਕਾ ਭਰਮੁ ਚੁਕਾਵੈ ॥
ਰਬ ਕੀ ਰਜਾਇ ਮੰਨੇ ਸਿਰ ਉਪਰਿ ਕਰਤਾ ਮੰਨੇ ਆਪੁ ਗਵਾਵੈ ॥
ਤਉ ਨਾਨਕ ਸਰਬ ਜੀਆ ਮਿਹਰੰਮਤਿ ਹੋਇ ਤ ਮੁਸਲਮਾਣੁ ਕਹਾਵੈ ॥

To be a Musalman is difficult, if one be really so, then one may be called a Musalman.
Let one first love the religion of saints, and put aside pride and pelf as the file removeth rust.
Let him accept the religion of his pilots and dismiss anxiety regarding death or life.
Let him heartily obey the will of God, worship the creator and efface himself.
When he is kind to all men then Nanak, shall to be indeed a Musalman.

Similarly to the Hindus Guru Nanak said:

ਜੋਗੁ ਨ ਖਿੰਥਾ ਜੋਗੁ ਨ ਡੰਡੈ ਜੋਗੁ ਨ ਭਸਮ ਚੜਾਈਐ ॥
ਜੋਗੁ ਨ ਮੁੰਦੀ ਮੂੰਡਿ ਮੁਡਾਇਐ ਜੋਗੁ ਨਾ ਸਿੰਙੀ ਵਾਈਐ ॥
ਅੰਜਨ ਮਾਹਿ ਨਿਰੰਜਨਿ ਰਹੀਐ ਜੋਗ ਜੁਗਤਿ ਇਵ ਪਾਈਐ ॥ ੧ ॥
ਗਲੀ ਜੋਗੁ ਨ ਹੋਈ ॥
ਏਕ ਦ੍ਰਿਸਟਿ ਕਰਿ ਸਮਸਰਿ ਜਾਣੈ ਜੋਗੀ ਕਹੀਐ ਸੋਈ ॥ ੧ ॥ ਰਹਾਉ ॥
ਜੋਗੁ ਨ ਦੇਸਿ ਦਿਸੰਤਰਿ ਭਵਿਐ ਜੋਗੁ ਨ ਤੀਰਥਿ ਨਾਈਐ ॥ ੧ ॥
ਅੰਜਨ ਮਾਹਿ ਨਿਰੰਜਨਿ ਰਹੀਐ ਜੋਗੁ ਜੁਗਤਿ ਇਵ ਪਾਈਐ ॥ ੧ ॥

Religion consisteth not in patched coat or in a jogis staff or in ashes smeared over the body.
Religion consisteth not in ear-rings worn, or a shaven head or in blowing of horns.
Religion consisteth not in mere words;
He who looked on all men as equal is religious.
Religion consisteth not in wandering to tombs or places of cremation, or sitting in attitude of contemplation;
Religion consisteth nor in wandering in foreign countries Or bathing at the places of pilgrimages.
Abide pure amid the impurities of the world, thus shall thou find the way of religion.

Guru Nanak was once questioned by a crowd about whether Hindus were superior of Muslims. His reply was, 'Without good acts professors of both the religions shall suffer[4]. When directly asked whether he was a Hindu or a Musalman, his reply was 'I am mere a human made of five elements'. The Adi Guru Granth shunned class, caste and creed and vehemently stressed the equality of mankind. Guru Nanak gave highest respect to the divinity of human beings - *'man tu jot sarup hain'*. Man is the embodiment of God. In his personal life he preferred sharing food with an honest carpenter than enjoying the best dishes offered by a feudal lord. To him purity of mind and soul had the best appreciation. He never distinguished between Hindus and Muslims. He had with him a constant companion, a Muslim Bhai Mardana who used to play on rabab.

The caste system has been described as the steel frame of Hindu society while Guru Granth Sahib exhorted his followers to defy the principle of caste-exclusiveness as it was the greatest obstacle in the path of integration. The Adi Guru Granth exhorted his followers to meet in congregation and take meals in the common kitchen (Langar) where they were to sit together, worship together and eat together irrespective of the castes they belonged to. In this way the Sikh Gurus through their hymns in the Adi Guru Granth as well as by their actions provided basis for integration of humanity on religious basis.

Unity of Hindu-Muslim : North-South Ragas

There are various strands of spectrum of ragas[5] in the Adi Guru Granth. It is not the music of single people. The thirty one ragas in the *Adi Guru Granth* make symphony of various ragas of different countries and melodies of various regions. Beside this a large number of folk tunes and metres from different regions and localities have been used[6]. According to an old tradition recorded in the Sanskrit text, six ragas were produced by Mahadeva and Parvati (five Mahadev and one Parvati).

There developed a schism between North and South Indian music. It was for Guru Nanak during sixteenth century[7] to bring the South Indian Ragas to North. In the Adi Granth, we find combination of ragas of both North and South India in Ram Kali Dakhani and Gaurhi Dakhani and Vadhans Dakhani. Guru Arjan Dev has included raga Yaman in the Guru Granth with the Indian name raga Kalyan. It is 29th raga in the Holy Granth. Among the chaukis of Kirtan at Hari Mandir Sahib, Amritsar, Kalyan chowki comes in the end as prescribed by Guru Arjan[8].

Another significant feature of the Guru Granth Sahib is combining music with the sacred verses. Pure composition unites music and poetry in a dissoluble bond. So indispensable the strictness of their union that rules of sense and propriety render them to be echos of each other.

References

1. Selections from the Sacred writings of the Sikhs, George Allen Unwin, London, p.17.
2. Ibid, p.10

3. The Adi Guru Granth, p.1383, Sheikh Farid Shlok Nos 70 and 97.
   ਫਰੀਦਾ ਬੇ ਨਿਵਾਜਾ ਕੁਤਿਆ ਏਹ ਨ ਭਲੀ ਰੀਤਿ ॥
   ਕਬਹੀ ਚਲਿ ਨ ਆਇਆ ਪੰਜੇ ਵਖਤ ਮਸੀਤਿ ॥
   ਫਰੀਦਾ ਮਹਲ ਨਿਸਖਣ ਰਹਿ ਗਏ ਵਾਸਾ ਆਇਆ ਤਲਿ ॥
   ਗੋਰਾਂ ਸੇ ਨਿਮਾਣੀਆ ਬਹਸਨਿ ਰੂਹਾਂ ਮਲਿ ॥
4. Bhai Gurdas, Var 1, Paurhi 33.
5. The word Raag was first used by Kalidas whereas concept of raag singing had already developed. V. Premlata, Music Through Ages.
6. For details see my paper Musicology in Adi Guru Granth, Guru Nanak Dev Uni., Perspectives on Guru Granth Sahib, Vol. 1, 2003, p. 123-132.
7. Emurie Te Nize Lidien Kopou, Indian Music History and Structure, p. 7-8.
8. Sarup Singh Alag, An introduction to Guru Granth Sahib, Ludhiana, 1999, p.293.

Global Consciousness and Guru Granth Sahib

Dr. Sutinder Singh Noor

We are in the post-modern age of global consciousness and every great classical text is being studied from this point of view. Guru Granth Sahib is a great holy text, full of global consciousness. The multi-cultural concept, the ideological, social and dalit consciousness makes this text most relevant for the contemporary age. It has the power to solve spiritual as well as materialistic crises of all sorts.

Guru Granth Sahib was compiled by Guru Arjan Dev with the available poetic-texts of Guru Nanak, Guru Angad, Guru Amardas, Guru Ramdas and that of his own, alongwith banis of Baba Sheikh Farid, Jaidev, Namdev, Tirlochan, Parmanand, Ramanand, Dhanna, Kabir, Pipa, Ravidas, Satta, Balwand and others. They were Brahmins, Muslims, Hindus and Dalits from Punjab, U.P., Rajasthan, Maharashtra and other states. This shows that Guru Granth Sahib is the first great holy Granth which presents the model not only of national integration but that of international integration too, aimed at a classless and casteless society, rejecting the egoistic and inhuman concepts.

To understand the Global Consciousness of Guru Granth Sahib, we have to understand its paradigmatic growth - paradigmatic not exactly in Saussurean linguistic sense, but in the Bakhtian dialogic sense. The paradigmatic growth also covers the shift in paradigm and transformation, as Thomas S. Kuhn discussed it in "The Structure of the Scientific Revolution." But before understanding this paradigm, I want to discuss the continuity of Indian spiritual tradition and also where the paradigmatic shifts occur in the tradition. Guru Granth Sahib rejected all kinds of yajnas, rituals and egoistic ideals.

The Pundit utter the Vedas, but lazes in doing deeds ,
He keeps silence and keeps aloof,
but within his heart is the knot of desire,
He has renounced the world,
but his outgoings (of the mind) cease not,
O, where shall I find the one to whom
I shall utter the inmost state of my soul,
And who, being himself emancipated,
will unite me with my God,
One becomes an ascetic and disciplines the body,
but the mind runs out and about,
And one remains chaste, but within one's heart is ego,
And one roams the pilgrim-stations, becoming a recluse,
But within one is wrath, born of ignorance.

No doubt Rig Veda, for God, used the word "Tad Ekam" also, but the concepts of Nirguna (Transcendent) and Sarguna (Immanent) distinctively appear later in Upnishads. Maitrya Upnishad says the *Brahm* has two forms: Kaal and Akaal (within time and beyond time). Prashan Upnishad also says that *Brahm* has two terms: *Par* (higher) and *Apar* (lower). *Paarbrahm* is *Nirguna* and *Brahm* is *Sarguna*. Brihdarnyak Upnishad associates Brahm with attributes of negation or 'Neti-Neti'. He is not fat, not thin, not small, not big, not red, not fluid, not shadow, not blackness, not air, not sky, not smell, not eye, not ear, not sound, not mind, not light, not mouth. He is not internal, not external. Kath Upnishad also says, He is beyond beginning, beyond end, beyond word, beyond touch, beyond form, beyond smell and beyond so many other beyonds.

We are conscious about the paradigmatic shift occuring upto the growth of *Ikonkar*. God is one, all gods, goddesses and deities have become mystic-signifiers. A transformation from Purana or mythic-structure to history is happening. In this sense, history is making a new concept of religiosity, a combination of reality and spirituality. Bhagats and Gurus in Guru Granth Sahib created a new concept of Society. Upnishads built a vast world of narratives to discuss various aspects of metaphysics created by Vedant, but philosophically these narratives were to establish the previous Grand-narratives. Guru Granth Sahib did not accept these Grand-narratives, techniques of mythical narratives and the genre of mixture of prose and poetry.

The poetry of Guru Granth Sahib is full of beautiful images of nature, imbued with all depths of cosmos. Guru Nanak rejected thematically the ritualistic *Arti*, as for him the real *Arti* is being performed in whole of the cosmos, which covers the beauty and aesthetics of the Universe. A globally conscious man or the post-modern consciousness is not grappling only with the complex materialistic problems but also discovering the realms of new aesthetics. Now, when we are in crisis of the failure of classical systemic theories, we have lost the sense of aesthetics. But this kind of poetry reminds us how we should understand and experience the cosmos.

Now, when we are also losing the meaning of human relationships, the metaphysical love-poetry of Guru Granth Sahib reminds us of the significance of depth of relationships. The poetry of Guru Granth Sahib creates the metaphors of bridal mysticism by way of which we are all brides and God is our husband. The man-woman relationship, marriage, home, family become more sacred and ethical. Says Baba Sheikh Farid:

I did not sleep tonight with my love,
My limbs all writhe with pain,

Go and ask the deserted ones,
How do they pass their nights.

Globally, we are facing another problem regarding human desire. In simple words, desire consists of love and erotic-impulse. We cannot disintegrate this complete signifier. Modern European thinker, Octovio Paz has defined this signifier in his *The Double Flame* as:

> *"The flame is the most subtle part of life, moving upward and raising itself, above in the shape of a pyramid.The original primordial fire, sexuality, raises the red flame of eroticism and this in turn raises and feeds another flame; the flame of love, eroticism and love: the double flame of life."*

The Sanskrit and Persian scholars developed the poetics of shringar. But the medieval Punjabi poetry, especially Gurbani goes beyond the poetry of shringar and this flame is transformed into the metaphysical consciousness. Guru Nanak has said in Raag Asa:

If the mind's pearl, like an ornament,
be weaved into the string of breath;
And the body's bride be decked
with the jewel of compassion,
Then the forsooth enjoys her spouse.
O Love, I am bewitched by Thy Excellences,
For, Thy attributes I find not in another,
If the bride wears her Lord like a garland,
And cleans the mouth with tooth-brush of damodara,
And wears the bracelet of the Creator in her hand,
thus, verily does she hold her mind.
If she wears the ring of Madhusudana,
and silks of Transcendent Lord;
And saturates the parting of her hair with patience,
And applies the collyrium of God's love,
And lights the lamp of the mind's temple,
and makes the couch of her body,

Then the Lord of Wisdom comes to her bed,
and enjoys her love.

Here the Lord of wisdom, knowledge, and consciousness reminds us that in Guru Granth Sahib we have binary of this consciousness and emotion (*Gian* and *Bhav*). A new kind of episteme emerges in the language of Guru Granth Sahib. Guru Granth Sahib rejects escapism from life and Shankar's concept of *Maya* (Illusion). It accepts the reality, it celebrates life. Even the metaphoric bridal mysticism creates the language of celebration. The modern global man is in search of this episteme. Guru Amardass wrote a Bani 'Anand' in Raag Ramkali to express this mode of celebration:

I am in ecstasy, O mother, for, I have attained to my Lord.
Attained have I to my Lord, all-too spontaneously,
And, within fairies have come to sing Lord's Word.
Sing ye the Lord's Word,
all those who have enshrined it in the mind.

Says Nanak:
I am in ecstasy, for, I have attained to my Lord.

To express the other dimensions of this ecstasy, Guru Arjan Dev worte a bani 'Sukhmani'. About 'Sukhmani', Punjabi critic Sant Singh Sekhon in *History of Punjabi Literature* wrote that it was composed in the situation of the Damocles' sword of the displeasure of the Mughal Emperor Jahangir, hanging on Guru's head, who was arrested, under Jahangir's orders, to be put to death after resorting to inhuman tortures. Sukhmani gives immense peace of mind and spiritual awakening to the reader.

In Guru Granth Sahib, this spiritual awakening is combined with social, cultural and political awakening as the Gurus were building a new paradigm of society and culture. The new thinking of Guru Granth Sahib rejected the concept of monarchy and feudalism. Guru Nanak opposed Babar when he invaded

India, as he criticised the contemporary kings, qazis, teachers and other corrupt men in unequivocal terms:

The Kali age is the knife, kings are hunters,
and justice has taken wings,
The darkness of falsehood is abroad,
And one knows not if everthere
will rise the moon of truth.
The subjects are blind, and submissive,
being unwise and live on falsehood.
The teachers dance to the tune of disciples
The Qazis do justice if their palm is greased,
And what bind men and women to each other
is greed, not love.

In Guru Granth Sahib, not only this political awakening is important but also the other systemic ethical concepts are treated as significant. Especially, two more concepts: the man who believes in Guru's teaching is Gurmukh and who does not is Manmukh; Gurmukh is ideal, conscious, enlightened, understands the vision of community, the relation with other communities and Manmukh is negative, egoistic, betrayer, cannot meditate on the vision of God. So, he is ignorant about the vision of community and the relation with other communities, which has become a social philosophy in this age of Global Consciousness.

The Sikh religious perspective denounced the morbid value system, as this was regarded as the major factor for the disintegration of the society. The basic argument in the Sikh scripture is: "Since all men have emanated from one primordial spiritual creator, so they are all equal." Sikhism believes in universal brotherhood where fanatic religious divisions have no meaning. Only Truth shall prevail, Guru Nanak said:

God is every where
He has created us all

He who realises this, is a true Hindu or Muslim,
All others are hypocrites,
All shall have to answer for their actions.
Good deeds will bring salvation.
Truth alone shall prevail in the end.
Nothing else will be a substitute for it before God.

In recent times, some people advocate that to achieve this equality, we must have one philosophy, one religion and even one political system in the world. Sikhism does not believe in this kind of monomania. Even comparative approach means we differ, and we are one at the same time. We believe in positive *difference*, and not in the negative one. We must be conscious that now we are living in a pluralistic, rather than a polymorphic age, where several cultures have to co-exist. We have to understand each other, and to achieve it, we must live in peace. If we understand religions, ideologies from this *difference* point of view, we would live in a dignified and harmonious co-existence.

Global Consciousness believes in this kind of philosophy which rejects the negative concept of war, inequality, caste system, all kind of fanaticism, fascism and apartheid. The ideology of Guru Granth Sahib advocates brotherhood, fraternity and a culture of love and aesthetics. This concept is not only epistemological, it is experiential too. That's why Guru Granth Sahib creates awakening, a new global atmosphere. In the age of globalisation, the secular, democratic and the pluralistic message of Guru Granth Sahib has become more relevant and significant. It has influenced the history and ethics of Sikhs as well as of other people in the modern world. It has already established the paradigmatic signifier to be realised in the future more forcefully.

Interfaith Dialogue and Guru Granth Sahib

Dr. Jodh Singh

Dialogical nature of man is the common theme of twentieth century philosophy in general. Sartre, Marcel and other existentialists as well as philosophers like Levinas, Derrida and Foucault have emphasized the dialogical character of human situation in particular. In fact, dialogue is an interpersonal and inter-subjective method of communication of oneself with the other. The existentialists do not accept the other as a transcendent reality, whereas the other is considered as Maya by Advait Vedanta and as a grand illusion by almost all the mystic poets and philosophers in India. Guru Nanak, however in his understanding of the 'other' considers both the supra-universal 'other' as well as 'empirical other' of the universe as real ones, though the latter one, in the limited sense due to its evanescent nature. Since existentialist thought of twentieth century is an effort to transcend the 'otherness' of the earthly 'other' with whom the dialogical nature of man is to interact, it will be in the fitness of the things to see as to what is the nature and the history of dialogue among the people of different denominations. Dialogue directly reflects conversation which, in the western parlance and history of intellectual rendezvous is that version which has been written in the form of conversation. Christians, through their political victories pushed further their strength and expansions and emphasised upon the authenticity and intellectual content of any information purporting to be truthful. They started the tradition of dialogue and took over the duty of putting up the seal of authenticity on any valid reasoning or dialogue. This dialogue instead of being among the equals came out to be between the ruler and ruled ones and hence the final outcome was always in the favour of the ruler. Being economically well-developed, the western countries had the competence of having and using maximum information about their own as well as other religions in their own favour. The works of most of the priests, seemingly done for other religions, somehow or the other accomplished the task of stabalization of the positions of the ruling class or the propagation of Christianity. Before the First World War (1914-18), words such as sympathy and fulfilment were profusely used to denote the lifestyle of the people of the Western countries.

The dialogues among the people pertaining to various customs, beliefs and rituals etc. have always been in vogue for hundreds of years. The tradition of written dialogues is also very old. The magnificent example of such dialogues is the Dialogues of Plato, in which much discussion has been undertaken on many intricate and complex problems of life and death. Though the dialogue between brother Yama and sister Yami pertains to incest but this dialogue in the Rigveda is supposed to be the oldest one. In the Upanishadic Age, the dialogues among the seers and their disciples have come forth but in such dialogues, by and large, the disciples considering themselves on the lower pedestal put up their querries and get the reply. In Buddhistic literature, the position is almost the same. In a very popular spirituo-ethical work the *Gita,* which is much acclaimed throughout the ontological circles, there is a long dialogue between Lord Krishna and Arjuna who was ready to repudiate fight in favour of his kith and kin. The religious history of medieval India is replete with debates full of refutations, rebuttals and affirmations wherein egotist tone and tenor occupies the main focus of dialogue. Universal victory and crushing defeat of the opponent seem to be the main motives of such dialogues. In the Judo-Christian traditions, most of the commands are in the forms of a dialogue.

Keeping in view some particular objective, the imaginary dialogues have also been created wherein dramatic elements are dominant. Among such dialogues David Hume's *'Dialogues Concerning Natural Religions'* (1799) and *'A Dialogue of Religions'* (1960) by Ninion Smart may be counted. An imaginary opponent is created in such dialogues and then the shortcomings of his religious beliefs are enumerated. In India, in order to help propagation of Christianity, the name of K.M.Banerjee's *'Dialogues on Hindu Philosophy'* (1861) may be named. In this work, the prominent Indian traditions have been placed opposed to each other in view of pushing up the propagation of Christianity. However, this method could not last for a long time.

After the two-three decades of twentieth century, Religion had to get ready for taking materialism head-on. The features of the concept of 'dialogue' in a factual form emerged after the first World War and its first declaration came in the form of work of Martin Buber's *I and Thou*. Buber was a Jew, who had from very near seen the religious and economic exploitations. He felt that the remedy of this exploitation was nothing but the identification and acceptance of humans. And this task could be accomplished only through man to man dialogue. The dialogue in the form of inter-religious dialogue however could become a vogue only after the second World War. In this post-war period, colonialism began to crumble and simultaneously the changes in value system became obvious. Though the relationship between man and man eased but nothing significant could be gained pertaining to the amity among the religious denominations. On the contrary, on the eve of division of India and Pakistan in 1947, the failure of politically-dominated religious dialogue was exhibited like day-light. India became a secular country, whereas Pakistan opted to be an Islamic country. Similar events occurred throughout the world at many places. In such circumstances, in order to remain associated with one and all, no other means except dialogue remains handy, and the dialogue, as the most helpful device is again emerging on the horizon of the globe. According to *Encyclopaedia of Religion* (volume 4, p.347) the Second Vatican Council (1962-65) inspired the Catholic Christian World that Church should ask people that its sons being full of wisdom and love through dialogue should accept the spirituo-ethical values of the sages of other religions and should further help maintain and develop them. Similarly, through another command, it was delineated that the followers of Christ, through their dialogue, full of honesty and perseverance, can know how much great treasure has been bestowed by God to the people living on this planet. Such proclamations set the Catholics free form all the age-old restrictions and consequently the dialogical literature stared flooding from all directions. Later on, the Protestants also contributed a lot in this endeavour.

However, in this literature the meaning and objective of dialogue differed variously. The real dialogue with other religions could be established scantily but much light on the doctrinal aspect of dialogue was shed by many a scholar. Under the name of dialogue, many procedures came into being. In the Debating Dialogue, mentally similar type of people gathered and put up their ideas. In this dialogue both the parties have implicit agreement about speaking and listening to the arguement. In Humanistic Dialogue of Martin Buber, one may find the element of meeting thc man as a man but in this process individualism is predominant. Man is discussed here, but the society of human beings who are units of society, is totally neglected. And this seems to be quite impossible as well as ludicrous. Its ideas are lofty but still it remains as an impracticable doctrine. In Secular Dialogue, such programmes are chalked out in which all the denominations of religions and their societies feel free to participate. Before the advent of Sikhism, the Spiritual Dialogue was practised in eastern countries and especially in India, where people, by living in monasteries, ashrams or hermitages would learn spirituality and extend the lineage of guru-disciple tradition.

Emmanuel Levinas, an eminent European philosopher of France, has also delved deeper into the problem of dialogue with the other. In this paper, while discussing the nature and form of dialogue envisaged four hundred years ago by Guru Granth Sahib, we will take up the works of Levinas (1906-1995) wherein we find him grappling with this problem of Dialogue. Before we come to look in detail into the Guru Granth Sahib for dialogue, it will not be out of place to know about the milieu and social background of Levinas.

Hegal wrote, "History itself is the final judge of History." "Emmanuel Levinas", as writes Susan A. Handelman in his "Fragments of Redemption", could perceive this 'universal history' as a grotesque spectacle of suffering and brutality. Born as a Jewish child in Russia in 1906, Levinas had witnessed the chaos and violence of the Bolshevik revolution and subsequent civil war. Levinas found his critique of history and philosophy in the sources of Judaism but he would locate the authentic and creative core of Judaism not in *Kabbalah* but in the *Talmud*.

Levinas left Russia in the year 1923 to study philosophy in Strasbourg and then later in Freiburg with Husserl and Heideggar. Getting enamoured of French Culture, in 1930, Levinas became a French citizen and was later on drafted into the French army. Captured by the German forces, he ultimately survived in a prisoner-of-war camp. In fact, his French uniform saved him from deportation to the gas chambers. Levinas writes in his biographical essay that his biography is "dominated by the presentiment and memory of the Nazi horror" (Signature,

177).During his captivity in the prisoner-of-war camp, his wife was hidden and saved with the help of a friend from his Strasbourg University days, Maurice Blanchot. All his family remaining in Russia was murdered by the Nazis.

Emerging from the camp after the War, Levinas gave a second thought to the work of Husserl and Heideggar he had studied in the 1920s and 1930s and gave a new mould to phenomenological thought. His philosophical critique now made ethics prior to and the condition of the metaphysics. In 1947, while producing his philosophical masterpieces, Levinas also became director of the Ecole Normale Irsraelite Orientale, a Jewish school which was part of the Alliance Israelite Orientale. The Alliance founded in 1860, was an organisation dedicated to spreading French and Jewish Culture throughout Jewish communities in France and its former Mediterranean empire. The Alliance was formed to respond to the problems of the emancipation and assimilation of Jews in France, protect their interests, help defend them from persecution and increase Jewish solidarity.

Emmanuel Levinas prolifically wrote on Judaism and the Jewish life. He delves deep into the disruption of the logic of identity by the irruption of the heterogeneous other. Working at the very limits of philosophy, Levinas has pondered over the 'end of Metaphysics' and above all has solicited the breakup of philosophical 'totality' by the 'other'. The connections between the historical horrors of the Nazi Period and the Philosophical idea of neutral, impersonal 'Being' is direct. For, as Levinas writes, the ontology as the attempt to reduce the other to the same or 'beings' to 'Being' is ultimately an egoism. "Philosophy is an egology" *(Totality and Infinity)* and "Heideggarian ontology, which subordinates the relationship with the others to the relation with Being in general, remains under obedience to the anonymous and leads inevitably to another power, to imperialist domination, to tyranny" (T.I.47).

The distinctive mark of Levinas's philosophy is the passionate search for a way out of this tyranny, 'this multiplicity of allergic egoism'. In his interpretation of etymology, Being or essence-the Latin *esse*-is rooted in *interesse* or 'interest',egoism,usurpation. 'War is the deed or drama of the essences' interest ....Essence is the extreme synchronism of war'. Sikhism holds that fight for righteousness and justice should be fought even if it is not in the case of one's own particular religion or social group. Guru Tegh Bahadur set a healthy model in the medieval period-fanatic scenario of India where he laid down his head for the safety of brahmanic society and faith of whose he neither was a member nor he ever accepted their tenets. It was the urge for ethical values, justice and religious freedom which inspired him to sacrifice his head defying the tyrannical ruler's sword.

The aspect of goodness of human reality also cannot be overlooked. That is also all-pervasive in man-to-man relationship. Vasily Grossman in his book *Life and Fate* takes a detailed notice of this human reality while he portrays the times of Hitler and Stalin. This book represents the society as being completely dehumanized. However, in the decay of human relations in that sociological misery, goodness persists, in human relationships. This goodness becomes a mute inner dialogue full of piety with the other. The whole passage is a long monologue in which Mostov is in prison and undertakes to read the writings of Onnikov who in fact expresses the author's (Vasily Grossman's) idea. He reads "Most of those beings who inhabit the earth do not take as a goal, the definition of the good. In what does the good consist? The good is not in nature, and it is not in the preaching of prophets either, or in the great social doctrines, or in the ethics of the philosophers. But the simple people bear in their hearts the love of all living things; they love life naturally; they protect life". And a bit further he adds : "Thus there exists side by side with this so terrible greater good, human kindness in every day life. It is the kindness of an old lady who gives a piece of bread to a convict along the roadside. It is the kindness of soldier who holds his canteen out to a wounded enemy. The kindness of youth taking pity on old age, the kindness of peasant who hides an old Jew in his barn."

Now this goodness is without any thought, because it is a goodness outside all systems, all religions, all social organizations. However, the tragedy is that the moment this goodness gets organised it vanishes into the thin air. Bhai Kanhaiya, serving Guru Gobind Singh practised his goodness of the heart openly when he, without even an iota of hesitation served water to the wounded soldiers on both the sides in the battle. When the Guru came to know about his such a task full of kindness and goodness irrespective of any calculation, he gave him a few packs of balm as well to apply on the wounds of the fighting troops including those in the enemy ranks.

Levinas also, after about two centuries of Guru period, while talking about unconditional friendship among the people holds that the idea of proselytism, propaganda and finding of some most-common denominator platform setting apart, and considering that in certain conflicts persuasion itself becomes a sort of violence and repression, one should go on searching for a proximity beyond the ideas exchanged, a proximity that lasts even after the dialogue has become impossible. To create the conducive atmosphere for positive dialogue, the parties concerned should allow the unconditional friendship to take shape and persist. Levinas asserts in *Beyond Dialogue* that no party should be pressed hard to enjoy the role of victim nor one should be allowed to be reduced by compassion. None should be made to realize that he receives friendship as commiseration or as a pardon, granted after long quarrel. Discussing the reciprocity of the *I-you* relationship, Levinas quotes Buber that when I say *you*, I know that I am saying you to someone who is an *I*, who says *you* to me. Consequently in that I-you relation, we are immediately in society, but in a society in which we are equal in relation to one another. I am to other what other is to me. In fact, "What seems to me to be suggested by the philosophy of Dialogue, is that encounter", says Levinas, "with the other man which takes place neither on side street nor a detour nor some parallel track of transcendence, and that the face of the other bears the trace of its straightest, shortest and most direct movement."

Levinas sounds prophetic when one finds him asserting in his work *Alterity* and *Transcendence* that the "piety of the ordinary human cannot be expressed on the basis of any category. For the survival of the humanity we will have to enter the era in which the good must be loved without promises. This should be the end of all preaching." A new faith of human goodness will have to be emerged where faith will be without triumph, where saintliness will be the only irrefutable value and the only right to a reward would be not to expect one.

The goal set by Levinas is very high but he himself undertakes to explain the technique for achieving the same. He says, "One is required to work on one's ownself and to go towards the other where he is truly other from whom for an insufficiently mature soul, hatred flows naturally or is deduced with infallible logic. The themes of historical rights, 'right of enrootedness,' 'indeniable principles' are required to be avoided." Levinas adds further by saying, "One must refuse to be caught up in the tangle of abstractions, whose principles are often evident, but whose dialectic, be it so rigorous, is murderous and criminal..." However, he recommended the proximity of the honest attentive and the vigilant person for tackling a tension but he feels that without any definite project before them and mutual dialogue, the proximity of such persons even may resemble sleep which is not going to solve any problem. Rather these persons will fade away into words, will get lost in technical questions, freeze up into institutions or structures only. A new solidarity and religiosity through meaningful dialogue is required to be evolved by recognizing and identifying those insoluble substances which have the potential of exploding in violence, guile or politics.

While discussing the conception of Levinas that ontology is an attempt to reduce the 'other' to the same or 'beings' to 'Beings' we can, on the basis of Guru Granth Sahib, feel that Guru Nanak's supreme Being is not neutral impersonal stuff, who has nothing to do with the wailing and sufferings of the beings created by Him. Guru Granth says that He is diffused profusely in all the three worlds and is always with the beings. When the human beings are butchered by the tyrannical opperessors of the mankind, He is not required to be neutral and is bound to take sides of the down-trodden and oppressed ones. Rather, full of anguish, Guru Nanak does not hesitate in initiating the dialogue with the supreme Being and in blaming the Lord for watching the mighty, shreding to pieces the weaker ones-*Khurasan khasman kia Hindustan draia...eti mar pai karlane tain ki daradu na aia* (GGS 360). Guru Granth Sahib out of the sense of 'goodness without any calculation', holds that fight for righteousness and justice should be fought even if it is not in the case of one's own particular religion or social group. Following the footsteps of Guru Tegh Bahadur, Sikhs in general and their Jathedars, the likes of Banda Singh Bahadur fought, got captured and tortured to death for the sake of the down- trodden. The Sikh history, particularly of the eighteenth century reverberates with the thought of promotion and diffusion of goodness without any calculation, ethical values, justice and religious freedom require the openness of heart and mind.

In Guru Granth Sahib, the dialogue is the wholesome process of knowing, saying and understanding each other earnestly (GGS, P. 1411). For the accomplishment of this goal, Guru Granth Sahib, while telling the people *jab lagi dunia rahiai Nanak kichhu suniai kichhu kahiai*, further stresses before establishing a meaningful and factual dialogue, one should first take care of the self-analysis and introspection. In fact, Gurbani is well aware of the human reality that whose mind is all dark, they do not stand true to their words. Their heart lotus is inverse and does not bloom. Therefore, their high verbosity notwithstanding, they exhibit their inner ugliness. The accomplished persons are of dialogical nature, and have the humble competence of saying something as well as of understanding a viewpoint in its proper context. Guru Nanak hails such persons by marking them as the competent persons *(sugharh)*.

manhu ji andhe ghup kahia biradu na janani.
mani andhai undhai kaval disani khare karup.
iki kahi janani kahia bhujani te nar sugharh sarup.

According to Guru Granth Sahib, samvad or dialogue is the effort towards understanding the genuineness of the issues posed. In this great Granth, the base of a worthy life is the doctrine that one should have partnership with the virtues of the people and should keep away from mischiefs - *sanjh karijai gunah keri chhodi avagan chaliai*. Guru Granth gives no recognition to the life lived in monasteries or jungles, it rather approves that life which prepares the individual to be of the world while not becoming worldly. Sikh life is the life of responsibility towards the surrounding and therefore its spirituality and spiritual dialogue have some distinction with other ways of life. Sikh religion gives due importance to man as an individual but it does not allow the interests of the society to be sacrificed for the sake of one man, whosoever he may be. It approves humanitarianism but not humanism of the West because humanism can flourish only in autocracy, apostasy and narrowness of heart and mind. Also the dialogue with others in view of conquering one and all absolutely does not fit in the thought frame of Guru Granth Sahib. Guru Nanak being fully conscious of the egoist personality likely to emerge from debating behaviour pattern of the society, says that the seeker flourishes whereas the debater perishes *-khoji upajai badi binasai hau bali bali gur kartara*. Debate creates suicidal ego known as the chronic ailment *(diragh roga)* in Gurbani. Only *seva* or the service can help get rid of this malady. Guru Amar Das furthers the view of Guru Nanak by saying *-badi binsahi sevak sevahi gur kai heti piari* - the debater perishes and the humble-servant of the Guru serves with love and devotion. Namdev also holds that if somebody is desirous of enjoying the Ram-rasayan, he should never indulge in polemics - *bad bibad kahu sio na kijai, rasana ram rasayan pijai.*

To save the self from polemical and disputational egotist mentality, the Sikh religion and Guru Granth Sahib talk of a meaningful, factual and introspective dialogue. Guru Granth Sahib clearly denotes two types of dialogue. The first form of the dialogue is the one with the self, the self- appraisal or peeping into the self. Before the external dialogue, Gurbani inspires first to look into one's own heart and mind. Getting face to face with one's own self, one comes to know about his or her own meanness, shallowness, the layers of self-interest, greeds and diplomacies. So long we do not cleanse out these propensities with the broom of knowledge emanating from worldly thoughts, we cannot become pure and unpolluted and our external dialogue cannot be meaningful.

Self-analysis or the dialogue with the self brings forth the stage of auto-suggestion. For auto —suggestions, one need not search for any guru in a person. The basic truths of the life are so simple and straight that every individual can realize it himself. When the world is not stable and everything is in a flux and perishable then why this fat ego? The realization that how much this ego has made me hollow and how much suffering I myself have created can be attained only by having dialogue with one's own self. Such a person understands that he, while not becoming obstruction in the deeds being performed around in the will of God, should allow the flow of the divine Will unhindered praying for the victory of the Wondrous Lord, *Waheguru*.

The self-analysing person becomes impatient for the glimpse of the divinity of the soul. He does not hesitate to ask himself as to what he should offer to see the light of truth, which is equivalent to the light of myriads of suns or in the religious language the court of the truth *(sacha darbar)*. For dialogue, what type of language should he use so that the court of the truth fills him with love to accept the greatness of the cognitive truth at the appropriate time *(amritvela)*. And to live the life according to that truth is the answer emerged from inside the question for which no external polemic is needed:

Pher ki agai rakhiai jitu disai darbaru.
Muhau ki bolani boliai jitu suni dhare piaru.
Amrit vela sachu nau vadiai vicharu.

The person capable of initiating dialogue with his own self can control mad race of thoughts with full confidence. He, with the help of repeated auto-suggestions realizes the divine truth: *manu tu joti sarup hai apana mulu pachhanu. mani hari ji terai nali hai gurmati rang manu. e manu meria tu thir rahu chot na khavahi ram.*

But from the points alluded to above, this hypothesis would be wrong that the mind is quite simple, is always eager to attain divinity and could be brought to the right track easily. In Guru Granth Sahib, Kabir is fully conscious of this fact when he says that mind knows everything but still it undertakes to doing evil. How is it that carrying lamp in his hand, he is still falling into the well of hell- *Kabir manu janai sabh bat janat he auganu karai. Kahe ki kuslat hathi dipu kue parai*. But even then, giving suggestion to mind cannot be stopped similarly as the tillage of the land cannot be abandoned because the animal would destroy it, or because of the fear of theft we cannot repudiate the purchase of the households. Guru Amardas, in his longer hymns *Anandu,* goes on to suggesting the mind by saying-*e man meria tu sada rahu hari nale, Hari nali rahu tu manu mere dukh sabhi visarana.* O my mind! be always with the Lord. O mind, be with the Lord and all your sufferings will vanish.

The man who ponders over the greatness of God by himself becoming broadminded, the man who inspires the mind towards understanding its true form, enjoys the virtues of one and all. Such a person wears the silken clothing of pure life, becomes partner in the virtuous enterprises, neither memorises the mischief of others nor reminds others their evils. Wherever he goes or joins a discourse, he thinks of welfare of others and joyfully tries to understand the crux of the problem raised. The qualities alluded to above, belong to a dialogical personality hinted at in *Raga Suhi* hymns by Guru Nanak:

guna ka hovai vasula kadhni vasu laijai.
je guna hovani sajana mill sajh karijai.
sajh karijai gunah keri chhodi avagan chaliai.
pahire patambar kari adambar apana pirhu maliai.
jithaijae bahiai bhala kahiaijholi amritupijai.
guna ka hovai vasula kadhhi vasu laijai.

The second type of dialogue delineated in *Gurbani* is the external dialogue. Guru Nanak knew it very well that the work of reclamation of the withered soul of mankind could not be done without undertaking the device of dialogue. The main objective of his four itineraries was dialogue with the so-called upper and low strata of the society, the religious pundits and the laity. While understanding their mental agony, he provided solutions to their problems. In the *salokas* of Kabir, recorded in the Guru Granth Sahib, the dialogue loaded with social responsibility and spirituality between saint Namdev and Trilochan is there wherein *bhagat* Trilochan asks Namdev as to "Why he is always busy in printing the cloth and thus by getting deeply involved with mammon has forgotten the name of Ram." Bhagat Namdev replies: "O Trilochan, on lips one should have the name of Ram; with hands one should go on earning his bread and butter, but the heart should remain deeply imbued with the Lord":

> *Nama maia mohia kahai Tilochanu mit.*
> *kahe chhipahu chhailai Ram na lavahu chitu.*
> *Nama kahai Tilochana mukh te Ramu samali.*
> *hathpau kari kamu sabh chitu Niranjan nali.*

The first *Var* by Bhai Gurdas puts forth the scene of the dialogue between Guru Nanak and different yogis. In this dialogue, the Guru generally maintains his composure and most humbly states to the yogis that he has no miracle with him, except the true Name of the Lord. But irritated *yogi* Bhangarnath under the guise of dialogue, sarcastically remarks that "O! Nanak, why you have forsaken the garb of *yogis* and have put on the clothes of the householders. By repudiating the guise of the *yogi,* you are trying to mix vinegar with milk and spoiling the pure *yogic* life." Guru Nanak, understanding his arrogance and sarcasm, in view of putting a small check on his inflated ego, replies in the same vein.

Says Nanak: "O! Bhangarnath your mother (teacher) knows nothing. You do not know how the vessel should be cleansed and hence the odour destroys the fruit therein. You having repudiated household life but still go to the householders for begging. But mind it, you will get nothing without putting in something (in the form of labour).

The hagiographical literature pertaining to Guru Nanak and his hymns in the Guru Granth Sahib make it explicit that the Guru was in continuous discussion with the pedantic *pundits*, the *maulvis*, the *yogis* and a host of *pirs* and *faqirs*. Not only that, flashed before the world a new idea of acceptance of the greatness and truthfulness of others irrespective of their caste, colour and creed. To see it through, he collected the hymns of spiritual personalities from different corners of Asia.

The acceptance fills others with love for one and all and then one enjoys the spirit of dialogue with the others.

In *Gurbani,* the best example of the external dialogue is Guru Nanak's longer hymns *Sidh Gosti* (GGS 938-946) in which, through a spiritual dialogue the philosophy of yoga vis-a-vis Sikh philosophy of life has been elucidated. What type of mental balance and stability of mind is required to be held by the discussants, the Guru himself becomes the best example of the same. Yogi Charpat asks: "O Nanak! The world is unfathomable expansive sea; give your considered opinions as to how one can get across it." The answer by Guru Nanak full of courtesy, self-confidence and truth illustrates the nature, form and tradition of dialogue in Sikhism. Says Nanak: "O Yogi, you very well understand the crux of the question you expect me to answer. What answer I can put forth. I sincerely hold that you have already swum (this world ocean) and how could I find fault in your way and technique. As the lotus, though living in water does not allow the water to wet its petals and the water fowl also keeps its wings unwet, likewise by merging *surati* into *sabad* the world ocean may be got acrossed."

> *Dunia sagaru dutaru kahiai kiu kari paiai paro.*
> *Charpatu bolai audhu Nanak dehu sacha bicharo.*
> *Ape akhai ape samajai tisu kia utaru dijai.*
> *Sachu kahahu tun pargrami tujh kia baisanu dijai.*
> *Jaise jal mahi kamal niralam murgai naisane.*
> *Surati sabadi bhav sagaru tariai Nanak namu vakhane.*

This constructive aspect of dialogue, which without hurting anybody, capacitates him to explain his own view-point is the basis of dialogue in Guru Granth Sahib. Unfortunately, we all have discarded such attitude and the results are obvious. The Sikh community is divided and almost everybody is playing on his own tambourine. In the *Sidh Gosti* whether the questions are related to the individual or the common man, whether they are philosophical or ethical, the level of the dialogue is full of serenity, sobriety and mutual respect. In seventeenth and eighteenth stanza, the *siddhas* inquire of the Guru as to what is reason of abandoning the household and why you have put on the garb of a *yogi*. The answer is not only sincere and respectful but candid too- *Gurmukhi khojat bhae udasi. Darsan kai tai bhekh nivasi* i.e. in the search of Guru-oriented persons I have donned this garb of an ascetic. In *Sidh Gosti,* the problems of life right from earth to sky have been discussed but nowhere the bitterness comes to the forefront. The reason for such a phenomenon is that persons involved in such type of a dialogue don't have any greed, nor they are internally hollow. They are truly contented people with their respective ways of life. In the words of Bhai Gurdas, in his first *var,* Guru Nanak considers the *siddhas* much more full of will-power and capacity and perhaps that is why the Guru is said to have told them that if the *siddhas* like you would remain confined to the caves of the mountains, then who would lead the people in the world below - *Sidh chhapi baithe parbati kaunu jagati kau par utara.* If the dialogue is initiated with the intention of giving proper recognition to the other person, the result of such a dialogue would be much more meaningful and affirmative in nature.

While referring to the philosophy of dialogue as the first philosophy, Levinas holds that "To address someone expresses the ethical disturbance produced in me, in the tranquility of the perseverance of my being, in my egotism as a necessary state" ... May be Levinas is not wrong and it is very true of the western philosophy where in the name of dispassionate study, everything is objectified, but that is not the case with the Indian philosophy. Here, everything is considered perennially infused with the eternal spirit. Here every object of empirical world is trying to transcend itself in order to achieve the realization by merging into the divine spirit. All philosophies here tend to create a sense of awe, wonder or in Sikh parlance *Vismad.* In fact, the person having reached this state finds his ego melted with all delusion and disturbances of mind getting vanished. He creates a dialogue with the Supreme, becomes more stable, tranquil and steadfast. His dialogue becomes a natural flow of love for one and all.

The Concept of Sahaj: A Transpoetic View

Dr Gurbhagat Singh

An eminent Sikh Scholar Bhai Kahn Singh, the author of Gur Ratnakar Mahan Kosh, an encyclopaedia of Sikh Literature explains Sahaj as "Jo nal jamian" (that which accompanied birth). Sahaj can also be rendered as cosmic equilibrium, spontaneity, or the normal natural state of humans and things. A religious sect, known as Sahajiyan have also dealt with this concept in their texts. Sashibhusan Dasgupta, the author of a well-informed chapter on Sahajiyan a in his book *Obscure Religions Sects*, is of the view that Sahajiyani waltenschauung has its beginning and primary elaboration in the Dohas and songs composed between 8th and 12th centuries A.D. Some of their authors belonged to a city near Midnapore in Bengal where there were about 100-200 Buddhistic monasteries in the 7th century A.D. visited by the Chinese traveller Fa Hein and then by Hieun Tsang.

Dasgupta cites a Buddhistic tantric text entitled *Hevajra Tantra* that says: "The whole world is of the nature of Sahajaṭ the Sahaja is the quantessence of all, quaintessence is Nirvana to those who possess the perfectly pure Chitta." But though this Sahaj in the form of Mahasukh in and through a physiological process, it should never be conceived as something belonging to the body. It is clear that Sahaj is innate, eternal and all-prevailing. To realize it consciously, one has to attain to pure mind or Bodhi Chitta, as has also been emphasized in the Dohas and songs. *Bodhi Chitta* is a combination of Shunayta (void) and Karuna (compassion). When the Chitta is attuned, its constituent material elements or *Sikandhas* disappear; the Chitta stays perfectly in vacuity," testifies the poet Kanhapada in a song.

Shunyata or vacuity is not nothingness. As the second century A.D. Buddhist-philosopher Nagarjuna says, it is the transmental realization of *Partityasamutpad* which can be translated into English as "co-dependent origination." It means that everything for its causation depends upon another of others. For that reason no self-assertion leads to knowledge or Gyan in the Buddhistic sense. Every self or being is voided. Nagarjuna's idea is partially close to what the Dutch-Jewish philosopher Spinoza says in the 17th century work, *Ethics*: "A body in motion or at rest must be determined for motion by some other body, which likewise was determined for motion or rest by some other body". Spinoza's contemporary Leibniz, German philosopher, also in his theory of "monads" accepts monads as simple substances out of which everything else is made, although he assigns an ontological unity with form to each unit. Leibniz's monad therefore is a paradox of individuation and otherness, while in the Buddhistic sense a paradox is particularity and vacuity. From the perspectives of Spinoza and Leibniz, Sahaj would be an intermediate state in which energies of several ontological units flow with their own flavours. This notion of intermediacy or dependence, as scholars acknowledge now, originates with the notion of monad in the Greek Pythagoreans and the Italian philosopher Bruno (1548-1600).

The difference between the Western perspectives of co-dependence and Buddhistic Sahajiyani perspectives is that whereas the former is God-centered, the latter is liberative from the theo-centre. The theo-centredness in the early

Buddhistics period which in Medieval India was hijacked by the Brahmaincal elite through the non-dualistic Brahmn of Upanishads and Vedantic thought. Dasgupta is not correct when he says: "This Sahajiyani Sahaja is the Brahman of Upanishads and the Vedanta". The final objective in the Sahajiyani Sahaj is not the realization of non-dual Brahman as Atma or Meta-self, but its *tthatha* or Suchness by awakening the four Lotus-plexes of higher nerve-centres, that is, *Nirman Kaya* (the subtle body of transformation), *Dharam Kaya* (the subtle unitive body), *Sembhog Kaya* (the Subtle body of bliss) and the *Sahaj Kaya* (the subtle body of Bodhi Chitta combining Shunyata and Karuna). The fourth *Kaya* was the Sahajiyani innovation. It leads to Mahasukha or Bliss. It is located in the *usmis kanal* or the supreme lotus.

Infact, behind the objective of Sahaj realization is concealed the context between the hegemonic Brahmanism and the hegemonized downtrodden. Sahaj tattava is revealed as a fully lotus-centered Kundalini, the effeminate energy, called Nairatma and Dombi. Dombi was a low and untouchable caste. In a Sahajiyani song, the poet Kanha-pada addresses the yogini Dombi: "I embrace the yogini......O yogini......I shall not live even for a moment without thee—I shall kiss thy life and drink the lotus juice."

The elaboration of Sahaj suggests that it is a complex sign with several signifides related to physiology, consciousness and the tensorial class contest. Sahaj can also be called ambiguous allegory, but an allegory not in the classical moral sense with a one-dimensional ethics. Allegory in our contemporary ethnographic, tearing apart the hegemonic meaning and denuding the socio-cultural content and polar visions. Influenced by Jacques Derrida and Walter Banjamin, an anthropologist, James Clifford talks of allegory that brings into the mind not just the hegemonic level but also the "other levels" by which he means the levels that have been repressed.

Unity that does not exist in the socio-historical structure, a Sahahjiyani endeavours to obtain in the "heart" as a *Sadhak fohthe* Buddha Chitta, the fully-awakened Kundalini Dombi is mediated by the Nirman Kaya, Dharma Kaya, Sambhog Kaya before entering the Sahaj Kaya. Several differential nerves or faculties are said to meet here. Idha (the left nostril nerve) and Pingala (the right nostril nerve) with their breath energies meet in Sushumna (the spinal centre) also called Avadhutika. The vital synthetic breath finally dies when Sahaj is obtained. It is in all Shunya. In a text entitled, *Panca Krama,* four Shunyas have been mentioned: Shunya, Ati-Shunya, Maha-Shunya, and the Sarv-Shunya in which Sahaj is realized.

In the *Hathyoga Pradipka* which is accepted by Briggs as a Hindu tantric text written by Chintamani in the 13th century, it is said in Chapter IV on Samadhi; "Raj Yoga, Samadhi,...... Jiwan Mukti, Sahaj, Turya, are all synonymous". Reverberating Patanjali's Yoga Sutras it is further said: "...when all *sankalpas* cease to exist is called Samadhi. When the great Kundalini awakens, then the Prana becomes absorbed in Shunya Samadhi".

In both Sahjiyan and Hath Yoga, through the physiological process of breath control or pranayam, the goal is to attain to the Sahaj Samadhi that is void, empty of all concepts and constructions of the mind. In the Hath Yoga, Atma remains behind, in the Sahajiyan it is just void or disappearance of any structure like Atma, but both agree that in the Shunya, whether atmic or noratmic, *anhad nad*/unstruck symphony is heard. The *Hath Yoga Pradipka* says that in this Sahaj Samadhi "ecstasy is spontaneously produced". In the last stage, the *Pradipka* says; "sounds, resemble those from tinklets, flute, Vina, bee". The English translator of the text Pancham Sinh adds: "By hearing these sounds attentively one gets concentration of the mind, and thence Sahaj Smadhi".

The realization of Sahaj, both in Sahajiyan and Hindu Yogic texts, is voluntary. Through effort, an ecstatic of samadhic state is obtained in which concepts are erased. A vital question to be asked is: Why this Shunayta or void that liberates and makes one a *jivan mukta* and frees in life? The question of freedom and liberation by awaking one's sleeping or repressed energies is related to the counter-semiotic/allegorical base of Sahaj. As mentioned above, the force that is to be aroused through Sahaj is the Dombi force, the energy of those who were marginalized. The counter or resurrectional aspect of Sahaj has been missed so far in various interpretations.

It was a thunderous or vajra idea in the ancient and medieval India that Nirvana was possible without reading or rational efforts. It can be obtained through a tranced consciousness in the Buddhistic Sahajiyani sense. In our times, Husserl has suggested that through noesis/intenationality, it is possible to concentrate when in a transcendental reduction, essences or objects are intuited directly, although consciousness remains in the lived world, i.e. *Lebenswelt.* But during this intuition the world remains bracketed. It is Merleau-Ponty, a French philosopher, who tells us that "all consciousness is perceptual. The perceiving mind is an incarnated mind......the roots of the mind in its body and in the mind". If the so-called higher consciousness is also rooted in the bodiated perception and the body is radiated by the world, then, the higher consciousness also would be guided at least partly by the existential worldly condition of the perceiver. Using Merleau-Ponty's light, then, the "freedom of consciousness" would be limited. In the context of this debate, it is possible to say that Sahaj Samadhi or the consciousness of erasure/de-scription was a consciousness for an alternate way of life, the way that could awaken the repressed energies, the Kundalini Dombi of the marginalized, and also simultaneously awakening the energy of the privileged who have put their humanistic self to sleep under their hegemonic aggression.

Erasure of the mind when it can hear the Unstruck Melody or the Creative Sound of total and integrative cosmic life, is the main theme of Sahaj. Void, therefore is needed to depress and liberate the sweeping energies and enable human beings to be part of the vast creative and enlightening consciousness. It is both to rise from marginalization and to stop marginalizing. This becomes clear when we get to the composition of Sri Guru Granth Sahib.

The Sahaj of Sri Guru Granth Sahib is simultaneously enlightened thought, quintessence of knowledge, manifestation of light *(jot)* and Sahaj Samadhi. It is listening to the *anhad dhuni* (unstruck/ceaseless sound) says Guru Ram Das in Rag Sarang. Bhagat Kabir says in Rag Gauri that the devotee becomes Sahaj-ecstatic. Sahaj is an ecstasy-giver or *kalalan*. But this ecstasy is a combination of transmittal bliss and knowledge that arises from being with Waheguru, the Guru of Wonder. The "sexo-yogic" joy of the tantric Sahaj, and the rise of the Kudalini in the *daswan duar*/tenth door integrating Siva-Sakti. The moon and the sun of the Hath Yoga, has been transformed into the joy and sacred meeting with the Guru of Wonder. It is a sense of "Bismad", says Guru Arjan in Rag Sarang. Sahaj thus is burst in song. Only singing the Guru of Wonder helps. Without this even all speech is vain, says Guru Ram Das in Sri Rag. The poets of the Guru Granth Sahib do not leave the liberative Sahaj to a state of emptiness or filled by mere rasa-giving Kundalini, they associate it with a meeting with the Guru of Wonder who is the creator of the Wondrous diversity. This diversity, according to Guru Nanak Dev in Rag Asa, is in accordance with His Hukam or Commandment:

Vismad/Wonderous Joy is sound, Vismad Vedas
Vismad beings, Vismad diversity
Vismad forms, Vismad colours

To associate Sahaj with the Guru of Wonder, the Causer of diversity that awakens sacred symphony is to advance the Sahaj and the Hathyogic counter sign/allegory of Sahaj to new dimensions. It is a fully setup countersign that not only wrecks in practice the hegemonic/unitarian mind and body affected by the imperial Sultans but also demolishes them as transient and false. In Rag Majh, Guru Ram Das says very strongly: "The kings and high officials of the subjects will not last, their shops, cities, bazars will all fall according to the divine commandment. The reason is given by Guru Nanak Dev in the same Rag asserting that these kings and high officials "suck the blood of human beings" and they do not have "pure minds" (Nirmal cheet).

The Sahaj of the Guru Granth also initiates a new "biopolitics." The body and mind that attain to Sahaj in Vismad will be guided by the Guru of Wonder and His wonderous, diverse creation. The de-scribing that this Sahaj works, is a further step in advancing the counter sign/allegory of Sahaj. The "biopolitics" shapes or reverses consciousness in which there is liberation from Maya or transient reality and one is weaved in the Sahaj of void, that is, one is not affected by the system privileging family, cast, says Bhagat Kabir in Rag Bhairo:

> *In this reversal are forgotten both family and caste.*
> *We are now weaved in sunna-sahaj (void of Sahaj).*

The new Sahaj weave of which Kabir talks here is very significant. In our contemporary idiom it can mean the total socio-cultural network that shapes a being and generates her biopolitics. The Gurus and Bhagats of the Guru Granth were not unaware of this aspect. The counter sign Sahaj of the Guru Granth has several signifieds that have not been made appropriately visible so far.

In Rag Asa, Guru Arjan Dev says: "Oh friends! Plant the crop of Nam. The quintessence of Waheguru/Transact the service everyday. At the shop of Bliss and Sahaj/Be in the network of Waheguru the Banker and trader. "The Guru poet is suggesting altering trade and agriculture alienated from Truth and Wonder. If trade and agricultural operations do not lead the bio-mental existence into the sacred wonder, then those need to be reorganized. In Rag Ramkali Guru Nanak Dev again relates the signifieds of Sahaj, truth and trade, when he says: "A Gurmukh's body is a shop the mind a trader." Says Nanak, the trade is a sacred transformation. In Rag Gauri Guareri Guru Nanak Dev gives the notion of Sabat Poonji or de-alienated/holistic capital. Apart from its spiritual and theological meanings, it has another signified also that suggests the possibility of generating sacred or de-alienated capital.

The Guru Says:

> *Sabat Poonji comes in the company of the True Guru.*
> *With this capital, wealth and wares will remain holistic.*

The same signified of sacred/de-alienated/holistic capital has been repeated by Bhagat Ravidas in Rag Gauri Bairagan when he says: "We are the traders of Ram transacting in Sahaj, I have loaded *Ram Dhan*/sacred capital, the world carries poison". This trade or transaction is of intelligence and enlightenment (*Budh Bibek*). Only this transaction makes one wealthy (*Dhanvanta)*, says Guru Arjan Dev in Rag Bhairo.

The qualitative difference between the Sahajiyani-Hathyogic and the Guru Granth Sahib is the whereas the former remains restricted to alteration of consciousness through physiological and meditational processes, the latter goes beyond. The Guru Granth poets are not simply directing phenomenological energies and urging "absolute union" with the universe as Professor Niharranjan elaborates. The Guru Granth poets are combining as well as directing all velocities including the historical and cultural ones. For this reason, Sirdar Kapur Singh has called the Sikh revelation and historical epiphany mental, physiological, political, economical, transactional. All energies are directed and harmonized in the Sikh Sahaj that initiated multiple praxis leading to the Sikh revolution. In a recent work entitled *Time for Revolution*, an Italian philosopher Antonio Negri has talked of Einstein's accomplishment as "the co-ordination of different velocities. The Sikh Sahaj is not only a co-ordination but also a teleological movement of different velocities. The counter sign or counter allegory of Sahaj, thus, has itinerated from the phenomenological to the multi-velocital and praxive.

Ethical Concepts in Guru Granth Sahib

Dr. Darshan Singh

Ethics is a method of theorising moral aspect of a group of people— group in the sense of race, religion or community. Sometimes, a political group is also relevant for this purpose. Every community or a group of people has some ethical perceptions according to which they desire to live. Therefore, when we talk of ethical concepts of a group of people, we mean how that group of people wants to live in different areas of life i.e. political, social and religious.

Broadly speaking, life, according to Sikh Gurus is a period in which one is expected to play a given role. The excellence of an individual life consists in how faithfully, meaningfully and efficiently one palys this role. The dichotomy of pre-determinism and free will is resolved by the Sikh Gurus in order to make their convictions workable. They are of the opinion that all the major decisions about an individual are taken by God himself. An individual is born with a definite amount of freedom to choose his actions but whenever he/she transgresses the given freedom, the Giver, the God, has the ultimate power to intervene and put the transgressing individual on the right path. Therefore, the freedom to choose action within a given paradigm is an inherent capacity given to every individual. Sikhism has its opinion on different aspects of life. It has a set of morals to be expected and practised in life.

Therefore, they have their convictions, relating to political, social and religious life of an individual and also of a group, which form the ethics of Sikhism.

Political Ethics

Politics means a theory, according to which a relationship between a citizen and state is to be determined. This relationship should be conducive to the fullest growth in all directions of life and should also be a guarantee for complete internal and external security. Unfortunately, it is not what we normally find in the actual life. It was particularly true during the period of Guru Nanak, who right from the beginning was committed to provide the type of political ethics which can provide meaningful relationship between the ruler and the ruled. Thus, Guru Nanak, throughout his writings makes a commitment to change the political system so that the oppressed, the slaves and the dishonoured could live an honourble life. His emphasis was on changing internal as well as external reality. He elaborates upon the system in which no transgression could be enforced. For this desired change, Guru Nanak started his struggle which continued during the succeeding Gurus too but the basic commitment, on which the struggle was started, remained the same. This struggle was actually to bring a discernible change in the political ethics of the time.

In his Babar Bani and at many other places, he has given the reasons for which the people suffered at the hands of the rulers. He is of the opinion that:

i. The political set-up was so irresponsible to the situation that it had no interest in the protection of the subjects. He says, "Kings and courtiers were like wolves and hounds[1]".
ii. Because of the indulgence in luxury in terms of wealth and women, the ruling class was reduced to inaffectiveness[2]. They were not in a position to deliver justice to the poeple.

iii. The total ruling elite was reduced to such a category of people who lost their vision. They could not foresee even the apprent threats in the prevailing conditions. Therefore, they could also not visualise the impending Babar's invasion and the resulting destruction[3].

iv. They were reduced to the status of a poor cow before a wolf[4].

Frequent references are available in Guru Nanak's Bani about the redundant political system. He is of the opinion that the ruling class was completely given to corruption. It had eaten into the vitals of all the institutions. Judiciary was manipulated, courtiers were bribed and other functionaries were irresponsive to the cause of justice. This situation was dominating to such an extent that the functionaries of the state were working against their declared duty and objectives. Instead of protecting the life and honour of the people they themselves were looting the both[5].

Luxury penetrated so much into the life of those functionaries that they lost all sense of proportion[6]. As a result of this the total value-system of the contemporary ruling class was degenerated[7]. Freedom of worship of occupation and of speech was assailed by will. Cultural suppression was committed without any fear. People were being forced and tempted to conversion and forced to adopt the life style of the ruler[8]. In the process, they were abandoning their language, dress and mannerism[9].

In order to perpetuate their rule, the contemporary rulers were attempting to divide the people also. This attempt was so apparent that a type of tax[10] (Jazia) was imposed upon non-Muslims. They were asked either to embrace Islam or to pay the tax. By introducing such laws, the government perpetuated the division between the followers of two religions and thus tried to prolong their rule. Most of the leaders of the contemporary society accepted this as their fate. Those who did not submit to subjugation, escaped to jungles and mountains in the name of attaining salvation. In the eyes of Guru Nanak, it was an act of betryal on their part. He severely criticised those who accepted it as their fate and also those who retired to jungles and mountains in the name of personal liberation.[11]

Guru Nanak resolved to face the situation. He decided to side with the suffering people. Naturally, his decision was to participate in the process of change which was to be brought about in the destiny of the people. He devised a kind of specific ethics to meet the situation and to seek the deliverance of the people from perpetual oppression. For this he wrote, sang, travelled and preached extensively. He worked on two fronts. Firstly, he tried to awaken and regenerate the life in the people and secondly, he worked out an alternative system primarily aimed at transforming the existing political set-up. Guru Nanak was convinced as he spoke about it in his Bani that change in the political system was very essential for bringing about a change in the life of the people. For this purpose he gave a vivid depiction of the corrupt political, social and religious institutions and tried to create awareness about this situation in the minds of the people, and thus bring about a change.

He was convinced that unless people were made aware to their impending miseries, there can be no meaningful resistance to this political order. He reminded them of their spiritual, cultural and political deprivation and inspired them to abandon the attitude of a defeated people. He not only awakened them but also presented before them an alternative model of government, which would leave no chance for the infringement into the peoples' rights, liberty and their choice of religion and language. The contemporary political system was that of monarchy. Guru Nanak advocated for a political system which ensures a fully grown, awakened and healthier society. For this purpose, he outlined a set-up of his vision. Frequent references to this effect are available in his Bani. Even in Japuji

Sahib, such references are available wherein the political system of his conception is outlined. For example:

Night, season, date and day
Air, water, fire (elements) and under regions,
In (the mutual gravitation of) these,
He has established earth (Dharam Sal),
A place for meriting religion.
On this earth there is a variety of life, colour and kind.
Endless is the variety in their names,
Everyone is judged by one's actions.
True is He and true is His court
In His Court, the accepted five sit in their grandeur,
They (five) are blessed with His insignia, (flag)
True and false are judged by them.
Saith Nanak: Those who repeat (His name)
are distinguishable. (Pauri: 34)

This stanza (Pauri) gives us the picture of Guru Nanak's mind on a political system. This I shall discuss in the following lines. But, before that, let us have a look at the terminology used by Guru Nanak in other parts of Japuji Sahib. He uses the words like: Padshah, Sultan (King), Hukam, Farman (order), Nashan (flag), Amar, Raj (rule), Diban, Darbar (court), Taksal (mint). This and the following points will prove his concern for a better political system; resulting into a change in political ethics:

a) **Sangat** (Congregation): Guru Nanak gave a concept of congregation. There are references to the fact that he established Sangats wherever he went. In this system, Sangat was rated as supreme body. Smaller Sangats were affiliated with the central Sangat.
b) **Individual**: An individual in Guru Nanak Bani is a sovereign and a respected member of Sangat having equal rights for participation in its proceedings irrespective of caste, colour, sex and religion.
c) **Ruler**: Sangat, in Guru Nanak Bani, is the only competent authority to select the ruler. The selection of a ruler will

not be on the basis of his divine rights, family rights or his birth rights, but it will purely be a choice based on merit. In Guru Nanak's concept, a ruler is not the owner or the master but only a custodian, given powers by the Sangat to function in a particular way. On the authority given by the Sangat to him, he may appoint his council of ministers. This position will also be given to a person purely on his merit. No other consideration will ever matter.

d) **Panj Pyaras** (Five beloved ones): At the centre of Sangat and an individual or the ruler, there is an institution of five-beloved ones (Panj Pyaras), who are again selected from amongst the Sangat. They represent the Sangat and also they guide the ruler. They are, in fact, the real executive power in the state. Their power is not limited to the politiccal matters only. They have the authority to guide and keep a constant vigilance on the functioning of every institution i.e. religious, social, political etc. Of course, they are selected by the Sangat, but once they are selected and are in office, their unanimous advice will be applicable to all. Every individual, as a member of the Sangat can aspire to be one of the five-beloved ones or one of the rulers.

This institution of five-beloved ones* was conceived by Guru Nanak as is evident from the above quoted pauri of Japuji Sahib. Their exalted position was kept alive by the succeeding Gurus and was strengthened by the tenth Master, as after baptising them with Amrit (Nectar), he

* *Guru Nanak says, "In Gurmat (Sikhism) five beloved ones are the sons of Guru". Maru M. 1*

- *The five beloved ones at the time of Guru Arjan Dev were: Bhai Bidhi Chand, Bhai Jetha, Bhai Langah, Bhai Pirana, Bhai Pera.*
- *The five beloved ones at the time of Guru Teg Bahadur were: Dewan Mati Dasa, Bhai Gurdita, Bhai Dayala, Bhai Ude, Bhai Jaita.*
- *The five beloved ones who were baptised by Guru Gobind Singh were: Bhai Sahib Singh, Bhai Daya Singh, Bhai Dharam Singh, Bhai Mohkam Singh, Bhai Himat Singh.*

bowed before them and requested them to baptise him in return, in the way he had baptised them. This act of Guru Gobind Singh explains as to how much important the institution of five beloved ones is, how much reverence the collective will of Khalsa is given and how the position of Guru and Sikh exchanges itself at times! Thus, the institution of Panj Pyaras was not conceived as new at the time of Guru Gobind Singh. It is part of the basic structure of Sikhism since the day of its inception. It was for the first time in the history of mankind that an individual was given so much recognition and importance.

Sangat has the authority to replace any functionary of the government as well as five-beloved ones. Therefore, all functionaries retained their positions subject to their ability and performance. In case of a non-performer or a bad performer, the Sangat has the authority to replace him. In each case, Sangat as well as an individual as a member of it, is the real power.

In this structure, only God is the supreme sovereign. Even a king is not sovereign. He is only a ruler, given to rule till he merits it. The ownership of every institution belongs to God. Sangat represents the real sovereign force. And as an individual represents and constitutes the Sangat, therefore, he is also sovereign. The procedure of appointing the functionaries shall not be by the majority but by consensus, depending upon the merit of the person. This model of a government, given by Guru Nanak in his Bani, caught the imagination of the people in such a way that most of the nations of the world adopted this system, after modifying it a little to suit to their local conditions.

Social Ethics

Social ethics demarcate the behaviour of an individual and also of a social group with another individual or a social group. Sikhism provides very strong foundation for evolving a social ethics, characterised by the founding principles of Sikhism. It offers a distinctive concept of social ethics based upon individual ethics, based on the following principles:

1. Each individual is the manifestation of God, the formless, one and same. Therefore, from this point of view, there is no difference between one and another individual.
2. Each individual is made of the same flesh, bones and blood.
3. Every individual has the same kind of body, consisting of the same five elements — fire, air, water, sound and earth — and is blessed with the same kind of inner and outer organisms, which means the basic instinct and the way to satisfy them are the same.
4. He takes birth and dies the same way.

   Guru Gobind Singh, the 10th Guru says:

   Someone has become Sanyasi
   And another one is Yogi
   Someone is celibate
   Someone wants to be known as pure
   Someone is Hindu
   Another one is believer in Islam
   But the humankind is same
   And it must be recognised so.
   The kind creator is same
   The merciful giver is same
   There is no difference
   None should be illusioned otherwise,
   One is to be served
   He is the only Guru of all
   One is the form
   All must be known as His light

   ....

   Temple and Mosque are same
   The worship and Namaz (Muslim worship) is same,
   All human beings are one
   But manifestation is diverse

....

The same eyes, the same nose, the same body and the same habits,
All are the combination of
earth, air, fire, sound and water.
Allah and unknowable are same
Puran and Kuran are same
There is only one form
All are made in the same way. (Akal Ustat)

Therefore, fundamentally and substantially, every individual is the same. Any argument or any theory philosophical or scientific, which perpetuates division between one individual and another individual, is outrightly rejected by Sikhism. It is in this context that the Sikh concept of social ethics is universal.

Practically speaking, Sikhism believes that there are three reasons which apparently induce one to believe in a division between different individuals and groups. This type of social behaviour is responsible for the devaluation of the human exsitence. The three reasons are:

1. Ignorance
2. Ego
3. Greed

1. **Ignorance**: It creates a false barrier, blinds the individual and divides the society into groups. Sikhism believes that only right type of education is the remedy for this disease. This education should include three stages for completing its process, that is, (i) to create curiosity to know more, (ii) to reflect upon whatever is learnt and (iii) to dedicate whatever is learnt and reflected upon to the service of the humanity.
2. **Ego**: It is traditionally considered to be a disease which paralyses the creativeness, inherent in every individual. The Sikh attitude about this is at variance with the western ethos. The western mind insists upon building one's ego,

treating it essential for promoting individualism. Even the state by giving more attention to an individual, particularly to a child fuels the individual ego. It feeds and grooms an individual into a totally alienated person. The Sikh ethics does not agree either with the eastern mind, which considers it as a disease and a means to create disorder, nor with the western mind, which treats it as existential reality. Guru Nanak has re-defined the meaning of word *Haumai,* the source of ego. Ego, according to him, is one factor which is solely responsible for individual's awareness about self-identity. Every thought and action is guided by it. Traditionally, it is considered to be an impediment on the way to self-realization. Guru Nanak agrees with it but at the same time he pleads that if given a correct perspective and canalization, it is also capable of remedying the said hindrance. Not only this, it creates wonders in almost all the areas of life. It is this force which, if rightly directed, animates the ability to create in the realm of art and culture, thus leading towards finer and higher levels of life.

This is the nature of ego, actions are due to it.
Ego is thus a bondage which commits
to the birth and death repeatedly.
Where does this ego take birth from?
With which discipline it vanishes?
Ego is under His order,
And it keeps the wheel moving.
Ego is severe disease,
But medicine is also in it.
If He (God) blesses, one meditates
upon the word of Guru.
Saith Nanak: listen with this discipline
the sorrows vanish.

Thus Guru Nanak distinguishes between the raise of I-ness (Haumai) and ego. If I-ness i.e. self is linked with ego, it is disastrous but if it is linked with the spirit, changed into superego, it is most creative.

3. **Greed**: It is also a reason for creating dissensions in the society. This results into a madrace for economic status. This attitude divides a society into different groups of Haves and Have-nots. It promotes, on the one hand, hoarding, embezzlement and a race for accumulating wealth at all costs and on the other hand, it generates poverty, frustration, sluggishness and a number of social evils. These social evils in the end prove counter-productive. If deprivation is the reason for degeneration, the affluence is also a kind of disease which may at times become the source of incurable handicaps. Therefore, the Sikh concept of ethics does not permit such tendencies to originate. It only discards those tendencies by saying:

   We cannot accumulate wealth,
   without commiting crimes (M. 1, SGGS, p. 417)

This concept of ethics also presents an alternative also. In this context, it says:

> *Those who accumulate wealth are in fact beggars*
> *And those in whose mind you (God) abide,*
> *They are the real treasures of virtues,*
> *(M.1, SGGS, p. 1287)*

In this way, Sikhism tries to provide a concept of ethics which would help in building a balanced society.

In modern times, religion is being accused for creating narrow individualism to divide a society. This allegation that religion divides is, at least, not applicable to the Sikh religion. On the other hand, it eliminates the grounds on which the people are divided. Thus, Sikhism has attempted to re-define even the religion. The Sikh religion is not a religion in the traditional sense. It does not confine itself to the worship of the deity, prostration before the deity or to pray for personal salvation. On the other hand, it is a commune. It works as a co-operational religion which concerns for the well-being of all. It has simplified its religious tenets in such a way that it believes in the unity of God and the mankind. Secondly, remembering of God and the physical work of an individual is combined into one action. It advocates for an active life, based on eternal truth. The journey of an individual, according to Sikhism, is from eternity to eternity.

In Japuji Sahib, Guru Nanak has detailed his religious ethical concepts through an individual whom he has termed as *sachiar* (one who lives a truthful living). He has used this word at three places. In the first place, he uses it in the form of a question mark. *Sachiar* is his ideal man, who embodies spiritual as well as physical powers in him. This is one word through which Guru Nanak is explaining his grand design of the total universal set up and an individual's place and role in it. He says:

Worrying brings no result even if
one worries a lac times.
(Idiomatic use of word soch)
Silence does not silence even if
one observes it continuously
Lust does not quench lust even if
one gathers in abundance
Wisdom of thousands and lacs kinds is of no avail.
How then to become a sachiara?
(one who lives a truthful living).
How to break the wall of falsehood?
By realising the Order,
By living by the will
Nanak writes alongwith (Pauri: 1)

It is clear that in Guru Nanak the ideal of *sachiara* takes the precedence over every other ideal even that of attaining salvation. *Sachiara* is really an emancipated person in this world and the world to come. At another place, Guru Nanak has illustrated his answer to the above question. He says:

> *True is Master, true is His name,*
> *Endless are the expressions of love,*
> *Beggars beg for more and more,*
> *Giver gives endlessly,*
> *Then, what to present before Him (God),*
> *In order to have an access to His court.*
> *Whic words should one speak that will attract His love for him.*
> *Get up early in the morning,*
> *Reflect upon the greatness of His true Name.*
> *Body is due to one's actions,*
> *But liberation is due to His grace.*
> *Saith Nanak: By believing (and acting) like this,*
> *Everyone will naturally be a Sachiara*
> *(one who lives a truthful living). (Pauri: 4)*

The use of the word *Sachiar* clarifies the daily code of an ideal man of Guru Nanak. In the third place again Guru Nanak uses this world in a conditional sense. He says,"If someone realises it, he becomes a *Sachiara*". (Pauri: 16)

While going through all the above quoted references, it can be concluded that in Guru Nanak Bani, especially, Japuji Sahib, *sachiara* is the highest position which an individual may strive to achieve. At another place, he says that truthful living is higher than even truth itself[12]. The use of this word signifies that Guru Nanak does not split the reality into units. His emphasis is upon transmitting secular in spiritual and thus bringing the spirituality into human actions. *Sachiara* is a living being, he is a social entity, he has a social role and he is a symbol of the desired change in the future social reality. He is invested with divine qualities at the same time. This was the concept which flowered into the concept of Saint-soldier at the time of Guru Gobind Singh. Guru Gobind Singh's ideal man is one who is in constant struggle against any kind of oppression and at the same time he is in tune with the Supreme Reality. An individual of Guru Gobind Singh's conception combines the traits of physical and moral discipline in him.

In this way Sikhism conceived of ethical concepts and pressed them through history to build a healthy and wholesome society. Guru Nanak has given a spiritual foundation to all his concepts. When we try to understand his concepts regarding political, social, economic or religious values, we find that the process the presence of God continues to remain as its quintessence. A close examination of the Bani proves the idea that the ultimate concern of Sikhism is the well being of every individual as well as of all the people of the world. Sikhism does not believe in discrimiation and deprivation. It is because of this that all its ethical concepts are directed towards the achievement of this goal, the goal which brings similar fruits for all.

References

1. Asa Di Var, M. 1
2. The dogs have destroyed their pearl (like country) and none will remember them after their death, Asa M. 1, page 360
3. If they could have given thought earlier, they would not have undergone this punishment, Asa M. 1, page 360
4. If this powerful wolf pounced upon the herd (of poor cows), M. 1, page 360
5. Greed and sin, both are king and his minister, falsehood has become the seeker. Cupidity is the assistant who sits on the judgement, M.1, page 468
6. By indulging in luxury, the kings have lost their sense, M. 1, page 417
7. The king is ruling like a ruler who has collected wealth by cruel means, M. 1, page 391
8. Self-respect and righteousness, both have disappeared. O! Lalo falsehood has gained prominence. The Kazi and Brahman (Muslim and Hindu priests) are no more in demand.

   Now hymns are read by the wicked, M. 1, page 722
9. The recognition was being sought by wearing blue clothes. The Puran (Hindu holy book) was being worshipped after receiving ill-gotten money, M. 1, page 471

- Everyone in the family has become a 'mian' (ruler's way of address) and has adopted the languages of other's (ruler's), M. 1, page 1191

10. You are imposing tax on Cow and Brahman, M.1, page 471
    - Peasant is dedicated to cultivation but he bears the punishment when king asks for taxes, M. 1, page 416
    - None will ask for Jazia (tax), M. 5, page 420
11. What are your looking for in the forests?
    I own a great forest withing myself.
    by repeating the Word, the truth will stay within.
    Where-ever I see, I find Him, I know none else
    By endeavouring to work for Guru, one enters,
    His place. — Asthtapadi
12. Sri Guru Granth Sahib, M. 1, page 62

Guru Granth Sahib and Religious Pluralism

Dr. Dharam Singh

Introduction

Guru Granth Sahib, the holy scripture of the Sikhs, is also the Guru-Eternal for them: they revere it as their living spiritual mentor but do not worship it as an idol on the altar. First compiled in 1604, it chronologically belongs to medieval times but an in-depth study of the faith reveals its critical attitude towards the medieval spirit and its responsiveness to several of the issues facing mankind today. One such issue is that of religious plurality. During the past hundred years or so the infotech revolution and development of fast means of transportation have transformed this big world into a small global village. As a result, people with different cultural, religious and racial backgrounds are now our next-door neighbours. Different faith-communities inter-penetrate and inter-act with one another on daily basis.

Attitude towards other Faiths

In today's pluralistic global village man cannot run away from or wish away the social reality of religious plurality and the social and theological issues arising from it. Gone are the days when one lived in his own tiny, isolated religious camp, blissfully ignorant of who existed or whatever happened outside. Today, people of different religious denominations have to live together and interact with one another. However, unfortunately, each faith-community is not in harmonious relationship with the other. This has been mainly due to the fact that each religious community tends to underrate the ideology and culture of the other. And this usually stems from the way leaders of each religion claim monopoly of truth or their faith. To them, only their religion, or only their prophet, can lead people on the path to God-realization and self-realization. Other religions are treated by them as fake or inauthentic, and other faith-communities as pagan. This exclusivist attitude[1] is doing much damage to our social fabric. We must realize that "the religious life of mankind from now on, if it is to be lived at all, will be lived in a context of religious pluralism....... This is true for all of us[2]".

And to achieve this - to enable different faith-communities to live harmoniously and peacefully - we need something like the pluralist model as formulated in the Guru Granth Sahib. In this model, the value and validity of multiple religions has to be duly recognized and appreciated. Such a pluralist perspective of religion holds that all religions share something in common: they make common reference to, or presume, a single transcendent reality as creator and preserver of the entire manifest phenomena[3]. Still, they have genuine differences, for each religion is a different historical manifestation of that reality and it presents visions of God, world and humanity from a localized, historically particular perspective. In order words, it can be said that the essence of divine revelation is universal but when shared by the received-prophet with humankind in a mundane language in a specific historico-religio-cultural context, it acquires limitations as well as differentiation.

To affirm the fact of diverse religions as finite manifestations of one infinite is in no way to diminish the significance of any particular religion; rather, such diversity reveals the richness of eternal and infinite truth. No doubt, one cannot put one's faith in parenthesis while trying to understand and examine the faith of the other and yet one must attend to the faith of the other as this is witnessed to by the believer, without pre-judging that faith and without abandoning one's own commitment. This is a very delicate undertaking because while doing so "our first task in approaching another people, another culture, and another religion is to take off our shoes, for the place we are approaching is holy. Else we may find ourselves treading on men's dreams. More serious still, we may forget that God was here before our arrival[4]."

Religious pluralism cannot be confined to the knowledge of other religious systems and their doctrines and teachings only. This would mean trying to confront a religious truth in the abstract. Pluralism presumes the effort to know and appreciate the historical-cultural context and the people themselves who make up other faith communities. This would involve our discarding the prevalent attitude of considering our neighbours, who are people of different races and religions, as aliens. We must not only live with our religiously diverse neighbours; we must also talk with, work with and learn from them.

It appears more and more difficult today to hold on to an exclusivist or inclusivist models for leading a peaceful and harmonious social existence. It has to be understood that there can be no one way to the realization of God and that there are many paths. It is necessary for different religions and faith-communities to meet each other and relate to each other, the objective being not to absorb or obliterate the other but to help and promote each other. This has become obligatory for humanity today because pluralism is no more just a textbook issue but has become a human existential problem.

Sikhism: A World—Affirming Faith

In the modern-day pluralistic world, the teachings of the Guru Granth Sahib can play a vital and constructive role, mainly because they tend to accept plurality. And then this acceptance is not passive; it is rather critical. This critical spirit is quite explicit on certain vital points such as the sanctions and safeguards favouring hierarchical division of social structure. In Sikh thought, all humans are equal and spiritually one with God and ethnically equal among themselves. Sikhism is also equally critical of certain prevalent religious practices which are contrary to the scriptural spirit of the given faith. The role of clergy, in both Hinduism and Islamic traditions, in misusing religion for the purpose of oppressing certain classes of society receives a severe condemnation in some of the hymns.

The Sikh faith integrates the world and worldly life with the idea of divinity. On one hand, it rejects asceticism and on the other provides reality, relative reality though, to the mundane world. This world cannot be considered simply to be sinful or mere *maya* or primarily a place of suffering; it is rather, the dwelling-place of the Divine. As the Abode of the God, the world need not be renounced; on the contrary, humans must strive to fashion the world into *Sach Khand* (abode of the Truthful). In this process, for Sikhs the spiritual is socialized, and the secular and social are spiritualized. The ideal religion, as says the scripture, is one which emphasizes upon man to perform concrete good deeds in this world and at the same time to constantly remember the Divine Name[5].

Sikh Attitude Toward Other Faiths

The lives of the Sikh spiritual teachers, the message of the Sikh scripture, and Sikh tradition stand witness to the constructive and positive Sikh response to interfaith relations. For example, if we look at the life of Guru Nanak, we learn that after his enlightenment[6], he took on four preaching odysseys in four different directions to share the divine message with the people at large. During these odysseys, he made it a point to visit any place of pilgrimage or of importance to both Hindus and Muslims which fell on his way to hold discourses with the holymen there. The idea was to listen to them and then convey them his own viewpoint. Instead of thrusting his view of Truth on anyone, he would listen to them and also share with them the revelation he had, had. Unlike the exclusivists, Sikhism acknowledges and appreciates other faiths with equal sanctity. The Sikh scripture clearly states that divine revelation cannot be religion-specific, region-specific or caste-specific.

Since each expression of revelation is considered an attempt to encounter and understand the Real One in a particular localized context, the Sikh Gurus advised everybody to be true to his or her faith: a Muslim should be a true Muslim and a Hindu should become a true Hindu. There is no instance in Sikh history or tradition of coercing anybody to convert to Sikhism. On the other hand, it holds that while mutual witnessing promotes mutual respect, proselytising devalues the faith of the other. Sikhism seeks to unite people, belonging to different religious traditions into a broader unity: Sikh theology holds that the object of religion is not to divide mankind, but to unite it; "not to act like scissor and tear as under the social fabric, but to act like a needle and sew it together[7]."

Similarly, Sikhism also rejects the idea of only one Savior. The idea that my prophet or my spiritual teacher is the only Savior to lead humanity on the road to salvation is alien to Sikhism which takes different religions as divine revelations made known by the prophets or spiritual preceptors at different times in different spatio-cultural contexts. In one of his hymns, Guru Amar Das, the third spiritual preceptor of the Sikhs, declares all religious traditions equally valid as he prays to Lord:

> *The world is burning in the fire of passion*
> *Save it, O Lord, by Thy grace;*
> *Save it the way Thou consider best*[8].

Such an attitude in the late medieval times was much ahead of the times and can very easily be taken as a precursor to the modern-day pluralistic model. The oft-quoted example in this respect is that of Guru Arjan who was once visited by a group of followers. They were confused by the diverse incarnations in which God was worshipped and they sought the Guru's advice. The Guru advised them: All forms and attributes are of God's, yet He transcends them. You should, therefore, worship only the Absolute One. At the same time, you must abjure rancor towards those who have a different way of worship[9].

Lest this understanding and appreciation of other religions should remain an abstract idea, Sikhism seeks to promote a dialogical relationship between different faith-communities. The Sikh scripture is quite emphatic in stating that "man throughout his worldly existence must seek to converse with others by first listening to others' viewpoint and then putting forward his own, for this is the only way to attain truth[10]". The notions of listening to the others' viewpoint (*kichhu suniai*) and putting forward your own viewpoint (*kichhu kahiai*) clearly urge for fruitful dialogue, aimed at searching for the truth. Such a dialogical relationship with other faiths leads to a much-needed deeper understanding and appreciation of other religions. The Sikh scripture categorically rejects polemics, insisting rather that only after polemics have been set aside can the real search for truth begin and bear fruit. "Polemics and argumentation causeṭ and are also caused by- "the ego which in the Sikh scripture is referred to as a 'serious malady[11]'; but humility, a pre-requisite for genuine listening to another, is the essence of all virtues[12]." There are innumerable references in Sikh scripture that stress the value of humility.

The best example of interfaith dialogue in the Sikh scripture is Guru Nanak 's *Sidh Gosti* which is a sort of spiritual dialogue on the Sikh philosophy of life vis-a-vis the philosophy of yoga. In this composition, the yogis put searching questions to Guru Nanak, who answers them with compassion and confidence. The dialogue is held without hurting the feelings of any of the participants, ever retaining serenity and sobriety and aiming at realizing the truth.

The vision of religious tolerance and affirmation of religious pluralism that are found in the message of the Gurus as contained in the scripture are also embodied in the lives of the Gurus themselves and Sikh tradition in general. This is evident from the very fact that Guru Nanak was revered by Sikhs, Hindus and Muslims alike. And, Guru Arjan was recognized by Emperor Jahangir for the way his message and conduct bringing Hindus and Muslims together to converse with him. Guru Tegh Bahadur went even further and laid down his life to protect all important religious freedom, by sacrificing his life in order to stop the Muslim ruler of the time from forcing the conversion of Hindus to Islam. It was clear that he would have done the same for Muslims had they found themselves in a similar situation under Hindu rulers. The Guru's sacrifice was clearly a manifestation of upholding the principle of religious pluralism - all persons have freedom of conscience and the right to choose their own faith.

When Guru Gobind Singh took up the struggle against the deceit and decadence of Hindu Rajput chiefs and the oppression and suppression by the Mughal Empire of the day, he could count many Hindus and Muslims standing on his side. One of the most moving Sikh affirmations of the value and validity of other religions can be found in Bhai Kanahaiya, as he looked out over the slain and wounded soldiers on the battlefield of Anandpur and honoured the same divine essence in all of them, no matter what their religion[13]. Treating all human beings as spiritually one and ethnically equal, no matter what their religious beliefs, is the pre-requisite for maintaining harmonious relationship in the modern-day pluralistic society, and the Sikh attitude towards other religions and religious communities can be taken as a model.

Looking Ahead

If we want a world free from the prevalent distrust and disharmony, hatred and violence, we must be able to see others as our brothers and sisters. This means that we have to discover how to affirm our own identity without threatening the identity of others. And we have to recognize and feel in our religious awareness that when we revile others' religion or desecrate another community's place of worship, we revile or desecrate the Divine Presence itself. This happens to be the central message of the Sikh faith in its teaching that if we truly believe in God's love for all the beings, we must affirm and value the others in their otherness. The Sikh acceptance of the cultural and religious plurality in human social existence is found expressed in several of its institutions and the Sikh way of life. The Sikhs conclude their daily prayer to God seeking welfare of all - *sarbat da bhala*. They see the love for God as the vis-a-tergo for love of mankind; and they express this love through *seva* or voluntary service rendered unto others and such other philanthropic activities. Sikhism is in full agreement with St. James's assertion that "faith without works is dead" (James 2:20); with their ethics of creative activism, they seek to realize the Gurus' vision of a society based on faith and love, tolerance and justice. This is the need of our contemporary, threatened world "that we do not limit ourselves to words alone but try to actively turn religious words into reality in our social lives."

References

1. For an understanding and detailed discussion on the concept and meaning of exclusivism and other related terms (inclusivism and pluralism), see Alan Race. *Christians and Religious Pluralism* (London:SCM), 1983. This phraseology was used by Alan Race for the first time and it has since been accepted and supported by almost all theologians including John Hick (*The Rainbow of Faiths,* London: SCM, 1985). Paul F Knitter (*The Myth of Christian Uniqueness: Toward a Pluralistic Theology of Religions*, Maryknoll: Orbis Books, 1987) and Harold Coward (Pluralism in the World Religions: A Short Introduction. Oxford: One word Publications, 2000)
2. Wilfred Cantwell Smith, The faith of other Men (New York: Harper and Row, 1962), 11
3. This is a general statement. A caveat to this claim must be entered in the case of certain traditions that tend to deny that religious language points to anything real.(e.g. the *sramanic* Indian traditions).
4. M.A.C Warren, General Introduction to the " Christian Presence" series (London: S.C.M. Press,1959), ff
5. Guru Granth Sahib, V. 266
6. For details, see the Bein episode in the janam-sakhis (the traditional life —accounts of Guru Nanak) wherein Guru Nanak, after leaving the house at Sultanpur where he was living with his sister and brother-in-law, to carry out his usual morning routine of bathing in the Bein rivulet, does not return and is missing for a number of days. It is believed that during those days he remained in meditation during which he was summoned by Nirankar (God) who offered him a cup of nectar and directed him to go into the world and spread his message.
7. Guru Granth Sahib,III, 853
8. Bhai Mani Singh, *Sikhan di Bhagat Mala* and *Varan Bhai Gurdas*, XI.20
9. Guru Granth Sahib,I, 1255
10. ibid., III,853
11. ibid., I,470
12. Bhai Kanahaiya was a devotee of Guru Gobind Singh; during a battle the Guru had to fight against the Rajput hill chiefs and the Mughal imperial forces, the Bhai served water to the wounded soldiers. One day it was reported to the Guru that the Bhai served water to the wounded soldiers of

the enemy camp as well. The Guru sent for him and asked him to explain. He told the Guru that he saw the same divine image in each face irrespective of the camp he belonged to. The Guru, on listening to this, was highly pleased and urged him to tend to the wounds of all.

13. Marcus Braybrooke, "Sikhism: A Religion for the Third Millennium" in *Perspectives on Sikhism* (Patiala: Punjabi University, 2001).

Guru Granth Sahib: Repository of Universal Values

Prof. Riyaz Punjabi

Intoduction

Guru Granth Sahib occupies a position of great distinction in the religious texts of the World. This unique document unambiguously underscores the unity of different religions on fundamental principles and brings forth the indivisibility of diverse spiritual experiences. In this age of rising fanaticism and religious intolerance, in which even cultures are sought to be polarized and divided, Guru Granth Sahib provides a beacon light to the beleaguered humanity. In this prevailing and predominant material culture of modern day world, in which the human beings are loosing their spiritual anchorage, Guru Granth Sahib provides a direction to anchor human mind into the bliss of spirituality.

The Inclusive Character

The holy Granth, in fact, is a blissful voyage in spirituality, compassion and human values. It reflects our shared spiritual, social and cultural values. The eclecticism of Guru Granth Sahib is clearly visible in its incorporation of not only the ideas and ideals but outright inclusion of poetic compositions of Hindu Bhagats and Muslims Sufis which are in harmony with the ideal and vision of Sikh Gurus. In this regard, Guru Arjun

Dev, the fifth Guru of Sikh order, who compiled the Granth Sahib for the first time in 17th century did not miss to incorporate four *shabads* and 114 *shlokas* from the hymns of Baba Farid in Guru Granth Sahib. It may not be out of place to mention here that Guru Nanak took great pains in collecting these hymns and after verifying their authenticity accepted them and utilized them in the dissemination of his mission. Guru Granth Sahib carries the hymns of Saint Kabir, the torch-bearer of the Bhagati movement in India. This aspect of Guru Granth Sahib endows it with the special characteristic of inclusiveness, a unique feature of the realm of spirituality apart from being the reflection of rich Indian religious and cultural diversity.

Guru Granth Sahib needs to be deciphered in the particular social, cultural and religious milieu of India, particularly in the 16-17th century. In this milieu, the currents of religious intolerance and antagonism and caste discrimination had held Indian society in its stranglehold. In this vitiated social atmosphere, Guru Nanak arrived with his gospel of *Awal Allah Noor Upaya Qudrat dey sab Banday* (God first created Light in which dwell all the Human Beings), drawing people of diverse faiths and orders towards him.

The Framework

The Sufi and Bhagati orders did prevail in India at the advent of the mission of Guru Nanak. However, most of these orders had been decomposed and had lost much of their sheen. Guru Granth Sahib provided a formal framework and laid down a well defined methodology to reach the goal of spiritual attainment. The framework provided in the Granth may be comprehended through its metaphors and similes which have broader connotations. Since the basic aim of the teachings of Granth Sahib is to prod the human mind to undertake an internal voyage to realize the ultimate reality, the absorption of metaphors becomes crucial to realize the meanings of the *slokas* in the Granth. In the same vein, Guru Granth Sahib persistently employs traditional Hindu mythological and traditional cultural terminologies. However, they acquire new meanings in tune with the core philosophy of the holy scripture. The rationale appears to make the message easier to understand for an average person to assimilate the communication from within.

The Light

Guru Granth Sahib, in essence, provides a new orientation in order to shape the human consciousness. Thus, it invokes the human mind to the basic reality of its existence which is common to all human beings universally. Therefore, when it articulates the concept of *Noor* - the Light, and stresses that the *'Creator created the Light first and all the human beings are the reflections of this very Light; how can we declare some beings as good and others not',* it establishes the first principle of spiritual unity and human brotherhood. However, the word *Noor or Light* as used in Guru Granth needs to be comprehended in its wider perspective of the Creator being the light and the perpetual quest of human beings to be absorbed in this very Light. Thus, it needs to be recognized that it is not the light in the physical sense but in the spiritual sense.The term that 'God firstly manifested in the form of Light as articulated in Guru Granth is akin to the Quranic concept of *Allah o Noor u Sammawat i Fi il Aradh Ṁ* meaning that God is the Light of the heavens and the earth.

Reflecting on the verse, the great islamic Scholar, Imam Ghazali, as quoted by the noted interpreter; of Holy Quran, Abdullah Yusuf Ali, writes:

> *The Ultimate Light is the final Fountainhead, who is Light in an by Himself, not a light kindled from other lights. The term 'light' as applied to any other than this primary*

> *Light is purely metaphorical. But these metaphorical lights have various gradations. So are their gradations in their opposites. There is no darkness so intense as the darkness of Not being. A dark thing is called "dark" simply because it cannot appear to anyone's vision; it never comes to exist for sight, though it may exist in itself. But that which has no existence for others no for itself is assuredly the very extreme of darkness. In contrast with it is Being, which is therefore Light. Thus God Most High is the only Reality, as He is the only Light.*

The concept of Light as elucidated in Guru Granth may be comprehended in the foregoing explanation. Again, the dictum of Guru Granth that 'In case every one is the reflection of that Light then who is good or bad' has larger spiritual connotations. Firstly, in the realm of spirituality every human being is presumed to be a pure soul. Secondly, this soul has to be guided to reach its ultimate destination. Thirdly, the voyage, to reach the destination is an internal process. The entire Guru Granth underscores this journey to within from without. Guru Granth provides:

> *Simple water cleanse the hands soiled with dust,*
> *the soap is used to cleanse the soiled cloth,*
> *conscious provides the method to cleanse the mind polluted with sin.*

Again, Guru Granth Sahib looks at the human beings with a positive approach and optimism. This optimism addresses the issue of distinctions, artificially created by the human beings to divide people. It provides:

> *All creatures are noble, and none is low*
> *All vessels have been designed by one Creator*
> *This Light manifest in all the three worlds.*

The concept of Light has a special emphasis in Guru Granth Sahib and it seems that this emphasis is to make the human beings conscious of spiritual unity in which every human being basks in the glory of that Light, which is eternal and all-pervasive.

Thy radiance is radiating all creation
O! Thou are the Light
All that exists radiates Thy Light.
Lord — The Only Master

Guru Granth underscores the faith in one Lord and monotheism remains the constant theme of the holy Granth. The faith in one God and devotion to Him is key to reach Him in terms of the Granth as provided in the following verse.

God is the treasure of all the virtues,
He is above this world (maya),
He is the sacred; Not born of anybody,
You can draw closer to Him by worshipping Him,
Shower praise on Him and listen to the praises for Him,
The fragrance through will spread from within, and
You will be relieved of all the sufferings, and you
will live in tranquility.

The above quoted *Pauri* (verse) from *Japji* in Guru Granth Sahib is akin to *Saura* Ikhlas in Holy Quran:

Say He is Allah
The One Allah, the eternal, Absoute
He begetteth not
Nor is He begotten
And there is none
Like unto Him.

And Guru Granth reiterates:

My Guru is that Who exists forever
Neither takes birth nor dies
Is imperishable Entity, All pervading.

It further provides as follows:

The One
Who is Infinite, Transcendent and Supreme,
Is the Guru realized.

The objective is similar that God is one and can not be comprehended in terms of human relationships, nor can he be perceived figuratively or through imagery. This concept is lyrically elucidated in Guru Granth in the verse *Ek Onkar; Satnam Karta Purakh.......*

God is but one Onkar, one Onkar-the truth
Away from fear, Lord of Universe
Unrelated to birth and death
He manifested himself
Center of all manifestations
Universe moves under His command
Pray and pray in His praise
He is the truth
From the beginning till the end
Nanak, the God, Onkar is a truth today
And would remain so ever after.

Again, Guru Granth Sahib provides that the basis of religion is to understand and realize God:

To accomplish knowledge is the religion of Yogi,
The religion of Brahman is to read Veda,
And that of Khishtrya is to show bravery,
The religion to understand the One God
is the religion of all,
Nanak is the servant of That (Lord)
who is without any blemish.

Guru Granth Sahib prods human beings to look around the universe and draw the inspiration from this creation as the living evidence of the bounties of the Creator. This experience would lead a person towards realization and ultimately be in a state of unison with the Lord. This wisdom finds expression in the Pauri (verse) *Aant na sifti.........* in Japji Sahib:

There is no end to your bounties, O Lord
They are everywhere and in every direction

So many earths, moons and suns and
stars created by you to decorate this universe.

Anchoring With Cultural Heritage

Japji Sahib is the core of Guru Granth Sahib. It is a song of devotion which underscores the love for the Creator and elevates the human spirit to a level in which Creator and the subject are merged in unison. However, it is this song of passion which is anchored to the Indian national cultural heritage. It incorporates traditional and classical Hindu cultural symbols, metaphors and mythological terms to drive home the message of the Guru Granth Sahib. The incorporation of this terminology is aimed at reaching to the common folk and integrate them to the core philosophy of Guru Granth Sahib. The following Pauri *Aakhey Brahmay Aakhey Ind......* provides an illustration to the point.

The entire Universe sings Thy praise,
Brahma, Inder. Gopies and Govind,
All are busy commending You,
Budhas praise you in devout reverence,
So do the Angels, Djinns, Saints and others,
Every one is in praise for you,
And yet Creatures can not comprehend your qualities.

The foregoing verse artistically uses the Hindu metaphors - the dieties worshipped by Hindus as Gods; and yet they reflect different meanings and provide a message in consonance with the core theme of Guru Granth - the theme of worshipping one Lord. Again, in order to reach out to common folks, Guru Granth speaks in the language of folklore *Eka Mayee Jugat Vihayee......*

It is said that Brahma and Maya gave birth to three deities
One creates, another sustains,
third one judges you in your deeds
However, the reality is that the World runs

according to the dictates of one God
He is the Lord and the Protector, though invisible but take care of everybody.

Guru Granth Sahib incorporates literary metaphors and similies as well, which adds another dimension to its distinctiveness and provides literary cultural richness to its content as is indicated in the verse *Jatt Pahara Dhiraj Suniyar*

In the furnace of piety, let your resolve glow
Make use of your intellect
Let the spiritual knowledge guide you
Fear the God and work hard
Raise the flame of love and raise it in your mind
Remember the truth that your love is eternal
You have the gold coins of true name
And you have the mint of truth
And the One who is stamped by the Lord
Gets the stamp of truth and gets through

Guru Granth Sahib is satirical as well in addressing the social evils as is reflected in this verse:

How are you Brahmin and we Sudra
How were we made of mere blood
And you of milk?

There could be no other way than this to expose the fallacy of caste system prevalent in Indian society. The message of Guru Granth Sahib is no passivity but action. The holy scripture no doubt underlines the reality of the world as an illusion (*maya*) but it does not preach so while performing daily choress. It envisages to learn to live in two spheres, outer and inner, and bring the harmony between the two. It reiterates the message of Bhagwad Geeta that you perform your Karma and leave the rest to the God. In the same manner Quran enjoins human beings to play their role in this world and not to ignore it. Thus, Guru Granth Sahib ordains not to be oblivious towards one's duties in this world.

Conclusion

The chief merit of Guru Granth Sahib lies in the fact that in its totality it emerges as a bridge among diverse faiths and brings together the followers of these faiths, particularly the Hindus and the Muslims. It brings forth the core spiritual aspects, setting aside ritualistic and dogmatic elements, which develop over a period of time, overshadowing the basic elements of the religions. It addresses humanity at large and not to any specific group of people. In this sense, the message of Guru Granth overarches an individual and assumes the contours of universality. In cultural terms, although it remains a repository of national culture, it incorporates universal cultural values and ideals.

The core message of Guru Granth Sahib has been summed up by the noted Historian, Arnold Toynbee in these words:

> *Yet, on both sides of this religious barrier (between Hinduism and Islam), there has been a minority of discerning spirits who have seen that, at bottom, Hinduism and Islam are each an expression of the same fundamental religious truth, and that these two expressions are therefore reconcilable with each other and are of supreme value when brought into harmony. The Sikh religion might be described, not inaccurately, as a vision of this Hindu-Muslim common ground. To have discovered and embraced the deep harmony underlying the historic Hindu-Muslim discord has been a noble spiritual triumph, and Sikhs may well be proud of their religion's ethos and origin.*

Guru Granth Sahib: A Common Treasure of Mankind

Dr. Jaspal Singh

All religious scriptures of the world deserve reverence. The message of these scripture guide our lives in one way or the other. But there is the least doubt that the place and position of Guru Granth Sahib is singular in the tradition of religious scriptures of the world. I intend here to share some points about the distinctiveness of Guru Granth Sahib.

(1)

Guru Granth Sahib is the only Holy Scripture in the world which occupies the status of the Guru. It is not looked upon by the Sikhs as only a scripture but as the visible body of the Guru. History tells us that the fifth Sikh Master, Guru Arjan Dev compiled and edited the collected compositions (*bani*) of Saints and Bhaktas before installing Guru Granth Sahib in Harimandar Sahib for the first time in 1604 A.D. Following this, the *bani* of Guru Tegh Bahadur Sahib was added to the *bir*, edited by Guru Arjan Dev, by the tenth Sikh Master, Guru Gobind Singh under his own supervision and direction at Damdama Sahib. This *Dadami bir* was then installed at Abchal Nagar, Hazoor Sahib by Guru Gobind Singh in 1708 and was given the exalted status of a Guru for all times to come.

Special religious guidelines have been prescribed to attend upon and serve Guru Granth Sahib due to its exalted status of the visible Guru. The tradition enjoins upon to enthrone Guru Granth Sahib on a specially raised plank with a canopy of cloth (*Chandoa*) overhead, with waving a fly-whisk (*chavar*) over it, and gracing it with the best of the robes. There are specific norms to open this sacred Granth in the early hours of the morning (*parkash karna*), taking it at night at a appointed place for retirement (*sukhasan karna*), holding special congregations (*diwan launa*) in its presence, performing holy music (*kirtan karna*), offering prayers in its presence, and taking the daily edict (*hukamnama*), establish the uniqueness of Guru Granth Sahib in the religious scriptures of the world.

In fact, the concept of paying reverence to the *shabad-bani* of Guru Granth Sahib lies ingrained in the Sikh tradition right from the beginning. The Gurus, through their discourses and preceptual practice always tried to teach their devotees and the Sikh congregation (*sangat)* the ways of paying respect to the *bani*.

In this context, it seems befitting to bring to light the remarkable historical event, mentioned in *Gur Pratap Suraj Granth* at the time of installing the Adi Granth for the first time in Harimandar. According to the great Sikh poet, Mahakavi Santokh Singh, Baba Buddha Ji placed the sacred Granth on his head and Guru Arjan Dev started waving the fly-whisk (*chavar)* over it. Reaching Harimandar Sahib, the sacred Granth was installed on a raised platform (*takht*) while Guru Sahib himself occupied a relatively lower seat. Henceforth, he started spending most of his time at the feet of Guru Granth Sahib and very rarely he used to visit his home. He spent the major time in the service and devotion of the Granth.

Buddhe līn granth sir dhārī
Chavar karhi Gur varaṅ vari
Tahan nivās Granth ko kīno
Sri Gur bhūtal nikt āīno

Kabi kabi sadan āpne jahi
Nāhi tān rahai Grinth ke pahi.

There is ample historical evidence that all the Sikh Gurus, who succeeded Guru Arjan Dev, followed the practice. Sarup Das Bhalla's *Mehma Parkash* also illustrates the sacred tradition of honouring and worshipping Guru Granth Sahib; though in a bit different way. According to him, after the compilation, Guru Arjan Dev was pleased to have its first glimpse in shape of a Granth. All the devotees and Guru himself paid their obeisance to Guru Granth Sahib by lighting earthen wares and incense sticks. In this way, a new tradition of worshipping and revering the Granth was founded.

Satigur dekh Grinth bigsāne
Nām bhandhār nij ghar mo jāne.
Ikant kothri bhitar rākhā.
Kar dhūp dip tekai sabh māthā.

There is an anecdote inscribed in *Mehma Parkash* with reference to Guru Har Rai Ji. The anecdote will, by itself reveal the fact that how much Guru Sahib himself venerated Guru Granth Sahib and how much he expected the same from the Sikh devotees: "One day the compassionate Guru was sitting on a cot. A recitar of holy hymns (*kirtankaar*) came to have the darshan of the Guru. After having the darshan, he thought that he should recite hymns in the presence of the Guru, as it would benefit him. He immediately started reciting *kirtan*. The Guru at once got up and sat on the floor. In a hurry to get down of the cot Guru's knee got hurt as it struck against the cot. The Sikh devotees present there started massaging his knee and entreated: "What was the need to get up in a hurry when the hymns and the sacred Granth are thine own?" The Guru then spoke. Thou are not aware of the importance of hymns. We should have reverence for it as much as we can. This *bani* is the bani of the Guru. It is the bani of God. If I don't pay reverence to it, how it shall redeem you. This *bani* and the Granth is the visible form of the essence of the person of the Guru. The knower of it achieves the zenith of my status. A true devotee of mine is expected to pay full reverence to these hymns. One who does not do this is not my disciple. All the Sikh devotees were amazed and were in the state of divine fear to listen to these words.

There is another historical event of great importance recorded in *Panth Prakash*. It is said that Sikh devotees once pleaded with Guru Gobind Singh to let his writings be collected and compiled into another Granth as the Granth of the Tenth Master on the pattern of Guru Granth Sahib. Guru Sahib outrightly overruled this proposal and said that Guru Granth was the only venerable Granth.

He Satgur tumrī jo bānī
Chahīe ikathā bīr bananī
Adi Granth Sahib sam Granth
Eh bhi banhai mānai panth
Eh sun dasme Gurū uchārī
Gurū Arjan badh bhe upkārī
Un kī nahi barabri chahie
Nā hum karain na tum phir kahie
Pujan jog Granth gurū rūp
Raihai soū sada anūp.

The author of *Twarikh Guru Khalsa* also takes note of same type of pronouncement of Guru Gobind Singh —"*Acknowledge and worship Sri Guru Granth Sahib as the only Guru and none else, who is your only spiritual benefactor*".

What I mean to say is that Guru Granth Sahib is the only sacred Granth in the world which reserves the status of the visible body of the Guru and for whose reverence special tradition has been evolved.

(2)

The distinctness of Guru Granth Sahib also lies in the fact that, in addition to the *bani* of Gurus, the *bani* of Bhaktas has also been included in it. Not only this, their hymns have been given the same degree of esteem as the hymns of the Gurus and this *bani* has the same status and reverence for the Sikhs. It comes out quite vividly that the range of contributors in Sri Guru Granth Sahib is quite vast. A contributor belonging to any caste, religion or occupation had the privilege to find space for his hymns in the Granth. He could be a Hindu, Jaidev, a Muslim, Sufi Baba Farid, a Brahmin, Parmanand, a low-caste Ravidas, Namdev of Maharashtra or Bhagat Kabir of Banaras. In fact, by including the hymns of Bhaktas belonging to different castes and faiths, Gurus tried to eradicate the caste system and inculcate the spirit of tolerance among the people.

It must be borne in mind that the hymns of only those Saints and Bhaktas has been included in Guru Granth Sahib, who happened to be the true followers of the thought and way of life, preached by the Gurus. C.H. Loehlin in his work, *The Sikhs and Their Scriptures,* very correctly points out that Guru Arjan Dev rejected hymns of self-deification; those derogatory to women; those which advised the concealing of God's message from man; those disparaging life and its struggle.

Historical writings tell us that contemporaries like Kahna, Chhajju, Shah Husain, Peelu etc. had approached Guru Arjan Dev with the request to incorporate their writings in Guru Granth Sahib. But the Guru rejected their plea on the ground that their writings lacked the spirit of holistic welfare, humility and universal vision, which were fundamental to the precept of Sikhism. There are several other instances and historical facts which make it clear that the criteria of choosing hymns of Bhaktas for inclusion in the Granth was adherence to those principles and tenets which were being preached and propagated by the Gurus.

The *bani* of 15 Bhaktas, who lived between 12th and 16th centuries, has been incorporated in Guru Granth Sahib. Thus, from the historical point of view it can be said that their influence spanned over to five centuries. Moreover, these Saints and Bhagats belonged to different parts and regions which stand a testimony to the fact that their geographical influence was traversing all boundaries.

One more point that needs to be understood is that how did the bani of Bhaktas reach Guru Arjan Dev. The traditional scholars have their own opinion about it. The writers, wandering in the world of their imagination, have treated this issue in different ways. They opine that when Guru Arjan Dev finished the task of compiling the *bani* of all the Gurus, the souls of the Bhaktas appeared before him and entreated him to include their *bani* in the Granth for the salvation of humankind. But on the basis of study of the *bani*, it can be affirmed that this episode can, by no means, be accepted as true. For example, a typical kind of similarity is found between the hymns of the Bhaktas and those of Gurus, which proves the fact that the *bani* of Bhagats was collected by the Gurus, all by themselves. And this practice had started right from the period of Guru Nanak Dev. I want to illustrate this point with a reference to Baba Farid's couplet:

Pahlai pehrai phulrā phalu bhī pachhā rāt
Jo jāganni lahanni se sāī kanno dāti

It means that those who get up in the early hours of morning (*amrit wele*) and meditate in the name of the Almighty are blessed with His Grace and all kinds of divine gifts. Guru Nanak endorses Baba Farid's thought with his couplet where he cautions the seekers not to feel proud of just being an early riser. The divine gift is unconditional, which a toiling early riser may miss and a relaxed one in deep sleep may be blessed with it.

Dāti sāhib sandīā kia chalai tis nāl
Ik jagande na lehani, iknā sutiā dei uthāli

Many such examples can be cited with reference to other Bhagats also, whose hymns are illustrated by the Gurus in Guru Granth Sahib. It is clear and obvious here that conscious efforts to compile the hymns of Saints and Bhaktas had begun right from the period of Guru Nanak which continued during the period of first four Sikh Gurus.

It can clearly be stated that to incorporate the hymns of Saints and Bhaktas in Guru Granth was a revolutionary step. This decision of the Gurus took the shape of a crusade to give a boost to the concept of religious pluralism in India. It should also be noted here that this historical step led to the preservation of precious *bani* of Saints and Bhaktas on one hand and added glow and grace to Sikh tradition.

(3)

The spiritual message contained in Guru Granth Sahib also has a distinctive touch of its own. In fact, *Bani* of Guru Granth Sahib is basically spiritual in nature. Let us first talk about the *Mool Mantra* in this context. It is a prologue to Guru Granth Sahib, and can easily be rated as the greatest divine message of Guru Nanak. This *Mool Mantra* is the seed form of the whole Sikh religious thought even as the whole spiritual discourse of Guru Granth Sahib can be understood by elaborating and interpreting the meaning of this great creedal formula.

The opening of this introductory thought of Guru Granth Sahib begins with the numeral '1' which carries a specific meaning and an extraordinary purpose. The numeral '1' denotes that 'one' is the definite and original form of this universe. In the history of religions, this is the first, foremost and the novel concept in which the existence of God has been described with the numeral '1'. The primary reason behind this is perhaps that meanings of words may change with the flux of time but the digits will continue to have the same bearing. Further, reading the numeral '1' right in the beginning leaves an indelible impression on the human mind. Further, if we deeply examine the form and structure of '1 Oankar' (ੴ), more revelations come to the fore depicting the existence of the Superconscious. Some scholars feel that in '1 Oankar', three derivatives of knowledge—digit, word and geometry—have been used to express the existence of God. '1' is the first digit, 'Oankar' is the first character and 'kār' is a form of geometry. While '1' and 'Oankar' represent the beginning of mathematics and the language of speech, respectively, 'kār' denotes the concepts of 'timelessness' and 'endlessness'. Thus, the entire spiritual thought of Guru Nanak Dev can be summed up in these words: '1' is the beginning of the entire universe but no one knows the beginning and the end of that '1' and that '1' is omnipresent, and has a common essence.

He then goes on to elaborate the word '*ik*': "The name of that 'one'(1) is The Truth (*sat*), He is the creator of the entire universe, He is fearless, foeless and formless. He is beyond life and death, self-created, and one attains to Him with the grace of the Guru." The concept of 'onenessness' in the *Mool Mantra* has been repeated at many places in Guru Granth Sahib and the diversity of material vastness has been regarded as the expansion of that 'one' force. Seen carefully, this principle of onenessness seems to be preparing the ground for the concept of human unity.

A number of other questions also come to the mind while talking of spirituality. What is this world? What is the existence of human being in this world? What is the relationship of this world and the human beings with Almighty God? The *bani* of Guru Granth Sahib has answered these questions in its own manner. This line of *Mārū Sohle*, '*Jān tis bhānā tā jagatu upāya*' makes it clear that the universe has been created by His Command. The aphorism in the *Japuji*, '*Kītā pasāo, aeko kavāo*' illustrates that the act of creation of this universe has happened by the will of God. It is also revealed in the *Japuji* that the mystery of the creation of this universe is beyond the petty wisdom of human beings. (*Jā kartā sirthī kao sāje āpe janae soī*).One needs to understand well that this universe is His abode and He resides in it. All the mysteries of the world are controlled by Him and He is present in each and every particle of His creation:

Balihārī kudrat vasiā terā ant nā jāī lakhiā

Artī is another beautiful composition of Guru Nanak Dev which is recited in every Sikh shrine. Nothing better can be written than this to depict the whole universe and its creation. These lines reflect the enormous and panoramic wisdom of Guru Nanak:

Gagan main thālu ravi chandu dīpak bane
tarikā mandal janak motī
Dhup malānlo pawanu chavro kare
sagal banrai phulant jotī
Kaisī ārtī hoi Bhav khandanā terī ārtī

(The sky is Thy salver,
The sun and moon Thy lamps,
The galaxy of stars as pearls scattered.
The woods of sandal are Thine incense,
The forests Thy flowers,
What a beautiful worship is this O Destroyer of fear.)

In fact, this world is a marvellous representation of the mystical design of God. And every human being, dwelling in this world is basically a physical and a conscious being and enjoys supremacy over all other living creatures because of His compassion. All other creatures are subordinate and human beings have been bestowed with a special and sovereign status. This verse of Guru Arjan Dev records this fact:

Avar joni terī panihārī,
Isu dhartī mehi terī sikdārī

Unambiguously, the *bani* of Sri Guru Granth Sahib clears all doubts about the relationship of human beings with the omnipotent God and also directs them to play a positive and constructive role in the life.

(4)

It is also worth mentioning here that the philosophy of *shabad-Guru* reserves special importance in the spiritual tradition of Guru Granth Sahib. The study of *bani* reveals that the hymns of the first Guru, Guru Nanak had the seeds of this philosophy embodied in them which thereafter continued to blossom in the Guru tradition. Guru Nanak's invaluable composition *Sidh Gosht* quite clearly illustrates this truth. His conversation with the Sidhs endorsed the idea that *shabad* can guarantee our salvation from this mundane world. *Charpat Sidh* had asked Guru Nanak as "The world ocean is said to be impassable, how can one cross it?"

Duniā sāgar dutaru kahiai
kiu kari pāīai pāro
Charpatu bolai audhu Nanak
dehu sachā bīchāro

Guru Nanak replied that as a lotus flower remains unaffected in water, and as a duck swims against the stream's current and becomes not wet, in the same way if one can keep his *surat* fixed to the Guru's *shabad*, one can cross the dreadful world ocean:

Jaise jal mahi kamalu nirālamu,
murgāī nai sāne
Surati sabad bhav sagar tarīai,
Nanak nām vakhānai

Guru Nanak has rendered exhaustive and matchless explanation of the principle of *shabad-Guru* in his *bani*. He has marvellously described the design of the *shabad* and the institution (*taksal*) where it is fashioned. The last *pauri* of

'Japuji' exhibits this view of *shabad* and *surat* in the following lines:

Jatu pāhārā dhiraj suniru
Ahrani matt ved hathiāru
Bhao khalā agani tap tāo
Bhāndā bhāo amrit tit dhāl
Ghariai sabad sachi taksāl
Jin kao nadar karamu tin kār
Nanak nadri nadari nihāl

(Make continence thy furnace,
Patience thy goldsmith,
Understanding thy anvil,
Divine knowledge thy tools,
God's fear thine bellows,
Practising of penance thy fire,
and Lord's love thy pot,
Where in filter the Nectar of God's Name,
Thus in the true mint
the Divine world (Shabad) is fashioned.
This is the routine of those
on whom casts His gracious glance.)

In fact, the whole Sikh theology is based on the principle of *shabad* in which lies the whole crux of the spiritual attainment. That's why a Sikh yearns for the support and refuge of *shabad*. A Sikh devotee starts his spiritual journey by chanting the hymns of the Guru. Thereafter, he goes deeper into the intrinsic realms of his heart with intuitive feelings of the *shabad* and becomes one with the all-powerful God. The Sikh devotee at this stage understands himself and his original source. His ego vanishes, the spell of ignorance goes off and he becomes an enlightened soul.

It should be well understood that to associate one's consciousness with *shabad* is to establish communion with God. But the fact to be kept in mind is that Guru is indistinguishable from the *shabad* and God, and that *shabad's* identity is revealed through the Guru; thus to unite with the Guru is identical to uniting with God. If we see minutely, it becomes obvious that with the common cord of *shabad*, the devotee can attain unity with the Guru and the Ultimate.

This fact should also be clearly understood that the *shabad* and the *bani* in Sikh tradition have the same connotations and both the words can be used interchangeably for each other. From a closer look, it seems that while the *shabad* denotes subtlety, *bani* symbolises its visible form. To some extent, it can be stated that *shabad* is formless and *bani* is its formative form. The transcendental aspect of *shabad*, as a result of the divine grace of the Guru, attains the form of *bani* in the garb of lyrics. The Guru becomes the poet, who composes the *shabad* in his own style to transform it into a lyrical composition. But it should be clearly understood that both are indistinguishable from each other. Both the *shabad* and the *bani* are two names of the same divine message.

In fact, the Guru tradition has always acknowledged the importance of *shabad* and the principle of *shabad-Guru* has consistently been prevailing uniformly in Guru's abode (*Guru ghar*). Though sacred Granth was compiled and edited afterwards, yet *shabad* and *bani* existed earlier too and enjoyed the status of Guru. The tradition of revering *shabad-Guru* was started by Guru Nanak. The compilation of the Bani in written form was also started from the time of Guru Nanak Dev, who then endowed the whole *bani* to Guru Angad at the time of latter's coronation as the second Sikh Guru. Following the footsteps of Guru Nanak, Guru Angad bequeathed the entire *bani*, including his own, to the third Guru, Guru Amar Das. Similarly, the *bani* of all the Gurus, Saints and Bhaktas was entrusted to Guru Arjan Dev, through Guru Ram Das. Guru Arjan Dev then, under his personal care and guidance got the whole *bani* written by Bhai Gurdas. The *bani* was compiled with brilliance of editing. Index of *shabads* and *ragas* was prepared. The whole *bani* attained the form of Guru Granth Sahib, and the luminance of the *shabad* found its way into Harimandar Sahib.

(5)

One more distinctive feature of Guru Granth Sahib needs to be viewed very profoundly. There is no doubt that the elemental theme of Guru Granth Sahib is spirituality and the hymns contained therein lay emphasis upon spiritual knowledge. But this does not mean that the wisdom contained in Guru Granth Sahib is confined only to spirituality. It, in fact, is a comprehensive exposition of the worldly affairs too, which includes community welfare, meditation, religion, ethics, patience, and service to humanity. Not only this, the *bani* also portrays a definite perspective of all the contemporary political and social systems and situations.

In fact, Guru Granth Sahib came into existence when a new cultural revolution was the dire need of the day. It was the time when the fanatic Islamic culture was expanding its network on one hand, and the Hindu ritualistic culture, on the other hand, was establishing its stranglehold. While on one side, there was excessive discrimination, superstitions and blind faith dominated the lifestyle patterns on the other. The rulers were mercilessly encroaching upon the fundamental rights of the people in the name of Islam and the Brahaminical system was trying to establish its supremacy by dividing the society.

Viewed from the historical perspective, it is explicit that the period of creation of *bani* is contemporary to the period of expansion of Islamic rule. The Indian people during this period were subjected to atrocities of the Islamic rule and non-muslims were facing a miserable and horrible time. The volume and details of cruelties of rulers of those times has been lucidly described in Guru Granth Sahib at a number of places:

Rāje sih mukdam kutte
Jāi jagāin baithe sutte
Chākaar lehdā pāini ghāo
Ratt pit kutiho chati jāho

(The kings are tigers
and the courtiers dogs.
They go and harass, and disturb
the sitting and the sleeping ones.)

Guru Nanak states that the protectors and interpreters of Islamic law offer prayers with rosary beads but, under the spell of political influence and taking bribe, they do injustice and do not hesitate to convert truth into lie. If some one endeavours to argue, they made him dumb-founded by citing examples from Holy Book:

Kāzī hoikan bahoi niā
Phere tasbī kare khudāi
Vadhi laike haku gvāe
Je ko puchhai tān parhi sunāe

All the rulers were engaged in promoting Islamic fundamentalism while the non-Muslims were facing the brunt of discrimination and partiality. On the other hand, all was not well within the Hindu society that was in majority. The entire social system was the victim of grubby caste system while hollow rituals pervaded the higher and lower lifestyle segmentations. The people of low castes were being badly exploited and humiliated. Taking the side of down-trodden people, Guru Nanak had stated:

Nīchā under nīch jāt nichī hu att nīch
Nanak tin kai sangi sāth vadiā sīu kia ris

Guru Nanak has also expressed his reaction against the declining cultural status in the society. According to him, the *Kshatriyas*, who considered themselves to be the saviours of Hindu society, had abandoned their sacred duty. They had become the advocates of those barbarians and foreigners, whom they earlier used to condemn and despise as cruel. Thus, the whole system witnessed a total chaos with religious tradition stooping to the sectarian cult:

Khatrīān ta dharam chhodiā malechh bhākhiā gahī
Srishat sabh ik varan hoi dharam ki gati rahī

Elaborating further, the Guru says, "the Primal Lord these days, is being called *Allah* and the turn of the muslim divines has come. A new law has been enacted to levy tax on temples of gods. The ablution-pots, calls to prayers (*Nimaz*) and prayer carpets are seen everywhere and the Lord appears in blue form. Peoples' language has changed and the word *Mian* has become dominant among one and all".

Ādi purkh kou Allahu kahīai sekhān aī vārī
Deval devtiān karu lāgā aisī kirat chālī
Kuja bāng nivāj Muslā nīl rup banvārī
Ghar ghar mīān sabhnā jīāṅ bolī avar tumrī

Under these circumstances, the Gurus initiated the creation of a new culture which was based on the spirit of human liberation, equality, a sense of self-respect, co-existence and mutual understanding among the followers of different religions. Creation of a broad-spectrum pluralistic society was the main objective of this culture. The Gurus expressed their views about this common and composite culture through their hymns and then placed them in Guru Granth Sahib. This whole design was aimed at streamlining the human society and giving it a unified form, illuminated by the radiance and halo of the *bani* of Guru Granth Sahib with the objective of creating of an ideal society.

(6)

Another point in this context relates to the global nature of the message Guru Granth Sahib. It is an important question to ponder over as to which composition can be identified as global and what its essential features are. I firmly believe that a global composition is one which has the capacity to bridge the gaps between human beings and the potency to cross all the hurdles and impediments of the world by talking about them in all its candidness.

An in-depth study of the *bani* brings out the fact very clearly that it is impregnable and invincible in nature. Every barrier and obstacle caves in before its forceful and spontaneous flow of words. The entire humanity is immersed into it. It's a gateway to resolving all kinds of problems inflicting the human society and the whole world and its concerns is the subject-matter of the *bani*.

Questions like what is the global scope of Guru Granth Sahib and who is covered in its ambit also come to our mind. Here, the following lines from Guru Nanak's *Asa-ki-Vr* seem to me quiet befitting as answering this question:

Purkhān birkhāṅ tīrthāṅ tattāṅ meghāṅ khetāṅh
Dipāṅ loāṅ mandlāṅ khandāṅ varbhandānh
Andaj jeraj utbhujāṅ khānī setjāṅh
So mit janai Nankā srāṅ merāṅ jantāh
Nanak jant upāi kai samāle sabhnāh
Jini kartai karnā kīā chintā bhi karnī tāh

The global contours of Guru Granth Sahib are immensely vast and gigantic. Guru Nanak says, "Men, trees, holy places, banks of sacred streams, clouds and fields, islands, spheres, universes, continents and solar system; The sources of creation, egg-born, womb-born, earth-born and sweat-born and oceans, mountains and sentient beings; He, the Lord, knows their condition, O Nanak, having created the beings, the Lord takes care of them all. The Creator, who has created the world, He takes care of it well."

I intend to share two points with regard to the global perspective of Guru Granth Sahib. The first point concerns the changing form of the contemporary world. Today's world has become multi-cultural and the centres of power are concentrating around various cultures. Feuds and conflicts among various peoples are happening on the basis of cultures, even as the political, intellectual and economic issues are losing their importance. The cultural diversity is the basis of divisions and alienation on various fronts. People are marching at a fast pace towards establishing their identities on the underpinning of a cultural group and cultural front. Cultural existence has superseded all other values. Scholars are of the view that chancy and breakneck strife henceforth in the multi-dimensional world will happen between groups of people, belonging to assorted cultural alliances instead of those defined by political, social and economic parameters.

The message of Guru Granth Sahib is fully capable of giving an affirmative direction to this world facing a grave confrontational situation. It is a crystal clear truth that the quintessence of *bani* corresponds to righteousness in a pluralistic society as it doesn't cater to any kind of casteist tendencies. The followers of *bani* also look forward to the emergence of a large, liberal and progressive world. It can be asserted that the *bani* has such an inbuilt blueprint which can most suitably guide us in the contemporary evolving world.

The second point is related to the progress of science which has seemingly generated all kinds of comforts as compared to what people had in the past. But this is not true. Wise people say that this world is full of miseries. The old pains and pangs end and the new ones crop up to take their place. It's true that science has phased out some of the human sufferings and found a solution to some of the problems but we all know that this advancement of science, at the same time, has created a glut of new despairs and despondencies of a higher magnitude. We are all in favour of scientific progress, which is scaling new heights everyday. But, it is a matter of great concern and anxiety that the level of morality is touching new ebbs. The speed of daily inventions of science has dwarfed and outpaced the values linked with decent human behaviour and a higher consciousness, which in turn is causing a state of imbalance between the two.

We should accept the fact that the progress made by science is of no use if the level of a human conduct and that of society is not simultaneously elevated. Everyone knows that all the inventions of science are ultimately proving disastrous for the society. The only saviour and the redeemer under these circumstances is moral probity of human beings which can pave the way for a utilitarian scientific progress. The *bani* explicitly advocates the cause of morality, good character and benevolent behaviour. Its whole emphasis is on inculcating the moral values both in the individual as well as in the society.

It is quite obvious from the above facts that the nature and scope of the *bani* of Guru Granth Sahib is global and its sensitivity is responsive to the global concerns.

(7)

To conclude this paper, let me cite some comments and observations of great scholars. According to Arnold Toynbee, 'The Adi Granth is remarkable for several reasons. Of all known religious scriptures, this scripture is the most highly venerated. It means more to Sikhs than even the Qur'an means to Muslims, the Bible to Christians, and the Torah to Jews. The Adi Granth is the Sikhs' perpetual guru (spiritual guide). It was formally invested with this function by the last in the series of the human gurus that began with the founder of the Sikh religion, Nanak.' Commenting on mankind's future Toynbee further adds, "In Sikh religion, and its scripture the Adi Granth will have something of special value to say to the rest of the world."

While expressing his views on the uniqueness of Guru Granth Sahib, Dr. Radhakrishnan has observed, 'We must appreciate other faiths, recognize that they offer rich spiritual experiences and encourage sacrificial living and inspire their followers to a noble way of life. The Sikh Gurus, who compiled the Adi Granth, had this noble quality of appreciation of whatever was valuable in other religious traditions. The saints belong to the whole world. They are universal men, who free our minds from bigotry and superstition, dogma and ritual and emphasize the central simplicities of religion.' He further states that the barriers of seas and mountains will give way before the call of eternal truth which is set forth with freshness of feeling and fervour of devotion in the Adi Granth.

Dr. Rajendra Prasad holds that the Sikh Gurus believed in accepting truth, irrespective of the source it came from. According to him, 'The Adi Granth contains the songs and teachings not only of Sikh Gurus but also of Hindu and Muslim saints who wrote between the 12th and 16th centuries. It is, therefore, a compilation of mystic poems by men of diverse faiths and social strata, hailing from various religions of India and speaking different languages.'

In his book *'Sarvotam Dharm Granth'*, Swami Ram Tirth, Dandi Sanyasi has highlighted the universal nature of Guru Granth Sahib. He remarks, 'Bani of Guru Granth is immensely blissful because its message is not selectively meant for any particular section of the society but for the whole mankind. It does not contain deceitful rituals for the benefit of any favourite section of society. Rather it teaches an easy and gentle way to achieve successful fulfillment of human life, to the whole mankind.'

Prof. Puran Singh's observation in 'The Spirit of Oriental Poetry' is also worth mentioning. He says, 'It (Guru Granth) is the scripture of all nations, for it is the lyric of Divine Love, and all people of thy earth subsist on such glowing lyrical prayer. Guru Granth is but one song, one idea, one life. Immensity is the substance of the sublime.' He further states, 'Guru Granth has the supreme quality of lighting our soul with love and freeing us from all bondage of sense in the light of self-realization. At every step eternity looks at us through each single star of a song.'

Undoubtedly, the embrace of Guru Granth is all inclusive. A diverse range of contributors belonging to different religions, caste and regions are given respective place in the ambit of the Granth. The vastness of vision and universality of message is also unparallel in nature. Truly, Guru Granth is a common spiritual treasure of the whole mankind, and a unique scripture, distinguishable from others.

Compilation of Sri Guru Granth Sahib

Dr. Rattan Singh Jaggi

To understand the mode of compilation of Sri Guru Granth Sahib, there is an urgent need to understand the then prevailing tradition and the prior compilations. When did the creation of Bani start and how was it collected, are the questions which demand our attention. These questions cannot be answered but an effort can be made to elicit information from the related sources to draw conclusions from these.

The concept of Bani originated with the verses of Guru Nanak. How did Guru Nanak create his verses and how did he keep these with himself ? These are the basic questions which we usually encounter. Unfortunately, we have not even a single writing or document of the Guru with us. It is not possible to know as to in which script he wrote his verses. He was a literate person and there is no doubt about it. The composition, namely, *Patti* in *Rāg Äsā* is a proof enough to suggest that he was conversant with the contemporary script and the language. The script used in *Patti* is the earlier form of the present Gurmukhi script. While completing this *Patti,* the words *Patti Likhi* are added, a fact, which indicates that this Bani was created in written form.

The next important point to be considered is whether the Guru himself wrote his whole Bani or he dictated it to some scribe or some other persons who played some role in it. The answer to this question is hidden in history. Some contemporary writings indicate that the Guru's Bani was put into writing by some of his followers. The *Puratan Janamsakhi,* which was originally written in 1588 A.D., has such a reference in episode (*Sakhi*) number 35 where it is indicated that during Guru's detention in Saidpur, his verses were committed to writing by Jharu Kalal, as is indicated in the episode:

> *Then the people of Saidpur became Guru's followers in large numbers. At that time Jhāṛû Kalāl was inside the prison and he carried the Guru's words in writing.*

Similarly in episode 43, during his sojourn towards South, the Guru had a dialogue with a Sarevṛā (Jain saint) and the *Mājh Kī Vār*, which the Guru uttered was taken down in writing by Saido Gheho.

In the same manner it was again Saido Gheho (episode 46), who was present during the Guru's dialogue with the Sidhas. It is mentioned that dialogue with Machhandar was scripted by Saido Jatt of Gheho Caste. In episode 47, which relates to Shivnabh, the *Pran Sangli,* was also completed by Saido. During Guru's sojourn to Uttarkhand, described in episode 49, two followers of the Guru, blacksmith, Hassu and Sihāṅ Chhīmbā, were his companions. While giving instructions and the need to follow the righteous path, the Guru uttered *Malār Rāg Kī Vār* which was put into written form by Hassu and Sihan. Similarly in episode 41, there is an indication that a Bania follower scripted the Guru's Bani, who stayed with him for three years. During his stay, he worked as a scribe and wrote a lot of Bani which amounted to a number of volumes (pothis). The Guru had a number of verbal encounters and dialogues with the Sidhas and his discourses were shaped into writing at a later date as the arguments and viewpoints of both the sides have been elaborated in a settled and detailed manner in his work called, Sidh Gost. It is also possible that the Guru himself put it down in writing.

An important point which needs to be understood is that the Guru always emphasized upon the need for writing the Bani, as he was of the view that attainment was not possible without having it in written form. The Guru says on page 566 of Sri Guru Granth Sahib:

Without writing, one is just not able to understand deeply and mere speaking is forgotten soon.

Not only this, in *Malār Kī Vār*, the Guru praises the scribe, the paper, the pen and the ink, which are essential ingredients of writing the Bani. On page 1291 of Sri Guru Granth Sahib, the Guru says:

> *O Nanak ! blessed is the paper, pen, ink and the mind which has got engraved on it the true name of the Lord and the person is equally blessed with the Truth.*

The above stated words and the contexts make it amply clear that the Guru used to script his verses himself, and whenever needed, his follower scribes helped him in committing his discourses to writing. He was deeply fond of writing the Bani. When a verse was available in writing, it was copied by the other followers and scribes.

Regarding the question of keeping such writings in safe custody, the first *Vār* (stanza 33) by Bhai Gurdas makes it amply clear that the Guru kept his verses in written form in a bag, and whenever needed he would read and recite from these writings. Besides this, in episode 57 of *Puratan Janamsakhi,* it is mentioned that while appointing Guru Angad as his successor, Guru Nanak Dev gave him a volume of his verses too. It is not clear whether the Guru had prepared this volume himself or had got it prepared by some other scribes. It is also not clear whether it was an anthology or a compilation but there is no doubt about the fact that Guru Nanak Dev's verses were in safe custody with Guru Angad Dev. During this period, a large number of people had got interested in the enterprise of writing, so much so that some people had started selling such writings for profit. The first Guru had cautioned such people in clear words as is mentioned on page 1245 of Sri Guru Granth Sahib:

> *Cursed is the life of the persons who write about the true name (of the Lord) and sell it for money.*

As per pages 184-185 of *Meharban Janamsakhi,* it is believed that Guru Angad Dev selected the verses for Japji from the written verses of Guru Nanak Dev available with him. Guru Angad Dev himself did not create many verses as he did not want to establish his reputation parallel to that of Guru Nanak Dev. He was contented to be the follower of Guru Nanak Dev and propagated the Guru's words among his followers. On page 150 of Sri Guru Granth Sahib, Guru Angad Dev says:

> *The person who has been blessed by Guru Nanak Dev and follows his teachings, does not need any further guidance.*

One thing is certain that Guru Angad Dev improved upon the script of *Patti* and gave it a form which is popular now. The need for reforming the script was perhaps necessitated for preparing copies of Guru Nanak Dev's verses for distribution among the masses. Guru Angad Dev, along with his own verses in shape of 63 Salokas, handed over Guru Nanak Dev's Bani to Guru Amar Dass. This fact of the whole Bani being with Guru Amar Dass gets corroborated by the fact that Guru Amar Dass's own Bani is deeply influenced by Guru Nanak Dev's Bani. The scholars dealing Guru Amar Dass's Bani agree on the point that Guru Amar Dass's verses are the reaffirmation of Guru Nanak Dev's ideas and concepts. The third Guru stressed upon the point that the followers of Guru Nanak Dev's faith should sing and recite the authentic Bani. As on page 920 of Sri Guru Granth Sahib it is mentioned:

> *O dear and true Sikhs (followers) come to me and let us sing the praises of the Lord through the Guru's word!*

> *You must bear in mind that only Guru's hymns are to be sung as these are the purest and highest forms of Lord's praises.*

Guru Amar Dass considered the Bani as the word of the Lord, coming direct from Him, matchless in every way. It is mentioned on page 515 of Sri Guru Granth Sahib:

> *This Gurbani (Guru's word), describing the praises of the Lord is really wonderful and none else is equivalent to this Bani of Nirankar.*

Obviously, Guru Amar Dass had great regards for the Bani. For the propagation of Sikh religion, he created 22 centres (*Manjis*) where the message of the Guru was disseminated through the writings and copies made from original writings which led to manyfold increase in the followers of the Bani.

In order to cater to the needs of these centres, a large numbers of scribes were available in the Guru's court. This fact is confirmed by the availability of *Babe Mohan Valian Pothian,* also known as *Goindwal Valian Pothian,* which were written by the Guru's grandson (Baba Mohan's Son) Sansrām (Sahansrām). It is clear that during the period of Guru Amar Dass, a tradition had got established by which the devotees used to engage in preparing handwritten volumes of Guru's verses.

Guru Amar Dass's decision to hand over the charge of the Gurudom to his son-in-law, Ram Dass, angered both of his sons, Baba Mohan and Baba Mohri. Baba Mohri later reconciled to the situation but Baba Mohan remained adamant, and to establish his position he kept these volumes in his personal custody.

Babe Mohan Valian Pothian

The first among these volumes is lying with Sri Vinod Kumar Bhalla, the grandson of Baba Dalip Chand Bhalla of

Ahiapur at 371, Lajpat Nagar, Jalandhar and the second is lying with the sons of Bawa Bhagat Singh Bhalla (Kanwaljit Singh, Jagjit Singh, Amarjit Singh) at Sunder Kutia, Pinjore (Haryana). These volumes have been examined and studied by various sikh scholars such as Bawa Prem Singh Hoti, Giani Gurdit Singh, Dr. Piar Singh, Dr. Gurinder Singh Mann and Prof. Pritam Singh. These two volumes do not contain all the verses of the first three Gurus. Similarly, the verses of Guru Granth Sahib, particularly the *Vār* verses are also not available. For these reasons, the scholars are of the view that there must be some more volumes.

While discussing these volumes, Bawa Prem Singh Hoti has, on the basis of internal evidence, stated that these were started in the month of Assu in Samvat 1627 (1570 AD) and were completed on tenth day of Bhadon in Samvat 1629 (1572 AD). In the *Ahiapur Wali Pothi*, verses are composed in eight *Rāgas* such as *Sûhī*, *Parbhātī*, *Dhanāsrī, Basant, Bhairo, Mārû, Kedārā* and *Tilang* by the first three Gurus and nine Bhagatas including Kabir, Namdev, Ravidass, Trilochan, Baini, Ramanand, Jaidev, Dhanna and Sain, and sufi Saint Farid. Besides these, one shabad each in *Rāg Gûjrī, Vadhans, Bilāval* and *Malār* and the first three salokas of *Āsā Kī Vār* are also included. One shabad of the fourth Guru and two of the fifth Guru are also penned but in a different handwriting.

In the *Pinjore Vālī Pothī,* the verses of Guru Nanak Dev, Guru Amar Dass and five Bhagat poets such as Kabir, Namdev, Ravidass, Trilochan and Bhikhan are included in four *Rāgas* - *Rāmkalī, Sorath, Sarang* and *Malār*.

By comparing these two volumes with Guru Granth Sahib, the researchers and scholars have pointed out a number of differences based on factual evidence such as :

(1) There are various textual variations.
(2) There are verses of mixed authorships.

(3) Somewhere the full verse, partial verse or additional verse is given under the names of the Gurus and the Bhagatas.
(4) Spellings are different. At one place, it is Mahalla, at the other it is merely Mahal. *Guru Baba, Baba Patshah, Babe Patshah Ka Bolna* are the different expressions used.
(5) The *Ghar* is not mentioned along with the *Rāgas*.
(6) There is difference in the full and precise Mûl Mantar.
(7) Figures are not used uniformly.
(8) There are differences of spellings of the names of the Bhagatas.
(9) The order of *Rāgas* is not according to the Guru Granth Sahib.
(10) Some papers are left blank perhaps with the hope of getting more Bani later.

The cuttings and crossings in these volumes indicate that whatever Bani was received, it was entered and added to the volume and what was doubtful, was revised or crossed out. Sometimes, the Bani is crossed because it was already there in earlier document. Obviously, the aim was to collect the Bani at one place. The scholars may be having their doubts but these volumes are of great importance to study as to why Guru Arjan Dev brought these volumes from Goindwal, examined and studied these for the purpose of compilation of Sri Guru Granth Sahib.

Guru Har Sahāi Vālī Pothī

Like the *Bābā Mohan Pothis,* this *Pothī* is also an early compilation. This Pothi was in safe custody with the Sodhi family of village Guru Harsahāi in Ferozepur district. This village was founded by Sodhi Jiwan Mall of Mīnā tradition in the name of his son (Guru) Harsahāi in Samvat 1899. This *Pothī* was passed over from one generation to the next, right from the elder brother of Guru Arjan Dev, Sodhi Prithi Chand. But this *Pothī* was lost in 1970, when Sodhi-Guru Jaswant Singh was returning by rail after exhibiting it at Delhi on the occasion of quicentenary birth of Guru Nanak Dev.

According to Sardar G.B. Singh and Giani Gurdit Singh, this *Pothī* was in a very poor condition. It was written by different scribes at different times and the last script was by someone from Mīnā sect. There was no uniformity between the text of this *Pothī* and that of the Guru Granth Sahib. There were many variations of the same verses. There was great similarity between this *Pothī* and the *Pothīs* of Baba Mohan. On the basis of these facts, various scholars consider this *Pothī* as the pre - *Bābe Mohan Vālī Pothī* while some regard it as post- *Bābe Mohan Vālī Pothī*.

In conclusion, it may be said that this *Pothī* had the verses scribed by different persons in an irregular manner. Guru Arjan Dev might have examined this *Pothī* at the time of compilation of Sri Guru Granth Sahib and which may have fallen in the hands of the persons of the Mīnā sect later.

Bhāī Bakhte Vālī Bīṛ

There are two more Bani compilations which need to be considered. The first is *Bhāī Bakhte Vālī Bīṛ* about which Giani Gian Singh has made a mention in his *Twārīkh Gurū Khālsā* (Vol. I, Languages Department, Patiala) as "the fifth Guru had issued directions in the form of edicts to the followers that whosoever had any word in written form should approach him." On getting the Guru's message, the Sikhs who had memorized the Guru's verses or had these in written form came to him. To this episode, Giani Gian Singh had added the following footnote in connection with *Bhāī Bakhte Vālī Bīṛ*.

> *The Guru's follower, Bhai Bakhta Arora from Jalālpur in Hasan Abdāl Pargana (sub-division) carried a big volume, which he had prepared while staying with the first four Gurus and showed to the fifth Guru, who noted down some Bani and returned the big volume to him.*

Now that volume is with his progeny, Buta Singh Pasārī at Rawalpindi, I have seen this volume. As the script was different, it could not be read but the volume is so huge that one could not lift it easily and these verses are unlimited source of Guru Granth Sahib. The signatures of all the Gurus are there because the sons, grandsons and great grandsons of Bhāī Bakhtā used to go to each Guru to obtain his signatures.

Nothing can be said with authority of the whereabouts of this Bir but one thing is clear that the fifth Guru must have used this Bir as the source material for the compilation of Sri Guru Granth Sahib.

Bahovāl Vālī Pothī

The second compilation requiring our attention is *Bahovāl Vālī Pothī* which is available as handwritten manuscript number six at Bhai Vir Singh Sahitya Sadan, New Delhi. This *Pothī* was brought from Pakistan to India at the time of partition by Baba Bachitar Singh Bedi of Village Bahovāl in West Punjab. He presented this Pothi to Bhai Vir Singh, which with the passage of time got preserved at the Sadan. It is a compilation of Gurbani. In the early pages, the script is quite old and towards the end, it is well developed and similar to the Gurmukhi of Damdami Taksal. It is obvious that the method of compilation of Bani in this volume is not as per the pattern of Sri Guru Granth Sahib. It seems that from time to time different scribes entered the Bani into this Pothī. Bābā Bachitar Singh was of the opinion that this compilation of Bani was available with Bābā Srī Chand and he had made it available to Guru Arjan Dev, when he attempted to prepare the holy Granth. Inspite of all the arguments, for and against, it remains a fact that this compilation was available prior to the compilation work undertaken by the fifth Guru.

It may be surmised that Guru Ram Dass had a number of compilations with him as he not only inspired and encouraged preparation of compilations, but he himself engaged in this activity. In the old *Bīṛs*, the *Japjī* is available under his signatures. The Guru considered those people, who wrote the Bani in their own hands as the blessed ones. On page 540 of the Sri Guru Granth Sahib this fact is made amply clear:

> *O my soul! Blessed and pure are the hands, which write the praises of Lord benefactor.*

For Guru Ram Dass, the Gurbani was personification of the Guru and he had great respect for the Bani as he states on page 982 of Sri Guru Granth Sahib:

> *The Guru's word is the manifestation of the Guru himself and the Guru is to be found in the Guru's word. Bani as the nectar of True Name lies hidden within it. In fact the devotee perceives and realizes the Guru in person and attains salvation by following His word.*

Similarly, Guru Ram Dass considers Gurbani as the storehouse of gems and diamonds. On page 442 of Sri Guru Granth Sahib, the Guru elaborates this idea in the following words:

> *Bani is full of priceless jewels, like the ocean with the Guru's invaluable thoughts which his followers receive from him. They now sing the praises of the Lord with the help of the Guru's word (Gurbani) as they are in the possession of the invaluable gem of true name.*

The third Guru has pointed out the existence of impure (*Kachi*) Bani in his composition namely *Anand Sahib*. During the very life time of the Guru, the pretenders had started reciting their own verses as is clear from the following words stated on page 304 of Sri Guru Granth Sahib:

> *The persons who speak the language of falsehood in trying to copy the Guru are forsaken by the Lord for being involved in false practices.*

When Guru Arjan Dev attained the Guruship, he planned for giving a formal look to the holy movement started by Guru

Nanak Dev. For this purpose, he considered the necessity of compiling an authentic holy book. Another reason for preparing the compilation was the unholy efforts by the Minas to adulterate the holy verses with their own unholy or false verses. The volumes indicating such reasons are *Bansāvālī Nāmā Dasāṅ Pātshāhīāṅ Kā, Mehima Prakash, Sikhāṅ Dī Bhagatmālā* etc.

In *Bansāvālī Nāmā Dasāṅ Pātshāhīāṅ Kā* , which was completed in 1769 (Samvat 1826) Kesar Singh Chhibbar writes about the reasons for compilation of Sri Guru Granth Sahib as the singers discarded by the Guru were taken into service by Prithi Chand and they started reciting the verses of his son, Meharban. And since he used the name of Nanak in his verses, the followers started accepting his verses as *Gurbani*. In order to save *Gurbani* from adulteration, the Guru asked Bhai Gurdass to collect the true Bani for preparing a compilation. Bhai Gurdass completed this job in 1601 (Samvat 1658).

Seven years after the appearance of *Bansāvālī Nāmā*, Baba Sarup Dass Bhalla prepared *Mehima Prakash* in 1776 AD (1833 Samvat). In its five episodes (11 to 15) relating to Guru Arjan Dev, it is stated that the Guru had an idea that an authentic holy book should be prepared for the Sikh faith. For this purpose, the Guru instructed Bhai Gurdas to procure and collect the authentic Bani of the Gurus and the Bhagatas for the purpose of preparing a volume. On a request from Bhai Gurdās, the Guru sent his purohit to Goindwal to get the *Pothīs* lying there with Sans Rām but the latter refused to oblige. Then, alongwith the singer Satta, the Guru with his followers, went to Goindwal, where they recited a hymn addressing Mohan the Almighty, who then willingly handed over the *Pothis* which were brought to Amritsar. The Guru made efforts to collect Gurbani from other sources also and got down with the onerous task of preparing the compilation of Sri Guru Granth Sahib which included the Banis of a large number of holymen. There are references in *Mehmā Parkāsh* to the controversy of Guru's refusal to include the verses of Kahna, Chhaju, Shah Hussain and Pransangli also. This original *Bir* is now called *Kartārpurī Bīṛ*.

When the *Bīṛ* was ready, a follower of the Guru, Bhai Bano came to see the Guru and the Guru asked him to prepare its hard bound copies. Bhai Bano started the job of copying when the Guru asked him to return the *Bīṛ*. Following this, Bhai Bano employed a number of scribes who carried the job of copying the *Bīṛ* on the way back. With the result the *Bīṛ* being prepared by Bhai Bano got distorted, as it lost uniformity too.

In this connection, *Sikhāṅ Dī Bhagatmālā* (explanation of Pauri 26) carries information which is worth consideration. There is no agreement regarding the period of its creation as different scholars place it anywhere between 1715 to 1790 AD. But the internal evidence suggests that the *Bhagatmālā* belongs to the period of *Bansāvalīnāmā* and *Mehimā Prakāsh* as there are various factors which show affinity between these writings showing one writer getting benefited from the writing of the other. Regarding the compilation, it is mentioned in *Bhagatmālā* as under:

> *Bhai Gopi Mehta, Bhai Tirth, Bhai Natha, Bhai Bhau Mokal and Bhai Dhilli Mandal came to see the Guru, where they told him that the Bani of the Gurus give spiritual peace but Prithimal, Mahadeo and other Sodhis had been reciting various other verses and were making additions and deletions. Moreover, they were promoting their own verses as Bani, which created discontentment. Following this, the Guru told Bhai Gurdass that the followers were now in a position to differentiate between the genuine and the fake Bani but the future generations would not be able to know which was and which was not real. Let us collect the genuine Bani and prepare a compilation in Gurumukhi script so as to help the followers. Thereupon all the holy verses were collected*

> *and placed in one room. The Guru asked Bhai Gurdass to procure the Gurus' Pothis from Mohan but Bhai Gurdās told the Guru that Mohan had refused to handover the Pothis to him and he might oblige if the Guru himself went there for this purpose. Then the Guru himself went to Mohan, who shut the doors of his house and the Guru sat outside the house and recited a hymn Mohan Tere Uche Mandir Mehal Apara.... Hearing the first stanza, Mohan opened the door, on second stanza he opened the door of the stairs. On third stanza, he came to wish the Guru and on the fourth stanza, he placed all the Pothis before him. The Guru handed over all the volumes to Bhai Gurdās, who scripted the Granth in Gurmukhi.*

Continuing with this description, there is reference to the Guru's refusal to include the verses of a number of other holy persons. Besides the above mentioned books, the references to the preparation of the compilation are available in the following writings:

Gurbīlās Pātshāhī Chhevīṅ

This narrative, related to the sixth Guru, is believed to be written by poet Sohan. Some scholars, however, are of the opinion that it was prepared by some unknown person. The author shows his proximity with Bhai Mani Singh but the internal evidence shows that it was created at a later date. In *Gurmat Martānd* (footnote on page 94), Bhai Kahn Singh has stated that the writing of this book was started by Bhai Gurmukh Singh Akal Bungia and Darbara Singh Chaunki Wale in 1833 AD (Samvat 1890) and it was completed in 1843 AD (Samvat 1900).

At Ramsar, the Guru examined sources of all the verses, corrected these wherever needed and gave the same to Bhai Gurdās who was preparing a volume (*Bīṛ*) in his own handwriting. During this period, there are references that the

Bhagatas visited the Guru and efforts were made by Bhai Ladha to obtaining Guru's pardon for Satta and Balwand. Efforts were also made by Kahna, Chhajju, Shah Hussain etc. to get their verses included. It is also mentioned that the Guru blessed Bhai Gurdās's Bani as the key to Guru Granth Sahib. The date for the completion of the Granth by Bhai Gurdās has been mentioned as Samvat 1661 Bhadon Sudi Ekm. In the sixth chapter, there is an episode of calling for *Pran Sangli* from Singlādīp. This way, all the information regarding the compilation has been included in the *Gurbīlās*.

Gur Prātāp Sūraj

This volume has been authored by Bhai Santokh Singh, who completed it in 1843 AD (Samvat 1900). In the third chapter (*Raas*), from Sections (*Anshu*) 32 to 50, this volume provides information regarding the compilation of the Granth but most of the information is almost the same as found in *Gurbīlās Pātshāhī Chhevīṅ* with a few fresh touches here and there. The author has given the same date of completion of the Granth but has related the creation of *Rāgmālā* to poet Alam.

Tvārīkh Gurū Khālsā

This book has been authored by Giani Gian Singh and the first volume was published in 1891 (Samvat 1948). Earlier to this writing, the author had published *Sri Guru Panth Prakash* in poetical form where the matter regarding the preparation of the Granth was dealt with briefly, which has been discussed and explained in detail in the *Tvārīkh* . In the *Tvārīkh,* it is stated that it was the Guru's own idea that a compilation was needed as he felt that a religion could not survive without an authentic Scripture. The rest of the information is similar to the information available in sources. The only addition is that the Guru had left some pages blank for including the Bani of the ninth Guru later. It is stated that Alam's verse *Rāgmālā* was approved by the Guru and thus included in the Granth.

The above stated books make it amply clear that the fifth Guru had a desire to maintain the purity of the Gurbani and he wanted to compile the same into a volume. For this purpose, he tapped all the sources to collect the verses of the Bhagatas and Saints, examined each writing and after confirming its genuineness included the same into the Granth. This way the Granth prepared by Guru Arjan Dev and scripted by Bhāī Gurdās became the authentic volume of this Granth.

In this connection, two *Bīṛs* deserve mentioning. One of the two *Bīṛs* is believed to be written in 1716 AD. According to G.B. Singh and Bhai Randhir Singh, this volume was available in the Dera of Baba Ram Rai at Dehradun but the present incharge of the Dera has taken it to an undisclosed place and the same is not available now. In this *Bīṛ,* after the hymn *Sukhsagar Suritar Chaintamani* by Bhagat Ravidās, it is mentioned that this hymn has been taken from the Granth of the fifth Guru. Same type of comment is added under *Salok Vārān te Vadhīk* of the fourth Guru. It is more than clear that Granth prepared by the fifth Guru existed at that time which could be used as the basis for preparing other volumes. This Granth is at present with the Sodhi family of Kartarpur, in District Jalandhar.

The second *Bīṛ* was written by Bhāī Rām Rāi in Samvat 1749, about which Bhāī Randhir Singh, in his unpublished book 'Gur Sabad Vigās', has stated that it was lying at Takhat Sri Patna Sahib. On page 1027 of this *Bīṛ,* gratitude is expressed for writing this *Bīṛ* and after quoting a verse, benefits of reading these verses have also been mentioned. Indications are given that some authentic versions or corpus of Guru Granth Sahib did exist at that time. It is clear that the version prepared by the fifth Guru was considered the authentic version and another version compared and corrected with it was considered equally authentic.

After Guru Arjan Dev, the sixth, seventh and the eighth Gurus did not compose any verse. The job of including 59 *sabads* and 57 *salokas* of Guru Tegh Bahadur in Guru Granth Sahib was undertaken by the tenth Guru in 1706 at Damdama Sahib and the revised version was scripted by Bhai Mani Singh. During his travels through Rajasthan and south, this *Bīṛ* remained with the tenth Guru, Guru Gobind Singh who before leaving his body, he bestowed the status of living Guru on Guru Granth Sahib on October 7, 1708. Thereafter, this Granth was brought to Punjab, which is stated to have lost during the mass massacre at Kup Rahira (near Malerkotla).

Guru Granth Sahib and its Formation

Dr. Gurnek Singh

The last decade of the 16th century and the first decade of the seventeenth century carry special significance in the annals of Sikh history for various reasons. Guru Ramdas got dug up the sacred pool of Amritsar followed by construction of temple in the middle of it, which ultimately evolved into a sacred centre for the Sikh disciples. But for the doctrinal and spiritual guidance, a Holy scripture or a Granth was needed.

To accomplish this task, Guru Arjan Dev sent his followers to scour the country to search for the *Bani* (hymns) for inclusion in the Granth. He took the raw material and alongwith Bhai Gurdas as the amanuensis meticulously scanned the whole medieval religious literature. Kahna, Chhajju, Pilu and Shah Hussain also brought their respective compositions for inclusion in the Granth. But their inclusion in the proposed Granth was denied, for these expressed contempt for women and were replete with ego, for which there is no place in Guru Granth Sahib. Gunindar Kaur opines that "whatever was in congruence with Sikh teachings, Guru Arjan included in the Guru Granth Sahib." Saints and their representatives were invited by the Guru to present their compositions. Only those hymns which were not wholly inconsistent with Guru's teachings were incorporated in the Granth[1]. Dr. Ganda Singh holds "Guru Granth Sahib, which includes the hymns not only of the Sikh Gurus but also of a number of Hindus, Muslims and so called untouchable saints and sages of India, may rightaly be called the Bible of the people[2]."

The Granth was composed in the language understood by the local people. As Dr. Ganda Singh says "the most remarkable thing about it is that it is written in the spoken language of the people[3]." Regarding the unique nature of Guru Granth Sahib, Harbans Singh says that "Guru Granth Sahib brings to a point of concordance the various thought-streams then current in the country, giving it a specific philosophic framework which sums up the ethos and experience of medieval India as no other work does[4]." The catholicity and originality of Guru Granth Sahib has been maintained over the years. Dr. Ganda Singh says further that "it is the only scripture which has come down through the generations in its original form without the change of a single letter or a vowel sign[5]."

Guru Arjan Dev arranged the whole *Bani* extant according to the Ragas (musical measures) which were a little different from the Indian classification of the Ragas. Indian Ragas, according to Gopal Singh were "expressive of excessive exuberance or unalloyed sadness[6]". The whole *Bani* was arranged on a systematic pattern, which, according to Pincott "is based, firstly, on the tunes to which the poems were sung; secondly, on the nature of the metre of the poems themselves; thirdly, on their authorship; and fourthly, on the clef or key appropriate to them[7]."

Guru Arjan Dev collected and edited the whole spiritual material and entrusted Bhai Gurdas the work of preparing the manuscript under his own guidance. After the completion of the Holy Scripture, Guru Arjan Dev installed it in the Harimandir Sahib at Amritsar and Bhai Buddha was appointed its first Granthi (Priest). In the beginning, it was called pothi or Granth. Its first version is said to be in Kartarpur in the custody of Sodhis and it consists of 975 folios[8]. However, Bhai Jodh Singh gives the number of folios as 974[9]. The contents of the Guru Granth Sahib are arranged in thirty Ragas from Asa to Prabhati. The present extant copy of Guru Granth Sahib consists of 1,430 pages in print. The tenth Sikh Master, Guru Gobind Singh made some additions in the Kartarpur version by incorporating 115 Sabads and Sloks of Guru Tegh Bahadur, the ninth Guru. In the Sikh tradition, the authorship of one Slok is attributed to Guru Tegh Bahadur in Raga Jaijavanti. In the Sikh tradition, the authorship of one slok is attributed to Guru Gobind Singh. Regarding the controversy, Sher Singh says, "in the absence of a definite proof why the couplet should not be assigned to the ninth Guru in whose name it stands, seems to be beyond reason[10]." The final volume of Guru Granth Sahib has been arranged into thirty-one Ragas.

The word Granth traditionally is used for the books, containing primarily sacred knowledge. Its meaning in Sanskrit is a knot which binds the book. According to Bradley it refers to the knot in the thong, which holds together a palm-leaf manuscript to form a crude book[11]. At present, Guru Granth Sahib is called variously as 'Adi Granth' and 'Guru Granth Sahib'. The term *adi* means primordial, and it came to be used after the Granth of the tenth Master came into being. The term shows its distinction from the latter Granth. The term *Guru* and *Sahib* came to be associated with the Granth as prefix and suffix and both refer to the reverence and respect attached to it. The term Sahib is from the Arabic root and means, master[12]. The term *guru* came to be associated with the Granth after the year 1708 A.D. when the tenth Guru bestowed Guruship on the Granth[13] and enjoined the Sikhs to regard Guru Granth Sahib as the only Guru[14], which is primarily Sabad as held in Sikhism from the time of Guru Nanak Dev. Henceforward, the personality worship came to an end and Guru Granth Sahib as revealed divine word came to be worshipped among the Sikhs. The world-known historian, Arnold Toynbee says in this regard that "of all known religious scriptures, this book is the most highly venerated. It means more to the Sikhs than the Quran means to Muslims, the Bible to Christians, and Torah to Jews. The *Adi Granth* is the Sikhs' perpetual Guru (spiritual Guide)[15]."

Emphasizing its universal character, says Sikh mystic poet Puran Singh that "of all the great gifts of divine poetry of the realized beings to mankind, the most fascinating is that we Sikhs in the Punjab call Guru Grantha. It is the scripture of all nations, for it is the lyric of Divine Love, and all people of this earth subsist on such glowing lyrical prayer[16]."

Guru Granth Sahib opens with the 'Japu' composed by Guru Nanak Dev, which has not been marked by any *raga*. It forms part of the daily Sikhs prayer. Every Sikh is enjoined upon to remember and recite it in the morning[17]. Every word is overloaded with meaning and is of philosophical nature. Traditionally, the composition is regarded as Guru Granth Sahib in miniature. It is regarded as the summary of whole of Guru Granth Sahib. It sums up the basic tenets of the Sikh faith. Next to Japu come the selected hymns of different Gurus which form the part of the evening and bed time prayers for the Sikhs. The evening prayer comprises nine hymns in toto, of which five are under the heading of *So-Dar* (That Portal) and four under the heading of *So-Purakh* (Supreme Being). The bed-time prayer, named *Sohila* (Paean of laudation) is composed of five hymns. These are daily prayers (*Nitnem*) later prescribed for the Sikhs to recite daily and these cover the first thirteen pages of Guru Granth Sahib.

From page fourteen starts the regular scheme of Ragas which continues upto the page 1351. The major *Banis* in third part contain Gatha, Phunhe and Chaubole by Guru Arjan Dev; Saloks of Kabir and Farid; swayyas by Guru Arjan Dev and the Bhatts (bards), saloks by Guru Nanak Dev, Guru Amar Das, Guru Ramdas, Guru Arjan Dev and Guru Tegh Bahadur, *Mundavani* (the seal) and in the end, is Ragmala, the index of the musical measures, which is believed to be used in the classical Indian compositions in general. The Ragas used in Guru Grath Sahib are Raga Sri, Majh, Gauri, Asa, Gujari, Devgandhari, Bihagaraa, Vadhans, Sorath, Dhanasari, Jaitasari, Todi, Bairari, Tilang, Nat Narain, Mali Gaura, Suhi, Bilaval, Gaund, Ramkali, Maru, Tukhari, Kedara, Bhairon, Basant, Sarang, Malhara, Kanra, Kalyan, Parbhati and Jaijavanti.

The contributors of Guru Granth Sahib cover about five centuries of Indian thought, i.e. from the twelfth to seventeenth century. The earliest being Jaidev and last, Guru Tegh Bahadur. The total number of the contributors of Guru Granth Sahib comes to forty-two, which include six Gurus, fifteen Bhagats, seventeen Bhatts, Satta and Balwand, Mardana and Sundar. One line of Surdas in Rag Sarang is also included in the Granth. There is a controversy regarding the number of authors in the Sikh tradition. Some scholars put the number at thirty-five or thirty-six. This confusion arises from the controversy about the Bhatts. The names of Bhatts have not been specifically mentioned as in the case of other contributors of the Guru Granth Sahib. Bhai Mani Singh gives the number of Bhatts as ten, Cunningham as nine[18], Ernest Trumpp as fifteen[19], Sher Singh as seventeen[20], Mohan Singh as twelve[21] and Sahib Singh as eleven[22].

The Banis of the second part indicate that Guru Granth Sahib has not been arranged subject-wise, rather the predominance of Ragas determines its order. Spiritual ecstasy and love reign throughout the entire Guru Granth Sahib. It is less logical and more emotional. The spirit, in tune with the Almighty, does not follow the rules of logic. It flows spontaneously. Its outpourings embalm the soul with perennial effect. Consequent spiritual elevation leads towards union with God which comes only through music and poetry. The music sublimates the soul which floats towards its destination, i.e., God. That is why music is inseparable part of Guru Granth

Sahib. The Gurus themselves were great musicians. The message given through music goes straight to the heart and mind of the seeker.

Guru Granth Sahib is written in Punjabi language in Gurmukhi script as it was the language of the common people at that time and the message given through it is easily graspable. Earlier, Lord Buddha also had chosen the contemporary language of the layman to propagate his message. As a matter of fact, Guru Granth Sahib is not in one language. We find about half-a-dozen Indian languages and many dialects are made use of in its writing. This mixture of the language is called *Sadh Bhasha* as popularly called at that time. Macauliffe says "the hymns in the Guru Granth are found in Persian, medieval Prakrit, Hindi, Marathi, old Punjabi, Multani and several local dialects. In several hymns the Sanskrit and Arabic vocabularies are freely drawn upon[23]."

Prior to the Gurus, Sanskrit was called the language of gods by the Brahmins to impart religious instructions and was not accessible to the common people. Unlike Brahmins, the Gurus' primary concern was to impart the religious teachings to one and all. To this end, they deliberately put into use the language of the people. The language used in Guru Granth Sahib contains words of almost all the languages of northern India. The basic teaching of the Guru Granth Sahib is the loving remembrance of God[24]. The whole purpose of the hymns of Guru Granth Sahib has been summarised in the concluding passage entitled *Mundavani*. Says Sher Singh "In this vessel (the Granth, some also interpret it as the universe) three things have been put: Truth, Harmony and Wisdom or Reason. These are seasoned with the ambrosial name of God, which is the ground of all. Whosoever eateth and enjoyeth shall be saved[25]."

Sikhism believes basically in one God. The unity or oneness of God has implicitly been explained in the very beginning of the Guru Granth Sahib. It opens with the *Mulmantar* (Creed formula) containing and explaining the nature of God as has been perceived by its founders. The *Mulmantar* translated runs thus : God is one, He is reality, He is the Creator, He is without fear and enmity, He is beyond time and is uncreated, He is self-existent and He only can be realized through Guru's grace.

References

1. Guninder Kaur, Guru Granth Sahib: Its Physics and Metaphysics New Delhi: Sterling Publishers Pvt. Ltd., 1981, p.16.
2. Sher Singh, Philosophy of Sikhism, Amritsar : Shiromani Gurdwara Parbandhak Committee, 1980, p.49.
3. W.H.Mcheod, Textual Sources for the Study of Sikhism, Manchester University Press, 1984, p.5.
4. Ganda Singh, op. cit., p.15.
5. Harbans Singh, "Scholarly Study of Sikhism," The Journal of Religious Studies, Vol. II, Patiala: Punjabi University, 1970, p.73.
6. M.A Macauliffe, The Sikh Religion, Vol.1, New Delhi :S. Chand and Co., 1963, Introduction, p. LIII .
7. Gopal Singh, Sri Guru Granth Sahib (English Version), Vol.1, New Delhi: World Sikh Centre, 1984, Introduction, p. XVIII.
8. Pincott as Quoted by Sher Singh, op.cit.,p.69.
9. Kahn Singh, Mahan Kosh, Patiala: Languages Department, Punjab,1974, p. 436.
10. Jodh Singh, Shri Kartarpuri Bir de Darshan, Patiala: Punjabi University, 1968, p.122
11. Sher Singh, op.cit., p. 49 fn.2.
12. Kahn Singh, op. cit., p.177.
13. Kahn Singh, Gurmat Martand, Vol.I,Amritsar: Shiromani Gurdwara Parbandhak Committee, 1978, p. 417.
14. Gian Singh, Panth Prakash, Patiala: Bhasha Vibhag, Punjab, 1970, p. 353.
15. Sir Arnold Toynbee in his 'Foreword', Selections from the Sacred Writings of the Sikhs, London: George Allen and Unwin Ltd., 1960,pp.8-9.
16. Puran Singh, The Spirit of Oriental Poetry, Patiala: Punjabi University, 1969, p.96.

17. Bhai Santokh Singh, Gurpratap Suraj Granth (ed.) Bhai Vir Singh, Amritsar: Khalsa Samachar, 1932, Vol. 4,p. 1207.
18. J.D. Cumingham, A History of the Sikhs, New Delhi: S. Chand and Co.Ltd., 1985, pp.324-25.
19. Ernest Trumpp, Adi Granth, New Delhi, Munshiram Manoharlal, 1877, intro., p. CXX.
20. Sher Singh, op.cit., p. 50.
21. Mohan Singh, A History of Panjabi Literature, Jalandhar: Sadsiva Prakashan, 1971, p.61.
22. Sahib Singh, Adi Bir Bare, Amritsar : Singh Brothers, 1970, p. 148.
23. M.A. Macauliffe, op.cit.,Vol.I, Preface, p.v.
24. Sabadarth Shri Guru Granth Sahib, Amritsar: S.G.P.C., 1964, Vol. IV, p.1136.
25. Sher Singh, op.cit., p.55.

The Poetics of Guru Granth Sahib

Indra Nath Choudhuri

Guru Granth Sahib is a multilingual text containing hymns of Sikh Gurus, compositions of the medieval Hindu Bhaktas and Muslim pirs or sufis. The most revealing aspect of this text is that it is not arranged subject-wise but according to the musical measure in which a hymn is meant to be sung. The ideas of unity and proportion in the writings of so many poets in so many languages and dialects are supplemented by rhythmic music which gives them a dynamic harmonious character. It builds a world of spirituality and establishes ever-new rhythmic relationship of notes, which reveals to us the universal mystery of the Divine, 1k Oaṅkāṛ. When we hear the *shabad,* the meaning of the divine poem dawns upon us and we realise that there is an empire within us, a vastness, and in that vastness the truth of one reality comes to the fore. So explains Guru Nanak:

The ultimate one who is Truth
One reality, truth is only one
The waves are many, the ocean only one,
but we see the unity, the oneness of the ocean,
we shall continue, wandering.

The text of the Ādi Granth is known as *shabad*, the Divine word, equated with the Supreme Reality. In the Indian epistemological tradition, *shabad* is repeatedly called *Brahm-*

Brahm Vaar. The *shabdatattva* or the power of the word, which is being the central point of all forms of phenomenal activity, is identified with Brahman. In other words, the supreme consciousness reflects in the supreme word and therefore *shabad* is Divine. The divinity of the word is brought out by song and music. Music helps an individual to get rid of duality and see unity in diversity. Music creates the power of concentrating the faculty of external sound *(Ahad Nada)* through the ears-creating unstruck melody *(Anahat Nada)* internally.

It is said in Ādi Granth, that through a harmony of *raga* and *nada*, song and instrument, transcendental realisation is attained in the *sahaj* way. Guru Nanak says, live the way He wants you to. If He has brought you sorrow there must be a reason behind it, some meaning, some mystery. In happiness or in sorrow let one tune play incessantly within you: I am happy the way you keep me. Your command is my life. Just let things happen by themselves. Do not swim, float. This is the philosophy of *sahaj*. The result is that eternal joy begins to manifest itself slowly and steadily by itself *(Sahaje)*. Just by thinking of Divine, a song will arise in you. Shabad is the creative power of God (the logos) the Divine Wisdom, realised through rhythm of music.

The name of the Lord is also a word but the Wonderful Lord, *Vahiguru* is called in many words like Rabb, Allah, Khuda, Ram, Damodar, Brahma, Vishnu etc. The name is a symbol that treasures within itself all that God is, and is not. The Name is not a mere word to be uttered mechanically without its essence being realized. Guru Gobind Singh says that the word is the embodiment of the Gurus. He, who searcheth me, findeth me in the Word. It is thus through the Word that the Name or the essence of Reality is realised.

Ādi Granth does not speak of monoism, but monotheism, not one of *advaita*, but unity with God. God as conceived by Guru Nanak is the Formless Absolute (Nirankar Brahm) which is manifested in this material world *(Sargun)*. This is the philosophy of the content structure of Ādi Granth. In Oaṅkār, Om is not a word but a resonance of a melody that is unique, having no source, no creation by anyone. God's name is the resonance that remains when music slowly fades away, when all dualities have faded and ceased to exist, when within the mind of a person Oaṅkār resounds that is the *anahat nadṭ*the frictionless sound, the unstruck sound. In fact, by following what Tagore has said, the highest unification that aesthetic experience can bring about is the sense of oneness with the Infinite. That is why, Tagore points out, in ancient Indian aesthetics the joy of union with God has been almost equated with the aesthetic delight (*Brahmsawad Sahodar*). The Sikh Gurus call in *Brahmagyan,* which is realization of the transcendental sense of unity. Says Guru Nanak:

> *Albeit all ever there is one Sole Creator, yet are one that realizes the Sole Creator pervasive within and without*

This Supreme state is called *Mahananda* or *Mahaṅ-Ras,* Joy Supreme. In poetics, the theme is accepted as the essence of art and literature but also the form which seeks to make the content yield its meaning. In art experience, however, as much as with the artist himself, content and form are practically inseparable. Creative idea and imagination involve the two-in-one co-functioning process and therefore any discussion about a literary scripture is possible only by looking at the thematic content and its form as one single integrated unit.

Guru Granth Sahib is a divine text. It upholds the creed of synthesis as against exclusiveness of form, symbols and ideas. Hence it is one personal and at the same time absolute God, who is invoked not merely through the way of action *(karm mārg)* or the way of knowledge *(Gyan mārg)* but through his love-worship *(bhagtī)* by dwelling upon and following the Way of the Name *(Nām mārg),* as enshrined in the Guru's word. It is said in Sukhmani, He who by the Lord's Grace is imbued with the Name, enters the Fourth State and attains Release.

There is a great emphasis in Ādi Granth on the *bhagtī* of the Lord. This is the devotion through love, therefore, it is known as *Bhai bhagtī* or *Prema bhagtī*. Sikhism has been rightly called the religion of love and service. Guru Nanak says that:

> *Those without taste of love or bliss with their Lord Are like a guest arrived at a departed home returning without entertainment.*

Without love man is an empty shell, which will crumble into dust. *(Ander Khali prem bin dheh dheri tan char)*. This devotion of *Prema bhagtī* has been given preference over other types of devotion by the Saint-poets. The Saint-poets, whose verses have been included in Ādi Granth, practiced this type of devotion:

> *In the lord was Namdev's heart deeply absorbed;*
> *So that the Dyer worth half a farthing was immensely exalted (1 pause)*
> *Kabir, discarding weaving and carding yarn,*
> *Into love of God's feet was absorbed;*
> *The low-caste weaver thus became store of merit (1)*
> *Ravidas who carried carcasses always, his worldliness discarded.*
> *In holy company becoming prominent, the Divine light be beheld. (2)*
> *Sain the barber was running errends, as known to all;*
> *The Lord in his heart taking abode, among the saints found the mention. (3)*
> *Lightening to such happenings, the poor Jat Dhanna too in devotion engaged.*
> *The Lord to him manifested Himself.*
> *Such was Dhanna's good fortune. (4) (2)*

Without devotion one is like a dog. He is like a stone in the water. *Bhagtī* is not a show. Dancing in the shrine is not the real *Bhagtī*. Real *bhagtī* lies in dying in the Name of the Lord. *Bhagtī* or devotion is the poetry of connection which connects the devotee with God. Love is the connecting factor, and hence, *bhagtī* is love. It is not worldly love which binds you in temporality. The love of *Bhagtī* unbinds you from your worldly state and leads you to eternity. It is a joyful openness to an unparaphrasable reality. It is said in Ādi Granth that the state of bliss and joy at the feet of the Lord is inexpressible. The Saint meditates at the feet of the Lord. He meditates on him because of the exuberance of love in his bosom for the Lord whom he considers as his beloved. He feels no comfort without him (Critical study of Ādi Granth, S.S. Kohli, p. 364).

Bhagtī is love, faith and humility, as opposed to discourse. Discourse is the practice of power that keeps society stable by delimiting a field, marking off its boundaries, legitimizing norms and perspectives. But there comes a point when such a world is felt to be radically insufficient. The heart, disturbed by love, moves towards a point outside the given boundaries when devotional poets like Kabir, Nanak and Meera worshipper of Sargun Brahm cross the boundaries of rules and authority and wander from place to place as they sing the love of God. Nanak made four great journeys in India and outside India to emphasize the value of love, Truth and Truthful living.

In the discourse-governed world, power dominates and *bhagtī* is against power. Power gives you *ahamkar* (ego) and it breeds tyranny. With *ahamkar* you cannot find God, you cannot find Truth. Faith in *bhagtī* breaks the boundaries of power and it stands outside discourse and addresses it in a wholly new and strange way. The complete surrender of self to God is the climactic achievement of his poetic personality. Whenever Guru Nanak introduces himself as a poet, he expresses his aspiration thus:

> *Thine is life and body, my whole self*
> *thou the deeply Beloved.*
> *Holy Creator! thus states the bard Nanak.*

It is the faith of complete surrender *(atmanivedana)* for union with the non-containable and non-finite, the 'other', the transcendent, and hence, a longing for completeness is the starting point of the devotional mystical way. It is a reversal of the Gita's model of *swadharma, nishkama karma* and *atmansamarparna* which is possible only in a state of equableness, harmony and balance or *samadarshana*. Here surrender is the first step because one cannot achieve the quality of *samadarshana* without surrender. We merge in Him whose sparks we are as only the sparks of fire merge in the fire, as the wave merges in the expanse of the sea (Adi Granth).

The intensity and complete devotion for an unqualified surrender to the object of one's love came to be sanctified. The poetics of *bhagtī* says it is not *kama* (worldly physical love) but *prema* (the divine love) which legitimizes everything substantial. To celebrate love between God and devotee, it was not necessary to evolve a new form. It was so easy to derive from the lyrical love poetry of the Indian tradition, but then the meaning started emerging differently. The earthen lamp was the same which lit the room of the lover and the beloved, but now the light pointed towards sky, presenting a transcendental meaning. The Guru's devotional poetry of *bhagtī* follows the Indian tradition in which the lover or the seeker is conceived as the female, yearning after the Divine Bridegroom, the Divine Spouse.

The very description in Ādi Granth, of the seeker or the bride who has a mind like a pearl which is woven into the string of breath and whose body is bedecked with the jewel of compassion and is turned into a couch for the Lord to come to her bed with her eyes looking bright. Ādi Granth creates a new aesthetics of the Divine. The Being and Personality of God is described in Sikh scriptures as Love, Beauty and Light out of which emanates the Unstruck Music of Life *(anhada shabad)*. The beauty of the words of God shows that He Himself is perfect Beauty. The contemplation of the Divine Beauty fills man's heart with love so that he longs to look upon the All-Beautiful:

In all creation Thy light, then who art light.
In all creation Thy light shines Thy effulgence.
By the Master's Word is this light made manifest.

While explaining the *mûlmantra* or the basic doctrine, Dr. Taran Singh explains *Akāl Murati* as beauty and whose Existence is unaffected by Time. He elucidates it by saying that a philosopher of the Guru's conception always looks for beauty, undying and eternal beauty in all aspects of life. The beauty of the philosopher's concept lies in the mind and spirit, rather than in the skin; it lies in the behaviour and attitudes; it lies in the cultured and integrated personality; it lies in the vision and idealism of man.

Now God is no more inaccessible, out of bounds—now he is brought to stay in the house from the temple, because *bhagtī* poetry is the poetry of sharing, touching, seeing the many in one. The bhagta and the God he worships become one. The most moving portions of Guru Nanak's compositions in Ādi Granth are suffused with the atmosphere of such devotion; and they are yearning cries of the soul-separated from the universal, the Divine for union with it. The bhagta needs to possess Him and be possessed by Him. But in reality, God does not come to stay with you. It only hints at a truthful living with God residing in you and also at the harmony of life which only love can bring. This is the unmatchable philosophy of Guru Nanak described in the Ādi Granth. "Truth is above everything, but higher still is truthful living." It brings the idea of the power of Truth and truthful living to the forefront of modern consciousness, which has been an important idea for millennia, under girding Indian morality. The basis of spiritual life is ethical conduct. The pure in heart will find God. Shun greed, give up calumny and falsehood, only then you will be rewarded by the Guru's teachings. "Keep me in the way that pleases Thee, O God! Thy servant Nanak will glorify Thee through the word" *(Sorath)*.

Truthful living means to go for *nam-marg*, to go on taking the name of 1k Oaṅkār Satinām, the one ever existent unchanging Reality, the ontological Reality. When this mantra 1k Oaṅkār Satinām penetrates your being, the fear or pain vanishes. Taking the name of 1k Oaṅkār Satinm or repeating it, infact, is called meditation *(Mannai)* or remembrance of the One Supreme. Guru Nanak says that God alone is the Truth and the whole universe moves around his *hukam* (Order) and the cosmic Law, the *rita*. And to understand that Order, one has to say good bye to 'I' . Guru Arjun explains this by a simile of a lotus in his famous composition, the *Sukhmani*:

The God enlightened ever are immaculate.
As the lotus growing in water is by it left untouched

Performing the Dharam gives one compassion or *Daya* and also *Santosh* or Satisfaction. *Daya* and *Santosh* bring balance in life and ultimately one has to dedicate oneself to the mercy of the Lord:

Jo tudh bhvāi sāī bhalīkār

Now, one can draw a practical framework of the poetics of devotion which gives the true meaning of *dharam* (Religion) or what one can say truthful living:

sat → hukam → mannai → (mann) →
satnam → daya & santosh → harmony in life.

Not through renunciation but by actively participating in the activity of life and yet not being attached to it, one can attain to salvation. *Nirban* is submission of one's ego to the God's cosmic order not that one may retire from the world's activity, but serve and share in a never-ending state of equipoise (*sahaj*). With love of *nām* one can clear one's wisdom from any sin and achieve balance.

Now, in *bhagti* poetry one hears a new kind of utterance that cannot be adequately described by any means. The Vedas describe it as are *surti,* the Puranas, epics and the Gita enunciate it as *smriti*. All these terms suggest passive or receptive modes. *Bhagtas*, however, prefer the active mode, where the emphasis shifts from hearing to speaking, from a religion and a poetry of the esoteric few to a religion and a poetry of anyone who can speak. It is like the natural highway (*gāddī rāh*) which is opened to everyone. Guru Granth Sahib is primarily written in Punjabi in the first language with all its varieties and also in a mixed language or *sādh bhāsā* known as *sadhukarī* with the then current vocabulary of Persian and Arabic included in it. The harmony of music brings unity in this variety of languages. By this time, Sanskrit had become the second language i.e. a language of culture, the inter-provincial lingua-franca, the preserver and a carrier of traditions. The *bhagtī* poets, whether it was Kabir, Tukaram or *Manikka-Vacakar* were all against the imposition of the elitist Sanskrit language on their mother tongues. In their view, God lives inside us as a mother-tongue does, and we live in God as we live in language, a language that was there before us, is all around us in the community and will be there after us. To lose this first language is to lose one's beginnings. Thus, the poet-saints created a poetry and a poetics of the mother tongue. They empowered languages which came to be known as "Guru's tongue" and toned down the influence of Sanskrit. In the dovotee's life, religion and language are one, and it is also an act and celebration, and, therefore, a language is used to sing and to hear the unheard words in the sound of the kettle-drum *(an hata sabadbajanta bheri),* which also announces the arrival of the Lord.

The idea of unifying the opposites is very crucial for Guru Nanak. The one supreme God is absolute yet personal. He is both immanent in His creation and beyond it. He is both *saguna* (personal and merciful) and *nirguna* (eternal one). He is the principle of continuity between opposites and differences. God is out there in the universe also resides in the *shabad* of Guru Granth Sahib, as well as in the devotee's heart. For Guru Nanak spirituality is complementary to earthliness, therefore he picks up small things of earthly life like seed, irrigation, peasant and tree from agriculture and uses them as metaphors to explain the intricacies of *nirvana* and create a spiritual revolution:

Make thy mind the ploughmen,
thy actions cultivator's vocation,
Modesty the water and thy body the field.
In this field sow devotion, make content the leveling plank,
And maintain the garb of humility.
By devotion and grace shall this crop sprout.
Where it grows, that home you shall see blessed.

Nanak discusses *bhagtī* with reference to its opposite, that is, *jnan*, knowledge again in very earthly way. There are five parts of spiritual upliftment. First is *dharam khand,* the law, rules of life, *rita,* the rules of nature, *jnan khand*, knowledge and realization. Guru Nanak, however, is anti-theological and also against any kind of conceptual erudition but not against knowledge, *jnan*. Then comes the *saram khand*, the domain of labour. One will have to drop one's ego and desire to make oneself empty for the *pahun* (Guest or Lord) to arrive as *sune ghar ka pahun*. This is followed by *karam khand,* where He comes to shower His *kripa* (Grace) on you. Separation is equally a condition for *bhagtī*. Guru Nanak also does not ignore this fact of life and depicts the pangs of the love-lorn bride as it is not only presence but the absence, not the bliss of union but the pain of separation is conveyed, which however can be dispelled by the Grace of the Lord. The fifth is the goal, *sachkhand* in which resides the *Nirankar*, the existential reality or the ontological Truth.

Bhagtī includes devotion to one's Guru. There are three types of explanation of the Guru to be found in Indian religious thought:

In Gita, the Lord is projected awesome and omniscient Guru and the relation between God and man is a one-to-one. Salvation is individual, a flight of the alone to the Alone.

In Buddhism, the initiates are bound to each other in *sangha,* a community, all related to the compassionate Buddha.

In Ādi Granth, the bhagtas are envisioned with each other as a part-whole relation with reference to God. Devotees become members of congregation *(sangat),* which in turn is related to a Guru. Directly or indirectly through a Guru, one worships and seeks for the Lord and the Guru's Word (*shabad*). Guru Nanak thus regarded the Guru as essential for the realisation of God.

The feeling of love or bhagtī is *brahmaswada* itself and not *bramaswada sahodara* as is said about the poetic sentiment of *sringara rasa*. It means that the experience of love in bhagtī is an experience of ultimate bliss, not limited by the adjuncts of time, space, objectivity, ignorance etc. But love and worship, human life and divine life, wordly and other worldly, beloved and the Lord are so mingled with each other, that it is difficult to understand, when on the pretext of writing poetry and creating music, they worship their lord, or when on the pretext of worshipping their Lord, they write poetry and sing. The poet's words are his own and of his God's too. His poetics is a poetics of possession. A Sikh is a part of the Khalsa order i.e., Sikh brotherhood. The idea of the brotherhood of man helped the weaker sections of community to assert themselves. Besides giving stimulus to the movement for equality and anti-casteism, the Gurus laid great importance not to have pride in one's occupation, in high birth, rather they discarded all superstitions and traditional beliefs in the false *dharma,* rituals and old customs while advocating such practices as *Kirt karnā, nām japnā and vand chhaknā*.

Sikhism showed due concern for the status of women too. Guru Nanak says, "Why denounce her, the one from whom even kings are born?" Guru Gobind Singh gave importance to heroic action and bravery for the sake of righteousness and for the protection of the oppressed people in the society. All these are enhanced by the power of Truth and truthful living and also augmented by the spiritual thesis of human life which is of man as a part of God. This is the poetics of spirituality and service to mankind and thus a graph can be reconstructed to map out the poetics of spiritual humanism of Guru Granth Sahib.

Saint Poets in Guru Granth Sahib

Dr. Maheep Singh

There are 15 Saint Poets whose writings have been included in the Guru Granth Sahib, compiled by Guru Arjun Dev. They belonged to different parts of the country, speaking different languages, having different faiths and different castes. Only one thing was common among them that all believed in oneness of God and equality of human beings. Here I am talking about five of them.

Baba Sheikh Farid

Sheikh Farid, who is reverentially called Baba Sheikh Farid, a 13th century Sufi mystic and teacher, commands great respect among the Sikh masses. His devotional writings, four hymns and 118 couplets are included in the Guru Granth Sahib.

Baba Farid was one of the founding fathers of the famous Chishti Sufi order in India. He became the disciple of Khwaja Qutubddin Bakhtiyar Kaki, who was a disciple of Khwaja Moinuddin Chishti. Baba Farid set up a centre of devotion at Hansi, in Haryana and later shifting to Ajodhan, now known as Pak Pattan (Pakistan), where he spent his entire life.

He was the first poet of literary Punjabi language. With his background in Arabic and Persian scholarship and his imagination and deep sensitivity, he transformed a rustic dialect. As a poet, he had to evolve the language and idiom in which he could express the subtle doctrines of Sufism. At the same time, it had to be the language of masses. For this, he employed images and symbols of rural life to turn people away from worldly pursuits and make them conscious of God.

Fully conscious of the limitations of human existence, pains, sorrows and failures, Baba Farid wove in his verses the recurring themes of transitoriness of life, the ravages of death, the grief and sorrow, the insignificance of worldly life and the brief span of life allotted to man. While on one hand he spoke of renunciation and asceticism, on the other, he insisted upon the involvement with God's creation. He believed that God manifests Himself through his creation, yet he rejected the needless wanderings in deserts and jungles. Renunciation for Baba Farid meant the rejection of material things and the sinful ways of life. One must live among the people, seek union with God and, if God is in the hearts of men, help them to find Him there.

In one of his verses, Baba Farid describes the whole journey of man and links up all the passages of life to the deeds he has performed in this world. It is only the good acts which will serve him in the court of the Lord. From the transitoriness of life, the permanence of empires and the fugitiveness of beauty, Baba Farid leads us on to the need of forsaking all pursuits which don't yield any spiritual benefit.

The poetry of Shiekh Farid, as preserved in the Guru Granth Sahib, is deeply sensitive to the feeling of pity, the subtle attractiveness of sin, inevitable death and the wastage of human life owing to man's indifference to God. The voice of human suffering finds in him as expression heard seldom and only in great poetry.

Saint Namdev

Thirteenth century Saint poet of Maharashtra, Namdev, in his great agony lodges his complaint in the court of the Lord:

> *In a cheerful mood to Thy temple, I came while performing devotion, was Nama (myself) pushed off from the temple O Lord, low is my caste why didst Thou give me birth in a dyer's home?*

Namdev was thrown out of the temple of Vitthala (Vishnu) in Pandharpur (Maharashtra) by the priests, because he was a low caste person. But his devotion to the Lord was so intense that it could turn the face of the temple. He made a mention of this truth in his composition:

> *Picking up my woollen sheet, back I turned*
> *And sat in the temple's rear*
> *while Nama the Lord's laudation was uttering,*
> *The temple door towards the devotee turned*

One of the most remarkable features of the phase of Bhagti cult was its awareness of social problems. It paved the way for the liberation of orthodox society. The old privileges of the higher castes could not be completely swept away, but the lower castes received a grudging recognition of religious status which had been denied to them for centuries.

Namdev composed poetry of fervent devotion in his mother tongue, Marathi as well as in Hindi. His verses and his extended visit to the Punjab carried his fame far beyond the borders of Maharashtra. Sixty one of his hymns were included in Guru Granth Sahib. These hymns or shabads share the common characteristic of lauding the one Supreme God, condemning the caste system, refuting the superiority of traditional Brahmin priest and message of the equality of human being.

Namdev performed a double function in the field of popularizing his views through his poetry. He built a bridge between the path of knowledge and path of devotion, between the language of mystic yogis and the rustic masses, between Maharashtra and Punjab. As he himself transformed from the idol-worshipping to the name-remembering spiritual self, he began to be frustrated by the fake preachers and masochist mendicants wandering all over the country. He found in the lowly the most sublime and he could experience the vanity and vacuity of the rich merchants and feudal lords and their pride in pomp and pelf. Namdev was a simple-hearted commoner who could prove in his life that single-minded devotion and sincere self-sacrifice can work wonders.

Namdev and other saints of that period were convinced that all virtues result from the prime virtue of devotion. They directly follow devotion. Namdev's work in the Punjab deserves a greater notice. His first pilgrimage with Dhyaneshwar is referred to in Tirthavali of Namdev. Both Dhyaneshwar and Namdev had gone right north beyond the Punjab. The Punjab accounts show that Namdev lived there for about 20 years. Namdev's shrine at Ghuman, in Gurdaspur district, is well known. It is a tribute to Namdev's work, a measure of his popular preaching that his verses had been accepted by the fifth Guru, Guru Arjun, for inclusion in the Granth, compiled by him.

Guru Arjan (1563-1606) had paid great tribute to Namdev when he mentioned in one of his compositions:

The mind of Namdev
became attuned with the Lord
That Calio-printer of little worth
became very precious

Saint Kabir

A rebel reacts with violent aversion to the injustice and discrimination from the powerful people in politics, religion and social system. In fourteenth-fifteenth century, saint-poet Kabir raised his strong voice against the religious hypocrisy, political tyranny and social injustice. He spoke out the truth which needed much courage, particularly in those days when rationalism was rare and an attack on established religious systems was deemed the worst type of heresy. But Kabir did it boldly and effectively.

Kabir was a bitter critic of all kinds of sectarian and narrow creeds and outlooks- "Neither the Brahmin is high nor is the Shudra low. Why hate one another? Hatred is folly." External rituals are meaningless. Besmearing the body with ashes, taking a ritual bath three times a day, keeping fasts and going on pilgrimage, floating rosaries, repeating God's name loudly, and indulging in physical mortification are a butt of great ridicule for Kabir. He could never accept the superstitious dogmas; however holy the sacred book that disseminated them.

In the fifteenth century Kashi, where he was born and lived, was the fortress of Brahmanic orthodoxy where the priestly elite held sway as masters. He took into task the so-called erudite pundits and their holy scriptures, the priestly pandas and their idols and the immense mystification and exploitation of the ignorant and credulous masses by them. No less was the satirical wit used by him on the superstitions of the popular religious faiths.

Kabir used very pointed and pertinent metaphors — "If by wearing a holy thread a person is called twice born (*Dwij*) why does the Qazi shout so loudly, standing on the top of the minaret at his morning prayer? Has Allah gone deaf?" In another couplet he said- "Look at these foolish people, who worship the dead. After cremating the dead body at the burning ghat, they make show of great love and attachment. They beat with stick the living elderly people, when dead they put Ganges water in their mouth. They starve the elders when living; when dead they feed the ancestors with rice-balls. The old while alive are always abused and cursed; when dead there is a ceremony of showing honour and respect (*shradha*)."

Kabir did not spare even the royal greed and political aggrandisement. He asked the question- "Is gathering forces and besieging castles and showing off his prowess the only job of a king? When he dies, what remains of this game? Crores of rupees and many elephants may be there with a king, such a miser's wealth is of no use." Kabir's castigation of narrow-mindedness and bigotry in both Hindus and Muslims puts him in the category of fearless social reformers. Condemning the idol worship, he said- "People are such fools that they go on worshipping stones. Why don't they worship the grinding stone which grinds for them the flour to eat." Kabir totally rejected the concept of Varna system based on the high and low castes, superiority of Brahmins and the utmost inferiority of Shudras. Kabir believed that the test of man's excellence is not birth but progress at the spiritual level. Birth, in his view, is an accident. He said- "While dwelling in the womb, man hath not family or caste. All men have sprung from the seed of Brahm."

From this follows Kabir's challenge to the Brahmin's claim to superiority:

> *Say, o Pandit, since when hast thou been a Brahmin;*
> *Waste not thy life in calling thyself a Brahmin.*
> *If thou art a Brahmin born of a Brahmin mother*
> *Why hast thou not come by some other way?*
> *How art thou a Brahmin? How am I a Sudar?*
> *How am I of blood and you of milk?*
> *Saith Kabir, only he who meditateth on God*
> *Is a Brahmin in my estimation.*

As a practical reformer, Kabir made a conscious effort for Hindu-Muslim rapprochement in the sphere of religion. The following sayings indicate the trend of his thought:

> "*All the men and women who are created are your form, Kabir is the son of Allah and Rama. He is his guru and pir. Hindus call upon Rama, the Musalmans on Rahiman. Yet both fight and kill each other, and none knows the*

> *truth." Because of his open condemnation of establishment, religious and political, Kabir became an object of the wrath of orthodox Hindus and Muslims, as well as of the ruling classes. The charge preferred against Kabir before Sultan Sikandar Lodhi by the priestly classes of Muslims and Hindus of Kashi was that those who paid heed to what he said remained neither Hindus nor Musalmans. His decision to die at a condemned place like Magahar in preference to holy Kashi was powerful blow at those rituals and conventions which dominated religion, both Hinduism and Islam in his age.*

Kabir would have been totally ignored and rejected by the priestly classes if Guru Arjun had not given an honourable place to his writings in the *Adi Granth* in which more than five hundred couplets composed by him were included. Kabir could hardly be said to have been honoured in his life time. Indeed, he was not only ignored because of his birth in a low caste, but jeered at for assuming a preacher's role. He was even physically maltreated. But he was a great fighter for the cause which was dear to him. Even in his spiritual approach, he used the metaphor of valour and bravery. In one of his very famous compositions he said:

> *The true hero is one who fights*
> *in defence of the humble;*
> *Is cut limb after limb,*
> *and flees not eh, field.*

(Sura so pahchaniye jo lare deen ke het, purja purja kat mare kabahum na chhande khet)

Saint Ravidas

Fifteenth century Saint-poet of Kashi, Ravidas was contemporary of Saint Kabir and both were said to be disciples of Swami Ramanand, who carried forward the Bhagti movement from south to north India. Both of these saints belonged to so-called low castes and they have mentioned this very fact in their compositions without any inhibition or complex. Ravidas said in one of his verse:

Low is my caste and status;
Low is my birth
Saith Ravidas the cobbler;
O, divine king: with thee
Have I sought shelter.

Although he followed the family profession of tanning hides and making shoes, gradually he started spending most of his time in the company of the saints. Many stories became popular about his devotion and piety. In the course of his spiritual quest, he reached a stage when he discarded images and idols and turned to the worship of the Supreme Being. In his vision, the greatest quality of his Lord is that He lifts the status of the low to the highest pedestal. In his own words:

Who else can perform such great deeds as thou
The cherisher of the humble,
Over the head the humble, places conopy of state
Thou alone wouldst show favour
to one whose touch the world defiles.
The Lord, exalting the humble of none stands the fear.

Ravidas acknowledged the omnipresence and omnipotence of God. According to him, the human soul is only a particle of the Divine. He rejects distinction on the basis of caste or creed, for, as he says that in the world beyond no such differentiations will be acknowledged. To realize God, which is the ultimate goal of human life, man should concentrate on His Name, giving up mere forms and ritualism. Birth in low caste is no hindrance in the way to spiritual development. The only condition required is freedom from duality; all else including pilgrimage and bathing in the sixty-eight centres is in vain. In his lifetime, he had thousands of followers, including the members of the higher caste, among them being Mirabai, a princess of royal family.

In Guru Granth Sahib, Saint Ravidas was given a very honourable place. His forty selected hymns, in 16 different Ragas, were included in this volume. Guru Arjun himself paid big tribute to him by remembering him in one of his compositions by saying — 'Ravidas, who always carted the dead animals, abandoned *maya*. He became renowned in the company of the saints and had the sight of the Lord.'

Saint Dhanna

It is said that when Guru Nanak was coming back to his native village in Punjab after a long journey of east and south India via Rajasthan, he met saint Dhanna on the way. Dhanna Bhagat, who was born in the village of Dhuan in Tonk district of Rajasthan in 1415 AD, was in advanced age of 90 years at that time. He brought a few hymns composed by Dhanna, which were later included in Guru Granth Sahib by Guru Arjun Dev.

Dhanna's father was a simple, God-fearing farmer, who frequently entertained holymen in his house. Dhanna as a child was deeply impressed by these holy visitors and his mind turned to the pursuit of spiritual grace. The most popular and oft-repeated story about his simple-heartedness is that he brought an idol from a Brahmin residing in his neighbourhood who was a regular worshipper of Thakurs. Dhanna took the idol with a dogged faith considering it as a deity. He offered it milk requesting to accept his offering, so humbly made. Nothing happened. Considering his inability to perform the prayer, he begged the idol again to accept his offering. Not getting any response, he took a pledge not to accept any food till his offering was accepted by the Thakur. It is said that the Almighty ultimately accepted the offering. This may be a myth but this certainly shows his strong devotion to the Supreme Being.

Dhanna was also said to be a disciple of Swami Ramanand, like Kabir, Ravidas, Sain and Pipa. In one of his hymns, he describes himself as an ignorant Jat and explains how he was attracted to the worship of God by the examples of saints like Namdev, Kabir, Ravidas and Sain:

In the Lord was Namdev's heart deeply absorbed
So that Dyer worth nothing was immensely exalted.
Kabir, discarding weaving and carding yarn,
Into love of God's feet was absorbed.
Ravidās who carried carcasses always,
his worldliness discarded.
In holy company becoming prominent
the divine sight he beheld.
Sain, the barber was running errands, as known to all:
The Lord in his heart taking abode,
among the saints found he mention.

Being a farmer by birth, he was very much down to earth. A devotee does not deny himself the needs of the body is attested by another hymn of Dhanna in a very frank way:

Lord, Thy servant am I in affliction
Those that to Thee are devoted,
Thou their objectives dost fulfil.
I beg for lentils, flour and some ghee,
Whereby may my heart be delighted.
Seek I also shoes and good clothing,
And grain grown over well-ploughed land.
A cow and buffalo in milk I see,
As also a good mare to ride
Thy servant Dhanna then begs also for a wife,
a good house keeper.

Bhatt Bani in Sri Guru Granth Sahib

Dr. Wazir Singh

The editorial pattern of Guru Granth Sahib is the gift of Guru Arjan Dev. The current volume of the Granth follows the main editorial scheme conceptualised by the fifth Guru, with addition of Guru Tegh Bahadur's verses in *Raag Jaijavanti*. The *Adi Granth* comprises three broad divisions: (a) the liturgical section with prayers of daily routine; (b) the musical section that is by far the largest part (1340 pages); and (c) the miscellaneous part of compositions, which are not set to *Raag* measures but dwell on various poetical metres. The contributors of the Granth include six Gurus, 15 *Bhagats*, 12 Bards (*Bhatts*) one *Dum* and a couple of associates of the Gurus, making a total of 36 authors.

(1) Place of Bhatt Bāni

The verses composed by eleven *Bhatts* in the *swayya* metre are found in the miscellaneous division of the Granth, which starts with sanskrit *salokas*, followed by *gatha*, *phunhas, chaubolas* and *salokas* of Bhagat Kabir and Sheikh Farid. These arc followed by Guru Arjan's 20 *swayyas* and 123 *swayyas* by the Bhatts. After these, *salokas* left over from the *vars* are placed, including 57 *salokas* of the ninth Guru, followed by *mundavani* and another *salok* by Guru Arjan Dev. The Granth ends with *raagmala* that bears no one's name as its author. One *Bhatt*, Balwand, together with his associate, Satta the Dūm, composed *Ramkali Var*, which praises the first five Gurus as it also refers to *Mata Khivi*, consort of Guru Angad, by name. This and a few other historical allusions are available in the *Bhatt* verses.

(2) The Number of Bhatts

Scholars are not in agreement about the number of *Bhatts* who composed panegyrics glorifying the Gurus. Some believe they were seventeen, while others hold them to be eleven. The names of the *Bhatts* are not explicitly stated at the head of their respective hymns, unlike the case of *Bhagat Banis*. But the internal evidence of the verses and their styles, as also the numerical figures state them to be eleven. Some of the names of the *Bhatts* do appear in the verses, for instance Bhikha, Kirat, Jalap, Mathura and Haribans. *Bhatt* Kalsahar mentions his own name in several verses, but sometimes he calls himself *Kal* and *Tal*. At least in six verses in reference to Guru Ram Das, the word *Kalchare* also signifies Kalsahar. In addition to these 11 Bhatts, the author of *Ramkali Var,* Balwand (in association with Satta) is also considered to be a Bhatt poet.

(3) Activities of the Bhatts

It is well known that the *Bhatts* used to keep record of their contemporary events and their *Bhatt Vahis* are believed to be quite reliable in this respect. Their descendants are still active at several centres of pilgrimage. Many of the *Bhatts* were poets, who roamed about the country and instantly composed verses and hymns, impressing the audiences. A group of *Bhatts*, possibly headed by Kalsahar, visited Goindval, as indicated by Nalh in one of his verses. Before this, the *Bhatts* were in search of some true saint, as is evident in one of Bhikha's verses, which expressly states that for one year the group of *Bhatts* moved from place to place but did not find any spiritual guide to their satisfaction. Bhikha confirms this in his praise of Guru Amar Das.

(4) Their Vaishnav Faith

The *Bhatts* belonged to Brahmin community and were followers of the *Vaishnav* faith. They held Sri Ramā and Sri Krishnā as Divine incarnates. And on meeting the Gurus in Punjab believed that Guru Nanak and his four successor Gurus were Ram and Krishna reborn. *Bhatt* Kalsahar says, during *Satyuga,* it was Guru Nanak, who overpowered Bali; in the *Tretayuga*, Nanak was Ramā of the Raghu clan; in *Duapar,* Nanak took birth as Krishnā who delivered Kans and in the *Kaliyuga* "You are called Nanak, Angad and Amar Das." He adds: "Your praises are sung by Ravidas, Jaidev and Trilochan as also by Kabir, Namdev and Beni, in addition to innumerable *Yogis*, *Jangams*, *Vyas* and *Brahma*. Guru Nanak placed his hand on the forehead of Bhai Lehna who became Guru Angad."

(5) Swayya: Their Favourite Metre

The *Bhatt Bani* as recorded in Guru Granth Sahib, is in the poetic metre *swayya*. It is a non-Raaga measure and has its own variations of style. At least three *chhand* metres are mentioned in the *swayyas: Radd* (in Nalh's praise of Guru Ram Das, 5th *swayya*); *Jholna* (Nalh's 13th *swayya*); and *Sortha* (in Kalsahar's praise of Guru Arjan). The numerical arrangement of *swayyas* is indicative of the authorship of particular verses and also of the change of style in a *swayya*. As for the names of *Bhatt*, interesting rhyme in pronunciation is noted, for instance Kal (Kalsahar), Salh, Bhalh, Nalh, Balh. Other names that do not fall in this category are Jalap, Kirat, Bhikha, Gayand, Mathura and Haribans. All of them, however, make use of the *swayya* metre for their verses.

(6) Language and Style

The language of *Bhatt Bani* is a mixture, deriving its vocabulary from Sanskrit and employing *Bhagat Bani* diction. The *Bhatts* used to sing odes (*Vars*) to brave fighters and eventually developed a specific lingo known as *Bhattashri*. Some of their verses recorded in Guru Granth Sahib are easy to follow by the Punjabi readership, but a large number of *swayyas* are not that easy. *Bhatt* poets often indulge in exaggeration and use of glittering phraseology in their verses. Quite often, two *Bhatts* follow each other in the same style. While entering their poetry in the Adi Granth, the rules of *Gurbani* grammar and word-endings were applied in order to bring the verses in line with the rest of *Bani* compositions. Some of the *swayyas* clearly indicate that their authors were familiar with the Gurus' and *Bhagats'* phrases and vocabulary. *Bhatt* Gyand's repeated use of *Wahiguru* in his verses is a proof of the popularity of the term during the *Bhatt* period.

(7) Praise of the Gurus

One major contribution of *Bhatt Bani* is the praises showered on the first five Gurus. Kalsahar who composed a total of 54 *swayyas,* devoted 10 of these to Guru Nanak whom he calls *Param* (Supreme) Guru. According to Kalsahar, Guru Nanak was bestowed with both *raj* and *yog* and as such he enjoyed *raj-yog* which characterized the lifestyles of all the rest of Gurus as well. Kalsahar composed ten *swayyas* in praise of Guru Angad Dev, who attained to the height of spirituality as *Jagat Guru* through contemplation of *naam.* The *Bhatt* insists that by having *darshan (*sight*)* of the Guru, all sufferings vanish. Similarly, he pays tribute to Guru Amar Das, who held all spiritual powers (*riddhis and siddhis*) by the dint of *naam bhagti*. Passing on to Guru Ram Das, the poet refers to the pool of nectar (*Amritsar*), established by the fourth Guru. Kalsahar regards Guru Arjan as the harbinger of *Janak Raj* in the region and the treasure of knowledge that is *Guru Bani*.

The *Bhatt* poets, who sang encomiums to Guru Amar Das included Jalap, Kirat and Bhikha. Salh and Bhalh also record one *swayya* each in praise of the third Guru. According to Kirat, God (*Narain*) descended on the earth for the salvation of humanity. *Bhatt* Kirat's *swayya* in reference to Guru Ram

Das is quite popular among the Sikhs starting with *Hum Avgun Bharai*. Nalh too chants his devotion to Guru Ram Das in his 16 *swayyas*. He prays the Guru for protection of his *laaj* (honour). Gayand composed 13 *swayyas* in praise of the fourth Guru whom he believed to be incarnate of the Divine. His *Wah-Wah* phrase is popularly recited by the Sikhs. Bhatt Mathura composed seven verses each in praise of Guru Ram Das and Guru Arjan Dev. Guru Arjan, for him, is *Hari* himself. Similar sentiments are voiced in the compositions of other *Bhatts*.

The praises sung by the *Bhatts* are to be seen collectively. All of them are one in holding the Gurus as the ship *(bohitha or jahaaz)* for ferrying people across the sea of mundane existence. The Gurus are *paaras* whose touch turns ordinary metal into gold. Guru Amar Das, says Kalsahar, has the sign of Lotus (*barif or kamal*) in his right hand which signifies him to be master of all spiritual powers, whereas the worldly powers sought by the folks are held in his left hand. In paying obeisance to the Gurus, peace of mind and spiritual satisfaction can be attained. No one can hope to win emancipation without the Guru's blessing.

(8) Historical References

Apart from the praises of Guru Nanak and the four succeeding Gurus, *Bhatt Bani* contains a number of references to the life history of the Gurus. Evidently, the *Bhatt* poets came into close contact with the Gurus and grasped their genealogy. *Bhatt* Nalh clearly mentions Goindval, situated on the banks of river Beas, where the *Bhatts* met Guru Arjan and experienced the bliss. Their verses repeatedly depict the sequence of Guru Nanak up to Guru Arjan, pinpointing the spirit or the divine *jyoti* passing on from the first Guru to the second and so on. *Bhatt* Salh pays tribute to Guru Amar Das 'Son of Tej Bhan' and the bard Kalsahar utters the praises of Guru Ram Das 'son of Har Das'. He sings the glory of Guru Arjan, who appeared in the 'Home of Guru Ram Das'.

(9) Classical References

The authors of *Bhatt Bani* seem to be great admirers of Raja Janak, whose reign had no parallel. Again, referring to Guru Arjan, he says *Satyug* like reign of Janak Raj has now prevailed. Guru Nanak is believed to have personified in various forms during the four *Yugas*, viz. *Satyug*, *Treta, Duapar* and *Kaliyug*. Bhatt Nalh seeks protection of Guru Ram Das, just as Daropadi's honour was saved by providing endless robes to her and as Sudama of modest means was honoured by Krishna. The names of harlot Ganika, Narad, Jasoda, Sanakas and several other angels and devils are mentioned in the verses. Even Nehaklank, Machh, Kachh, Brahma, Vishnu, Indra and Shiva figure in the classical-mythological references in the *swayyas*, which are composed to eulogize the Gurus.

(10) Significance of Bhatt Bāni

Gurbani is the outpouring of the divinely inspired spirits. Similarly, *Bhagat Bani* is an independent entity, collected and selected by the Gurus and incorporated in the holy Granth. But the *swayyas* composed by the Bhatts are unique in the sense that they are testimony to the spiritual heights of *Gurbani*. The *Bhatts* did not belong to the family circle of the Gurus, nor were they associate of the Bhagats. They came to realize the divine essence, present in the Gurus in person and in their sacred Word.

Bhatt Bani has ideological affinity with *Gurbani* as well as *Bhagat Bani*. All the three centre around the vision of *Naam*. The *Bhatts* share with *Gurbani* their faith in the efficacy of *Sat-Santokh-Gyan* as the vehicle of deliverance. Their firmly rooted faith in the immortal character of *amrit bani* brings out their Sikh spirit. The linking of Guru Nanak and other Gurus with

Raja Janak, may be an off-shoot of the *Bhatts*' way of looking at the historical-mythodological tradition of India. Eulogising is their own unique way of expressing their sentiments. They adopted the poetic metre *swayya* for paying tributes to the Gurus, even though they were quite familiar with the use of classical r*aagas* in *Gurbani*. Whatever the methods and means they chose for their poetry, their dedication to the Gurus is evident and crystal clear.

Editorial Techniques in Guru Granth Sahib

Dr. Mohinder Kaur Gill

Guru Granth Sahib is the largest collection of spiritual hymns in the medieval period. No other language has the honour of having such a prestigious collection in this period. It is not only an ideal collection but it also establishes high standards. It comprises the Bānī collection of the littêrateurs of five centuries. Shaikh Farid (1173 AD) lived in Pakpattan, Multan, while the last Guru of the Guru tradition was born in Patna and passed away in Nānded, South India. The Guru family and Gurus travelled from Sheikhupura (Nankana Sahib) to Nānded, and advanced from the Punjab (now Pakistan) towards Deccan to spread the mission of the Gurus. The Bānīkārs (the contributors of the hymns) were linked with the multifarious tradition of saint devotees stretching from Maharashtra to Pakpattan, and the inquisitive roaming singers and musicians, the Bhattas, who came from various parts of northern India. Their Bānī included in Guru Granth Sahib has been given as much respect and prestige as that of the Gurus.

It may be asked what technique was used to collect and systematically compile the Bānī of so many spiritual beings and then to make it possible for people to get to know it. Answer is simple — the genius and its planning. Guru Granth Sahib is the best example of the combination of brilliance and planning. Guru Arjun Dev collected the works of the earlier saints as well as those of the contemporary ones. Moreover, when the rendering of the Bānī of the contemporary devotees did not fit into his thought pattern, he just left it, like that of Saint Dādū Dyāl, Shah Hussain, Chhajju, Peelu, et al. The fifth Guru gave preference to the gurmati thought process while preparing this collection. Gurmati enjoins to worship the formless as well as the Brahm with form. The Bānī of the Bānīkārs of Guru Granth Sahib was recorded with a proper arrangement of heading and proper planning. From the viewpoint of this arrangement, the fifth Guru emerges as a philosopher, a littêrateur, a conscious editor and an efficient planner. It seems relevant to think over the above mentioned observation in order to understand the planning of the Gurbānī.

The Arrangement of the Bānīkārs

The thirty six Bānīkras of Guru Granth Sahib can be divided into four categories:

1. Gurus: Guru Nanak Dev, Guru Angad Dev, Guru Amar Dass, Guru Ram Dass, Guru Arjan Dev and Guru Tegh Bahadur.
2. The Sikhs close to the Guru's House: Baba Sunder (the grandson of Guru Amar Dass). The musicians and instrument players: Mardana, Satta and Balwand.
3. The Sufi saints and Bhaktas from 12th to 16th century: Sheikh Farid (Multan, Pakpattan), Kabir (Benaras), Namdev (Maharashtra), Ravidas (Benaras), Ramanand (Prayag), Jaidev (Bengal), Trilochan (Maharashtra), Dhanna (Rajasthan), Sain (Reeva-Madhya Pradesh), Peepa (Rajasthan), Bheekhan (Lucknow, Kakori), Sadhna (Sindh), Parmanand (Pandharpur, Rajasthan), Surdas (Awadh, Uttar Pradesh), Baini (Rajasthan Asni).
   Thus it is obvious that these Bhaktas came from different parts of India.
4. The Bhatts — 11 in number

Guru Arjan Dev adopted three ways to denote the details about a particular Bānīkār. For the Gurus, it was the serial order of the Mahalla which has been given in the beginning of the Bānī. At the end of the hymn, as was the custom those days, the word Nanak has been used after the name of the specific Guru Bānīkārs, which depicts the same emotion for the same harmony of one supreme light. The names of all the Sikhs close to the Guru's House, those of the musicians and bhaktas have been given at the beginning of a specific composition. This is another way of introducing the Bānīkārs.

Savaiyyas have been composed by the Gurus as well as the Bhatts. The Savaiyyas of the Gurus have been named as Savaiyyas Sri Mukhvāk, and those of the Bhatts of the first, second, third, fourth or fifth Mahalla. In the Savaiyyas pronounced by the Gurus, the word Nanak has been used at the end. Because of the number of Bhatts, the name of the specific Bhatts has been included in the last line of the verse. Thus the Mahalla arrangement has been adopted for the Gurus, names have been specified for the Bhaktas, and the *Savaiyyas* of the Bhatts have been grouped under a single heading like 'Savaiyyas Sri Mukhwak'. Thus the whole arrangement has been made absolutely clear.

The Compilation of Bānī

The entire Bānī of Guru Granth Sahib has been rendered in thirty one musical modes. It begins with Bānīs of daily prayers, and ends with Bānīs free of musical modes of specific poetic forms called Chhands; like Sloka Sahskriti, Slokas of Kabir etc. The Bānī in musical modes rests in a specific pattern. Guru Nanak Dev's composition of Bānī occupies the first and foremost place in every musical mode. Alongwith this, the poetic mode has been mentioned in the beginning. The stanzas (*Padas*) also have been registered according to their form. For example, a *Pada* can be just one *pada*, two, three or four *padas* (stanzas). This means that the first concern while recording a *pada* is the serial order of the Guru, and then alongwith it, the stanzas uttered by the Bānīkārs are registered according to the number of *padas* after the *padas*, the preference to Ashtpadis (stanzas of eight lines) is considered if they have been created in any specific musical mode. After this is the lengthier Bānīs like Sukhmani, Anand, Bawan Akhrī, Oankār in their specific musical modes, provided that a Bānīkār has created the vār in that style. If more than one vār has been created in the same musical mode then the preference is given to the order of Gurus. The Bānī of the devotees (Bhaktas) has been registered at the end with a special reference to their period except for Shaikh Farid. For example, in the Bānī of the Bhaktas Kabir, Shaikh Farid, Ravidas, Namdev have been registered in a specific order. After the Bānī in musical modes, the Bānī free of the musical modes has been registered according to its mode and the serial order of the Gurus. A Rāgāmālā (a necklace of musical modes) has been added at the end of Guru Granth Sahib, which is indicative of the family systems of the musical modes.

The Mūl Mantar

In Guru Granth Sahib Mūl Mantra has been incorporated under the following five various headings:

1. Ik-Onkār, One Oaṅkār
2. Ik-Oaṅkār, Satgur Prasād
3. Ik-Oaṅkār, Satinām Gur Prasād
4. Ik-Oaṅkār, Satinām, Kartā Purakh, Gur Parsād
5. Ik-Oaṅkār, Satinām, Kart Purakhu, Nirbhau, Nirvairu, Akāl Mūrati, Ajūnī Saibhaṅ, gurprāsdi.

In the entire Bānī of Guru Granth Sahib from 1k-Oaṅkār to Mundāvanī and Rāgmālā, wherever a new Rāga begins, the Mūl Mantra has been placed in the begining. The basic reason for this is that the Gurus placed this creedal formula to invoke the divine aid. In the Guru Granth Sahib, through its use in the above mentioned various forms, the emphasis is placed on devotion and on seeking His Divine Grace which helps the seeker to attain realization. It explains His qualities. We come to know about the qualities of the Absolute Brahm through it. Obviously, these words are used at the beginning of the Bānī and the Bānī being the form of God, explains His features and specifications.

The Arrangement of Musical Modes

Guru Granth Sahib has thirty one basic musical modes. Out of these, Guru Nanak Dev has composed the Bānī in nineteen rāgas, Guru Angad Dev has uttered only slokas, Guru Amardas has written in 17 rāgas, Guru Ramdas and Guru Arjan Dev have composed Bānī in 30 musical modes or rāgas, Guru Tegh Bahadur in 15 rāgas. Out of the Bhaktas, Kabir and Namdev have composed their Bānī in 18 rāgas, Ravidas in 16, Trilochan and Beni in 3, Dhanna, Jaidev and Farid in 2, Bhikhan, Sain, Sadhna, Surdas and Parmanand have written 2 *padas* each in only one rāga.

In Guru Granth Sahib, the Gauṛī, Vadahañs, Tilang, Sūhi, Ramkalī, Nat, Mārū, Basant, Kalyān, Prabhāti, Bilāwal and Gond rāgas reflect a pleasant combination of more than one musical mode. In the same way, the rāga Gauṛī Pūrbī, Dīpakī, and the rāga Gauṛī Guarerī, Sri etc. figure in a narrower class. These râgas are rendered according to the seasons and timings.

The Tune Script of the Musical Modes

The tune script of the musical modes incorporated in the Guru Granth Sahib is not available. So the distinctive quality of the particular rāgas is not reflected, but there are some modes which have got their specific tunes like Vadahans. Mārū, Jaijawantī. The Āsā, Sorath, Dhanāsrī and Bilāwal create an atmosphere of happiness. Tilang has words of Arabic and Persian languages and Basant denotes blossoming while the Malhār and Sarang create the effect of spring.

The basic difference between the Gurmat music and classical mode of music is that Gurmati lays emphasis on the Sabad of Bānī whereas the classical music is more concerned about its technique. The efficiency of music of Gurmat lies in singing of the Bānī. The reference to the name of *rāga* is available, but the notation of a particular *rāga*, and the time for its singing is absent. The classical music makes the idea of music more interesting by its *taans* and *paltas*. In the Gurmat, it is the meaning of the words which is more important.

Singing of the classical modes was restricted to the royal courts. The Guru turned this rich heritage towards the common people. The musical modes took a turning towards the people in general from the royal courts. In the same way, the effort was made to create understanding in the human minds. The musical mode or music does not belong to anybody in particular; the use of this common heritage is the speciality of the Bānīkārs. All said and done, the arrangement of the musical modes in the Guru Granth Sahib is quite complex. It has many different types of the musical modes. It is related to the literary forms as well as the folk styles.

The Arrangement of Numerals

It has been pointed out that Guru Granth Sahib contains Bānī of the Gurus as well as the Bānī of the Sufi saints. A larger part of the Bānī in the Granth is linked with the arrangement of the rāgas (musical modes). Each *rāga* has its own further divisions like the stanza form, the *ashtpadis* (para comprising eight lines) etc. Such divisions are further divided into classes of two, three, four, five or six sub-divisions. Thus whereas each *rāga* has registered the Bānī of more than one Bānīkārs, it also has utilised more than one creative form. In order to understand this, the arrangement is the only way by which the specific creator (author), the form of creation, and its correct count can be established.

The *Mahalla* number tells us about the author, but how much Bānī he has composed in that specific *rāga* can be judged only by the number of the hymns composed by him. The form of the stanzas is not uniform in Guru Granth Sahib. The same variety can be seen in the *ashtpadis* and the *slokas* too. The musical Bānī can be in stanzas, *ashtpadis*, *chhants* (a poetical form) or in any other form. This much detail is certainly examined as to how many stanzas are contained in one *pada*.

Alongwith that, it is also suggested as to how many lines a *pada* has. That is the reason why the external Bānī could not be mixed up in the Guru Granth Sahib.

Here, I would like to clarify my point with an example.

Page	*Rāga*	*Contributor*	*Total*	*Explanation*
14-25	Siri	Mahalla 1	4/33	Here 4 denotes the units and 33 denotes the total
26-39	Siri	Mahalla 3	4/31/64	Here 4 denotes units. 31 denotes the number of compositions of Mohalla 3 with 33 compositions of Mohalla 1. The total comes to 64.
39-42	Siri	Mahalla 4	4/6/70	Here again 4 denotes units. 33 compositions of Mohalla 1, 31 of Mohalla 3 and 6 compositions of Mohalla 4. The grand total comes to 70.

The same technique of the number is prevalent in all the *rāgas*. It becomes clear at the end of every *rāga* as to how many *padas* have been registered by a particular Bānīkār. That the number keeps on increasing is pointed out at the end of every *pada*, and then added up at the end, not only for one Bānīkār, but for all of them. This way the entire detail of the formation of the *pada*, the specific Bānīkār, the number of strokes can be ascertained. The same technique is perceptible in the *ashtpadis* too. In the lengthier Bānīs, as at the end the *Bārāhmāhā* 14/1 has been registered. It is clear that 14 pertains to the number of couplets, and one to the Bānī. At the end of *Sukhmani Sahib* 8/24 has been registered. 8 is the number of lines and 24 the number of *Ashtpadis*. The number 17 at the end of Gauṛī Thitī signifies the number of *paurīs*. In short, the Bānī in Guru Granth Sahib has been given in the name of the creator, the types of *padas*, the number of words, the poetic forms, the types of *rāgas*, the total number of the contributory verses of a specific Bānīkār in one *rāga*, and the requisite number. This technique of numbering has made unique contribution to maintain the original form of the Bānī in Guru Granth Sahib.

The Arrangement of Titles

Although the main arrangement of the Bānī in Guru Granth Sahib relies on the gesture towards the Rāgas, but at the same time the gesture of the Gurus and the sub-titles have been registered too. These sub-titles have been given along with literary forms as well as peculiar recognition of their forms. For example Gaurī Sukhmanī, Mahalla 5 in the Gaurī Rāga points to all three forms, first is the musical mode, second is the Bānī specific and third the Bānīkār himself. In the same way, Gaurī Guarerī Mahalla 1. Gaurī Chetī Mahalla 1 refer to the beautiful combination of two rāgas. The *ashtpadi* is symbolic of a specific form. The folk styles have been referred to by the use of the particular name.

The Management of the House (ਘਰ)

In Guru Granth Sahib, the Houses (ਘਰ) from 1 to 17 have been registered with primary titles. In order to understand these, it is imperative to keep in mind the seven musical notes: *sa re ga ma pa dha nee*

All seven of these are in pure form. The notes *ma* and *pa* are fixed, and do not ascend or descend. They always remain stationary. The rest of the five notes are:

re, ga, ma, dh, nee

Out of these *ma* is *Tībr* (sharp) the other four are purely soft. It is clear that these five notes can increase or decrease, so are they variable.

> *Re ga dha nee* are soft, softer and pure soft.
> As a result 4 x 3 = 12 soft
> 1 x 3 = 3
> 15 sharp, sharper, soft + 2 = 17 stationary notes.
> Total notes of houses = 17

All said and done, the house points towards the main note of the musical mode. However, more research needs to be done on the arrangement of the house.

Arrangement of Rahāu (ਰਹਾਉ) (Pause)

Rahāu occupies a special status in the Gurmati music. Rahāu can mean many things but largely speaking, it is accepted in two ways. One, that it is the main refrain of the *shabad*, or the basic line where the singers come back again and again. It is the line which is sung again and again after the Aṅtrā (ਅੰਤਰਾ). Secondly, rahu lays stress on the central idea of the shabad.

Sukhmani is psalm of the nectar of God's name. The minds of the devotees attain peace through it. In Guru Granth Sahib, there are more than one Rahāu (pause) in a *shabad*. Where one finds two 'rahāus', the former one poses a question, and the rahāus explains the answer. Where three rahāus figure, the first one comes for inspiration, the second for the helplessness of the seeker and third formulates a suggestion. Where we find four Rahāus. Here the first three stand for the same feeling while the fourth confirms the system of daily prayers.

Each 'Rahāu' denotes its unique tune where six of them occur. In Vār Rāmkalī, Mahalla 3, rahāu has figured again and again to mean singing. Actually Rahāu is largely connected with the musical mode. Its corroboration has neither been used in the form of Jāp (repeating God's name) nor in the creations devoid of the control of the musical mode. And yet the corroboration of it being the central idea is done many times.

It may be concluded that two types of study are necessary for the understanding of the arrangement of the form of such a large collection as Guru Granth Sahib. First, one is systematization and second the method of its formation (ਰੂਪ ਵਿਧਾਨ). The technique of its collection cannot be understood without the editorial method. It is through the method of the editorial technique of Guru Granth Sahib that one can understand the basic rules working in it. The arrangement of the recording of Bānīkārs in Guru Granth Sahib, the method of recording the Bānī, the arrangement of Mūl Mantar, systemisation of musical modes, numbers, titles, houses and the Rahāus reflect the awareness of the fifth Guru as a great planner on one hand, and an expert artist on the other. His insight reaches its climax when he points not only to the musical mode, but also to the different categories of Rāgas of the musical mode, alongwith the main notes of the musical system. In the same way, he not only suggests the beat etc. but tells about the Partāl (search) in order to make the singing more enjoyable. The arrangement of Rāgas (musical mode) is closely connected with the arrangement of Rahāu, and its title. The Gurmat music has progressively become very serious and artistic because of these four ways: such as the use of poetic modes and techniques. They present the poetic skill of the fifth Guru. To bring followers of various belief systems together determines that he was swayed by the desire of unifying the country.

Conserving Guru Granth Sahib Manuscripts

Dr. Mohinder Singh

One of the greatest achievements of the fifth Sikh Master, Guru Arjan Dev, was the compilation of the *Adi Granth* and its installation in the sanctum sanctorum of the Golden Temple in 1604. The Sikh community is singularly fortunate in so far as its scripture is concerned. The Guru not only supervised the compilation but also authenticated the first copy by inscribing the *Mool Mantra* (the primal creed) on its first folio in his own hand. Its first copy (in original) is preserved with the Sodhi family in Kartarpur near Jalandhar in a place known as Quila Sodhian.

According to a popular tale after the completion of the Adi Granth, Bhai Bano, a devotee of the fifth Guru, was asked to take it to Lahore for binding. It is said that on the way Bhai Bano was tempted to make a copy which he got hurriedly done. This resulted in some mistakes and additional hymns finding their way into it. On coming to know about this act of Bhai Bano, the fifth Guru expressed his displeasure and the *Bir* (volume) so copied did not find approval with the community of believers.

Since printing or any other mode of making copies of the scripture was not available in those days, making handwritten copies of the Bir was considered an arduous task of religious merit. Devotees spent months together in copying the Birs neatly for the benefit of the congregations. However, a survey of some of the rare Guru Granth Sahib Birs pertaining to the seventeenth and eighteenth centuries shows that in spite of Guru's disapproval of the Bir copied by Bhai Bano some of the devotees also made its copies along with the Kartarpuri Bir. It may be mentioned here that in terms of length, the Bir consists of 974 large size folios (1948 pages).

Since the original Kartarpuri Bir was not given to Guru Tegh Bahadur by the Guru's rivals, including Dheermal and his supporters, the tenth Sikh Master, Guru Gobind Singh, had to prepare another version of the Guru Granth Sahib, popularly known as the Damdami Bir, which also included a few hymns of his father, Guru Tegh Bahadur. It is this version of the Granth that provides the authentic text of the printed Guru Granth Sahib.

II

As regards the hand-written *Adi Granth* manuscripts, it has been an established practice of the scribes to compare their copies with the original Granth, popularly called *Vadda Granth* (Great Granth) inscribed by Bhai Gurdas. It was believed that a Granth corrected against the *Vadda Granth* becomes *Shudh* (correct and acceptable). Those who did not have access to the original Granth did so by comparing their copies with another Granth popularly called Jagana Brahamin's Granth, which is considered more accurate than others.

With the tenth Guru's decision to elevate the *Adi Granth* to the status of Guru Eternal for the Sikh community before his death in Nanded in 1708 A.D., the *Adi Granth* came to be popularly known as Guru Granth Sahib and became a subject of veneration like a living Guru. Though the Guru Granth Sahib is not worshipped like an idol or a deity, it occupies a central place in any Gurdwara and is shown utmost reverence by the devotees visiting that place. In fact, reverence for the Granth started from the days of Guru Arjan Dev. After the installation of the *Adi Granth* in the Golden Temple, he devised a practice whereby after the day's service the Granth was ceremoniously closed and taken in a palanquin to a place called Kotha Sahib in the Golden Temple precincts and rested at night. It is important to note that while the Granth was kept for rest in the palanquin, the Guru himself slept on the floor to demonstrate respect for the scripture. Similarly, the next morning the Granth was carried with great reverence to the Golden Temple and installed therein with due reverential ceremony.

With the passage of time, hundreds of handwritten copies of the Guru Granth Sahib were made for installation in the gurdwaras or for use by individual devotees. With the establishment of Maharaja Ranjit Singh's rule in Panjab and induction of eminent Pahari and Kashmiri painters and scribes into his court, some of the beautiful illustrated copies of the Guru Granth Sahib came to be prepared. Therefore, we find many illuminated Birs available in different repositories. The National Museum, New Delhi, has a number of illuminated copies of Guru Granth manuscripts.

One manuscript with 52 x 74 cm folio size is dated 1839 A.D. and is believed to have been got prepared by Sodhi Bhan Singh for presenting it to Maharaja Ranjit Singh. This Granth also has a sister Bir minus the illustrations presently in the custody of a private family in Quila Bagrian near Patiala. Takhat Patna Sahib, birthplace of Guru Gobind Singh, has the largest collection of Guru Granth Sahib manuscripts. Some of them are also illuminated. While the Granth in the National Museum is very well conserved, the one with the Bagrian family and the large collection in Patna Sahib need urgent attention of those looking after the rare manuscripts.

While a large number of Guru Granth Sahib manuscripts were available, including some very rare ones such as the Kartarpuri Bir prepared under the direct supervision of Guru Arjan Dev, the Damdami Bir prepared under the direct supervision of Guru Gobind Singh and various other copies duly signed by the sixth, seventh, ninth and tenth Gurus, no catalogue or any such account of the Guru Granth Sahib manuscripts was prepared and kept under the control of Akal Takhat or any other central Sikh authority. As a result, with the passage of time some of the rare volumes either changed hands or simply disappeared. No one knows the fate of the first five volumes of the Damdami Bir which were got copied by Baba Deep Singh and sent to different Takhts (seats of temporal authority). Similarly one does not know for sure which is the Guru Granth manuscript, which was bestowed *Guruship* by Guru Gobind Singh before his death at Hazoor Sahib, Nanded, in 1708 A.D.

III

The first serious attempt at locating and cataloguing rare Guru Granth Sahib manuscripts was made by Sardar G.B. Singh, a high ranking official of the Indian Posts and Telegraph Department. As an outcome of it, he published a book called, *Sri Guru Granth Sahib Dian Prachin Biran*, popularly known as *Prachin Biran* (rare manuscripts). In his preface to the book, G.B. Singh writes that he became interested in the study of rare Guru Granth Sahib manuscripts when the Sikh *sangat* of Dhaka presented him with some rare *Hukamnamas* of Guru Tegh Bahadur during his visit to that place in 1915 A.D.

Druing his long tenure in the postal service, he tried to locate and study some more rare Guru Granth Sahib Birs while traveling to different parts of India. Since facilities like xeroxing, microfilming or digitization were not available then, G.B. Singh took exhaustive notes in his own hand. Whenever he found any writings in these manuscripts in the hand of the Gurus, he tried to make their copies faithfully by using the tracing paper and has reproduced these rare writings in his book referred to above.

In part II of his book, G.B. Singh mentions about the rare manuscripts that he was able to go through during his research. This includes such rare manuscripts as the Kartarpuri Bir, the Damdami Bir, Bhai Bano Bir, Bura Sandhu Bir, Pindi Lala Bir (destroyed during the army action in the Golden Temple in 1984), Dehradun Bir and other rare manuscripts at Agra, Mirzapur, Lucknow, Ayodhyaya, Allahabad, Burhanpur and Patna.

Even though the fifth Guru did not approve of Bhai Bano's action of copying the Adi Granth, it is interesting to note that the devotees kept on making its copies since the original Bir, now known as Kartarpuri Bir had gone into the hands of the descendents of Dheermal, who did not allow its access to anyone. Under the circumstances, the devout Sikhs were left with no option except to make copies from the Bano Bir which was easily available. Therefore, we find many manuscripts of the Bano recession. According to popular belief, the original Bhai Bano Bir was kept with a family of Bhai Bano in village Mangat, District Gujarat (now in Pakistan). After partition, this Bir was temporarily kept in the house of one Bhai Mastan Singh in village Barot, District Meerut (U.P.). It was here that this Bir was examined by Bhai Randhir Singh, a Gurdwara Inspector of the Shiromani Gurdwara Parbandak Committee. Later on, this Bir was installed in a Gurdwara, built in the memory of Bhai Bano in Jawaharpur, Kanpur. Bhai Vir Singh Sahitya Sadan, New Delhi, has six manuscripts of Bhai Bano Bir pertaining to different periods.

IV

While no one knows the exact number of Guru Granth manuscripts, presently available, whether copied from Kartarpuri, Bano or Damdami Birs, there are scholars who have tried to locate them and have worked on different Birs available with different institutions and individuals. Most notable among them are Prof. Pritam Singh, Prof. Piar Singh, Dr. Pashaura Singh, Prof. Gurinder Mann and Dr. Jeevan Deol. While these scholars have done commendable work in their own fields, none of them has prepared a detailed catalogue of the extant Birs available at different places. With a view to filling this gap, the National Institute of Panjab Studies, New Delhi, has taken up a project — "Locating, Cataloguing and Digitizing Rare Guru Granth Sahib Birs" with the help of the National Mission for Manuscripts, Department of Culture, Government of India. As per a preliminary survey, apart from different individuals, the following institutions possess various Guru Granth Sahib manuscripts, which need to be catalogued and digitized on an urgent basis:

1. **Takht Sri Patna Sahib, Patna (Bihar):** This is perhaps the biggest repository of rare Guru Granth Sahib Birs and Hukamnamas, including some illuminated Birs, signed by Guru Tegh Bahadur and Guru Gobind Singh.
2. **Takht Sri Hazoor Sahib, Nanded (Maharashtra):** It was at this place that Guru Gobind Singh, the tenth and the last Sikh Guru, bestowed *Guruship* on Guru Granth Sahib before his death in 1708. As per Sikh tradition, Baba Deep Singh prepared five copies of the Bir for five Takhts and it is believed that one of the copies of that Bir is still preserved in the collection of Takht Sri Hazoor Sahib in addition to various other Birs.
3. **Takht Damdama Sahib:** As per popular Sikh belief, it was at this place that Guru Gobind Singh prepared the Damdami Bir, which has since become authentic and the accepted format for printing Guru Granth Sahib Birs

throughout the world. Many rare Birs are lying at this Takht.

4. **The Golden Temple, Amritsar:** The Museum of the Golden Temple, Amritsar, has many rare Birs. In the *Toshakhana* of the Golden Temple is lying the *Shahidi Bir* of Nankana Sahib. On the first floor of the Golden Temple one handwritten Bir is being used for daily service.
5. Guru Nanak Dev University, Amritsar has nearly 23 rare Guru Granth Sahib Birs.
6. Punjabi University, Patiala has three rare Birs including two illuminated ones.
7. Dr. Balbir Singh Sahitya Kendra, Dehradun, has some rare Birs.
8. Language Department of Panjab has some rare Guru Granth Sahib Birs.
9. Punjab State Archives, Patiala has a rare Bir pertaining to the period of the ninth Guru.
10. National Museum, New Delhi, has some rare Birs including some illuminated ones.
11. Museum of Union Territory, Chandigarh

In addition to the above institutions, some rare Birs are also believed to be available with various individuals, prominent among them being the following:

1. Collection of Giani Gurdit Singh, Chandigarh
2. Collection of Prof. Pritam Singh, Patiala, which is being taken care of by the National Manuscripts Mission.
3. Collection of Prof. Vikram Singh, Patiala
4. Collection of rare Birs with Capt. Amarinder Singh, New Moti Bagh Palace, Patiala
5. Rare Birs and the Gutka (prayer book) of Guru Gobind Singh with the Bagrian family in Quila Bagrian.
6. A rare Guru Granth Sahib Bir in the Dera of Mahant Ram Kishan, Patiala
7. Some rare Guru Granth Sahib Birs in the Dera of Guru Ram Rai in Dehradun.

8. Sethi family in Delhi has a unique Bir which has Banis not according to Ragas but according to Gurus and Bhaktas. This also has the Dasam Granth appended to it under the Bani of tenth Guru.
9. Bhai Vir Singh Sahitya Sadan, New Delhi has a number of Guru Granth Sahib manuscripts including a very rare Bir popularly known as Bahowal Bir which is believed to be one of the drafts of *Adi Granth* prepared by Guru Arjan Dev. The Sadan also has a mini Bir of 1"x1-1/4" used by the Sikh soldiers during World War I.
10. Recently a reference has been made by the National Manuscripts Mission that as per message received by it from the Indian High Commission in Dhaka, a rare Guru Granth Sahib Bir corrected in the hands of Guru Arjan Devji himself is lying in a Gurdwara in the Dhaka University area.

The Concept of Faith in Guru Granth Sahib

Dr. Satnam Kaur

In Sikh religion, many different words have been used in the context of the life of faith: *ot, tek, bharosa* (or *bharvasa)*, *adhar, as, asara, sardha* (or *sraddha*). But for faith itself, as distinguished from what it means to cultivate and hold on to faith in actual life, one could say that the right word is *sardha*, a variant of *sraddha*. *Ot* and *tek* (or *adhar*- refuge, *asara*- support) may be said to stand for the *objective* side of the relation as experienced, indicating how *God* here appears to us, as a shelter and as an anchor or support, or as the foundational reality, and *bharosa* (or *bharvasa* or trust) and as (or steadfast hope) may be said to characterize what or how it *feels* to have *faith* in God.

The word *tek* can be taken in two senses: as a source of repose to which we turn occasionally as an abiding support. In the second sense *tek* is indistinguishable from *adhar*. So we are perhaps justified in taking *tek* and *adhar* as one. *Bharosa* (or *bharvasa)* must be taken as *reverential* trust or in the sense of trust in Reality as compared to which we appear quite humble in our own eyes. To look on a friend as *adhar* is simply to feel assured that the trust will not be betrayed. But the *bharosa* which is incidental to *sardha* (as trust in *the Lord*) is no mere loving trust in a fellow-being, but trust as touched with a measure of reverence (for the Supreme Being). It is all right to speak of having *bharosa* in a subordinate; but we do not ordinarily speak of having *sraddha* for those who are inferior to us in rank. As for the word *asra*, it may be taken to mean either that (Reality or Being) which serves as a support or the (more or less) confident expectation of assistance, tinged with a moving dependence on the source of assistance. Finally, we must remember that God as *adhar* is the fundamental and *abiding* support; it is no mere *pre*-condition, but an *under-running* determinant or sustainer of whatever is or happens.

The Sikh view of faith from the viewpoint of philosophy requires us (a) to clarify the concepts relating to the life of faith; (b) to discuss the traditional philosophical questions of knowledge, reality and truth in relation to faith as projected in the Sikh scripture; and (c) to carry out the discussion in the context of the life of religion taken quite generally.

If we go by the dictionary meaning of faith, it may be taken in (at least) three senses: as belief in the truth of revealed religion; as the living reception of religious belief; and as genuine trust and confidence in God. It seems that in the Sikh scripture the last of these meanings dominates. However, it is hardly enough to say that faith is trust in God or *sardha* (*shraddha*). The real is what faith requires us to do. We may begin by considering the ways in which faith is commonly spoken of by ordinary people, by philosophers and by saints or sages.

As for *ordinary people,* the more important ways in which they talk about faith may be roughly put as follows:

(a) I do not have any faith in God.

(b) I do try to pray, but my faith in God is *still quite weak.*

(c) I do not understand all this talk about faith. How can one have faith in something that is not visible?

(d) Faith in God - how is it at all necessary? Why should we not depend on our own efforts, instead of leaving everything to God?

Now it is easy to see how philosophical reflection is set aside by such ways of speaking about faith. To begin with (a) if faith is a kind of *having*, what is this precise kind? Surely, it cannot be the same kind of having as the owning of some property; for, whereas such ownership does not usually bring about any qualitative improvement in the life and conduct of the owner, the acquisition of faith is known to have transformed even sinners into saints. The distinction which Marcel draws between *being* and *having* is surely no disjunction, for there *are* some invasive experiences, like prayers of soulful petitioning or confession, which enrich or deepen our being with their very incidence. Faith, too, is a having *and* exaltation or steadying of being. To *have* faith in God is at once to be bound to God in the relation of love. The word 'bound', however, may at once suggest a question. If faith is a kind of binding, does it deprive us of all freedom? Interestingly, the Sikh answer here is that real faith in God can certainly make us *free from* all apprehensions (*andesa*) and the bondage of the senses - may, even from the birth-death cycle. But the *Gurus* do not discuss, they do not even pose the question if a man of faith has freedom to do anything without the aid of, if not in opposition to God. Philosophy is troubled by a different question too. May faith be said to provide for cognitive *freedom*? The common answer here is that one cannot be *compelled* to really believe in God.

As for the Sikh *Gurus*, they would readily agree with Vivekananda's insistence that consummate faith is acceptance of *apratikulya;* that a man who is blessed with it is convinced that *everything* that happens, because being handiwork of (a benevolent) God, is bound to be somehow good for him... (and that) the highest reaches of faith are not mere interpretations.

In respect of (b), some philosophic remarks may be made at once. If faith can be more or less steadfast - as only seems proper to believe, for men of religion are freely seen to pray for a *deepening* of faith - it must be regarded as a kind of vital, personal relation, and not as a merely inert one like contiguity of things in space; and it if is a vital relation, it cannot be said to merely fall *between* the two related terms, but must be taken to affect their inner being too and as standing in need of careful nurture. The Sikh *Gurus* speak of being suffused with, and being dyed in love of God; and the way they are found to look on faith, praying in earnest for its maturation (*sardha puri*), is indistinguishable from Kierkegaard's fervent utterance that faith as a commitment of one's whole life and being, and that there is only a single prospect of victory that keeps one glued to this commitment: the consummation of faith into utter self-effacement.

The question projected in (c) is perhaps the most natural expression of the average man's skepticism about faith. But to this the religious man's ready reply would be that it is precisely because God is not a visible object that faith is necessary. Praying to a God who is directly seen would be a merely human kind of petitioning; and acquiescence in what is given to sense is mere belief, not religious faith. Nor should be suppose that just because God is not visible, faith in His reality is wholly unwarranted. The warrant of faith, as one sets out on the path of religion, is no immediate evidence, but the accumulated testimony of saints of every religion. The Sikh *Gurus* however freely recommend recourse to the *tek* or *ot* of saints. Finally, a *realisation* of God is possible; and this realisation, though it is supersensuous, can be so comprehensive and immediate that one may find it impossible to shake off the feeling that God is present everywhere.

The question that comes in (d) doubting the utility of faith as against that of human effort, is relatively easy to answer. Saints, including the Sikh *Gurus*, do not underestimate the value of human efforts; they only enjoin a measure of change in its disection. Our efforts, they suggest, should be directed not only at the attainment of merely empirical ends, but also at the subjugation of innate evil propensities like anger and lust; and, above all, at the supreme end of curbing self-will and commitment to the Will (or *hukam*) of God. The truth indeed as one's own experience may bear out that it is extremely difficult to abstain from dependence on such earthly sources of help as friends and our own financial resources.

Saints and scriptures speak of faith quite differently. The Sikh Gurus, like saints everywhere, proclaim that faith in the Name of the Lord is the surest way to dissipate sinfulness (*kil bikh*), and so to put an end to the sorrow which results from acts. They also hold the view that faith is essentially a fascination of the heart. The Bible declares that 'all things are possible to him that believeth', or that the true believer is an irrepressible optimist. If all these views are taken together, it would be clear that faith is a blend of the gentle delight of contentment and assuredness, and of love and undying hope.

To turn, now, to the Sikh view of faith, we may begin with *sardha*. *Sardha,* or the actual having of faith, is not the experience of a simple and isolated state. It is rather an intricate fabric of some attitudes, feelings and relations. On the inside, faith is no simple dependence on God, but is also (a) kind of incessant, if implicit, thirst for closer approximation to Him. Further (b) it is accompanied by a measure of felt detachment towards what the family and the world in general have to offer by way of help and solace. And, on the outer side, faith (or *sardha*), is related (c) to the kindness or judicious guidance of the Guru and (d) to God-realization as our spiritual destiny though (e) the immediate or proximate cause of attaining to this end is only His grace.

Harijan ke vadbhag vadere
jin Hari Hari saradha Hari pias.

Hari Hari Namu milai triptasahi
mili sangati gun pargasi

Supremely fortunate are such of the Lord's servants who have faith in the Lord and a thirst for Him. They are fulfilled by the Name divine and by holy company they are endowed with the light. [(GGS, 14), for more quotes see GGS, 444, 149, 95, 493].

If a question be put as to how faith develops, the Sikh answer would readily be the same as those of other religions: it is, in the main, faith that enkindles faith (*sardha sardha upai milae*). It is the living example of other men of faith - aided, of course, by the inherent, if dormant impulse of one's own devotion to God, and the teacher's revelation of the mysteries of the life of faith - that enables a man to progress on the path of faith. One could say so in the light of the following:

gram gram nagar sabh phiria
rid antari Harijan bhare
sardha sardha upai milae
mo ko Hari gur guri nistare.

"Though I have wandered over villages and cities but I have found that God's devotees, alone seek Him in their hearts. Arousing in me devotion conducive to my emancipation, the Master has united me to the Lord." (GGS, 983)

God as the *Haven: Ot*

God as *pritam* is the loving assurance of absolute protection. Faith is indeed a trust not only in His Reality but in His infinite attributes. In the Old Testament, we may note, faith in God:

> "*Includes the whole relationship that exists between God and man. It has for its object God's Omnipotence, His purpose in choosing His people, His love for them. His constancy, fidelity and the fulfilment of His promise.*"

Contemplation of, and faith in His *attributes* enables us to steady ourselves in *specific* situations. We must also remember that the Providence that God is, for one and all, is no dead weight on our individual freedom. His work is only to provide the general pre-conditions of life, and what we make of the years granted to us, a life of ascendant nobility, or of deepening hellishness, is left wholly to us. The outer, material bases of life may be said to proceed essentially under the *ot* of the Name of the Lord. But, in the main, these material conditions of human existence flourish of their own impulse *according to the average man of the world;* and under the *ot* of the Lord, *according to the man of faith.* However, we repeat, this provision of the material basis of life by the Lord is as such that there is no compulsion on us to be good or bad. The provision is just a bundle (*pot*) or the possibility (*bij*) of vice and virtue (*pap punn*). But, because his being is riddled with the innate defects of desire and anger, what the human individual tends, in general is to choose a life of utter indifference to the Name, and when he passes away his state of being so to say, is freckled with impurity:

> *kheti vanaju navai ki ot*
> *papu punnu bij ki pot*
> *kamu krodhu jia mahi chot*
> *nam visari chaley mani khot.* (GGS, 152)

However, the crises in which man turns to God not only call for protection, relief and material replenishment, but at times for proper guidance. The 'shelter' divine can also be a light that may relieve the gloom of a desperate situation or show us the way out of the dark and burning pit of worldly attachments.

Turning now to a fuller account of our understanding and experience of god as *ot*, which (we have said) is involved in faith or *sardha*, we may proceed along the following lines:

1. *God's appearance* as *ot* to a man of faith

2. The subjective *pre-conditions* of availing of God as our *ot*.
3. Our experience of God as *ot*.
4. *The need* to turn to God as our surpassing shelter.
    1. In view of the above, I find it reasonable to suggest that a Reality which is to serve as an unfailing shelter (or *ot*) should itself be changeless or eternal - *asthiru karta tu dhani tisahi ki main ot.* (GGS, 936)
    2. This experience, however, is not easily accessible. It can be had only by the man who fulfils some essential pre-conditions. If he is sincere in seeking the shelter of God he must do so out of deep love for Him, or in utter self-surrender so that, his concern for self is wholly dissipated (*hau mui*) - *gun ki mari hau mui sabadi rati mani chot.*
    3. But, whatever be the ways of evoking the self-effacing love demanded by turning to God as our *ot*, once such love is lit up in our hearts it cannot but be returned by Him, forthwith overflowingly, because outgoing love for His *bhaktas* (it is held) is the very essence of His Being. And once the individual in question comes to develop such sensitiveness, he finds it easy to make his contemplation of God steadfast.

> *tu mero meru parbatu suami ot gahi mai teri.*
> *na tu dolahu na hum girte rakhi lini Hari meri.*
> *ab tab jab kab tu hi tu hi*
> *hum tua parsadi sukhi sad hi.* (GGS, 969)

In spite of the fact that holding on to the *ot* of the Lord is something of an effort, it is by no means a joyless enterprise. Like the act of creating a rich and fascinating work of art, the endeavour to keep oneself continually under the wings of God is at once to revel, so to say, in the inhaled presence of an object of love and beauty. The devotee who puts himself under the *ot* of the Lord focuses on His lotus feet (*charan kamal*), and he feels impelled to sacrifice his all at the sweet fellowship vouchsafed to Him - *charan kamal basiaa rid bhitri sasi girasi uchario Nanak ot gahi jagdisur punah punah balihario*. (GGS, 534)

The 'fellowship' is an approximation to a Reality which not only relieves one of fear (*bhai harani*), but gratifies the inner eye which intuits the presence of the Lord, and relieves the devotee of all his pains. Be it noted that we have spoken of the devotee-deity 'intermingling' as a 'sweet fellowship that is *vouchsafed* to (not attained by) the devotee.' Indeed, if cognitive freedom be understood as the individual's own ability to identify God, the Sikh scriptures may be said to deny it to man. Their view is that He comes to be known only by those to whom He graciously decides to reveal Himself: *jisahi janavahi tini tun jata.*

4. In spite of our discussion above the final question still remains unanswered. Why should we at all think of turning to God as our *ot*? To this a ready and brief answer would be that taking refuge in the name of the Lord conduces, on the one hand, to a refinement of our sense of values, and ultimately to spiritual liberation, on the other. The need of cultivating the love or of resorting to God as our *ot,* is heightened by the fact that the raging fire of worldly passions (*agani sagar bikral*) is matched in its extent only by our utter inability to face the challenge on our own. For the average man, however, who likes to give may to fleshly passions rather than to overcome them, there are some more obvious and appealing reasons for turning to God. God, say the Gurus, is not merely the sovereign controller, but also the ever faithful ally of every human being, so that it is plainly absurd to turn to other sources of help, and to refrain from His unfailing assistance.

What is more, the Lord is not only Omnipotent, and the admitted redeemer of numberless people in the past, but also the immanent knower (*antarjami*) so that, we may add, He can be expected to see and relieve even such problems as trouble the innermost depths of ourbeing, and so cannot be objectified and put in terms of words. This is why the Sikh sages insist that the realisation of God as one's true support (or *ot* or *adhar*) is the only true source of happiness and ultimate victory; and indifference to the Lord, a guarantee of pain and perdition. However, finally one could say that though philosophically very thin difference might be scrutinized among *ot, tek, adhar, bharosa* etc. but religiously these words convey almost the same meaning of reverence or *sardha* in the context of the supreme reality God:

> *ek tek Gobind ki tiagi an as.*
> *sabh upari samrath prabh puran gun tas.*
> *jan ka namu adharu hai prabh sarani pahi.*
> *Parmesar ka asra santan man mahi.*

Translated into English, it would be:

> We have sought shelter with Lord only, and hope from others has been discarded. Almighty Lord is perfect repository of merit. The divine *nam* is the prop of the devotees and they worship Lord's feet. The shelter to the devotees' heart is the Lord Himself. (GGS, 812)

Sri Guru Granth Sahib: A Source of Sikh Values

Dr. Harbans Kaur

The historicity, authenticity, universality or catholicity of Guru Granth Sahib, gives it a unique place amongst the world religions. As our life is a part of the society we live in, therefore, religion provides the moral and ethical values, which binds a man with the society and the world at large and provides way of his relationship with the Absolute. If Sikhism is a way of life, then there must be some code of conduct or values to be followed. The essence of this code of conduct is ordained by the first Guru, Guru Nanak Dev in Guru Granth Sahib:

Truth is higher than all else,
Higher still is truthful living.

Multi-culturism is inherent in Sikh values. Sikhs do not merely tolerate other cultures and religious traditions, but give genuine respect to them. The authors of Guru Granth Sahib preached that "there is one father: we are all His children". The qualities of valour, self-dependence, fearlessness without enmity, service to mankind, spirit of freedom and democracy were imbibed in Khalsa.

We have to seriously think that why inspite of all the scientific and material progress the world has made, we are today standing on the doorstep of a volcano which may at any movement erupt and lead to annihilation of the human race. I would like to invite your attention to the saying of Guru Arjun in Guru Granth Sahib *'Sarab Dharm me sresht Dharam, har ko Nam jap nirmal karam'* i.e. of all religions, the best religion is to utter the name of God and do pious deeds. With all the scientific progress, the selfishness, attachment and desire of acquisition of all that is material, has so increased that by and large we have ceased seeing God in humanity. Bhagat Kabir says:

> *God first created light;*
> *all else to His might subject.*
> *Since from one light is the whole world created,*
> *who is noble, who inferior?*

Let all the well-meaning people of the world apply their mind to find out a solution to the burning problems. Talking aloud about the service to the humanity with selfish motives is going to aggravate the problem. The need of the hour is action with speed, suited to the atomic age. In this age, the philosophy of Guru Granth Sahib can guide us, make us better human beings with teachings of truth, contentment, tolerance, mercy and community service. The concept of world citizenship can be realised as it carries all the requirements of a World Religion and contains almost all the features of United Nations Organisation.

The Sikh Gurus advocated that instead of denouncing the world as unworthy it was possible to live pure life among the impurities of world. Guru Nanak says:

> *As the lotus liveth detached in water*
> *Or as the duck floateth carefree on the stream*
> *So doth one across the sea of life by attuning himself*
> *To the holy word and enshrining the Lord in the heart*

They disapproved the practice of those who were unwilling to fight the battle of life under the pretence of cultivating spirituality and shied away from worldly responsibilities. The combination of 'piety and practical activity' is exemplified in the life of Guru Nanak and other Sikh Gurus as according to them the concept of righteous living is meaningless except in the context of society. The ideal is to achieve saintliness as a member of society, to have a spiritual existence with the necessary material requisites — *'raj mein jog kamayo'*. The Sikh Gurus enjoined upon their devotees that while living in the world, they should maintain an absolute purity — purity of thought, word and deed. Guru Nanak has said, 'those who work hard for their livelihood and give something in charity to the deserving can alone recognise the path leading towards the Lord.'

Guru Nanak's whole life was based on the ideal principles of ethical, spiritual and professional living. This is exactly what he taught to his disciples and this became in course of time, the main characteristic feature of the new fraternity. Exploitation in any form he detested, because it cut at the very roots of human equality and dignity.

The Gurus worked for a society in which there was no economic inequality and exploitation. They were also against human parasites. Guru Nanak preached necessity of labour for the maintenance of one's own livelihood. Each was to get his due and no one was to encroach upon what belonged to the other. "That which belongs to another is unlawful, like the flesh of a pig to the Muslims and that of a cow to the Hindus". Guru Nanak expected from the rich, love, affection, care and better working conditions for the poor labourer by saying:

Where the lowly are treated with loving care,
There do Thy Mercy and Thy Grace descend.

The ideal of equality found practical expression in the common meals (Langar) as well as the corporate worship (Sangat) at Kartarpur. This reflected both secularism and socialism in the true sense of the word. For sometimes Guru

Nanak himself lived and dined with the so-called low caste Bhai Lalo.

Gurus laid emphasis on the adoption of ethical values, to discard pretence and hypocrisy, to cultivate inner devotion and a truly religious attitude by recognising the greatness of God by reflecting upon his revelation and by meditating on The Nam. Guru Nanak told his disciples not to attach any importance to external forms, formalities and rituals. Although born in a Hindu family, he revolted against the meaningless Hindu customs and ceremonies. He tried his best to wean people away from all the impediments and formalities which stood in the way of purity of true religion. He told people that spiritual awareness could not be attained without noble actions, selfless service and truthful living.

Gurus also advocated equality for women. They raised their voice to get them an equal status with men in the domain of religion and society. Guru Nanak's appreciation of a householder and placing a woman at par with man was a significant deviation from the medieval values. She was placed at par with man, just as the Sudra was placed at par with the Brahmin. In 'Asa di Var' he poses the question why denounce her who gives birth to the kings?

For Guru Arjun, she is not only equal to man, but is the best. "In all the family she is the noblest. She is the counsellor of her husband's younger and elder brothers. Blessed is the house, wherein she has appeared. O' Nanak, she passes her time in perfect peace".

Guru Nanak enabled women folk to win recognition as an independent social entity and laid the foundation for their education and social development. Women were not only allowed to listen the hymns of the Gurus but could also sing them and participate in the preparation of langar. For the first time in India, men and women of all faiths, castes and creeds could sit together and eat in the common kitchen of the Guru. Bhai Gurdas says,"*Lok ved gur gyan vichari ardh sariri mokh duari*", i.e. "A woman is one half of the complete personality of man and is entitled to share his secular and spiritual knowledge equally with him. She is the gateway to his spiritual liberation." Without her participation in social and religious activities man is incomplete and so is society.

The social world, based on ethical values, which the gurus were seeking to create was one of complete understanding and equality between men and women, high and low, rich and poor, black and white, one that was realistic and free from rituals. The people of such a world were not to be guided by imposters, they were not supposed to cling to superstitions or social prejudices. For them the mind was to be the only lamp that illuminates the dark path of ignorance and this lamp was to be kept eternally lighted. Thus the Sikh Gurus opened a new road for the society and built a new social order. "He who lives with dishonour, does not deserve the food he eats", Says the Guru.

Perennial Oriental Wisdom of Adi Sri Guru Granth Sahib

Anurag Singh

The Sikh religion emanated from the revelation of Truth to Guru Nanak, and was organised by him and his nine successors in the light of their fresh and unique experiences and realistic knowledge of social, ethical, spiritual and political problems of humanity. It is popularly known as Sikhism: Discipleship of the Divine Enlightener but Guru Nanak calls it by the name *Gurmat*: Guru's Wisdom[1]; a word used over two hundred times in the writings of the Master and explained by Bhai Gurdas in his *Vars* and *Kabitts*. It is also called *Gurmukh Marag*: Religion of the Enlightened, *Nirmal Panth* Community of the Pure, Sach Ka Marag: Path of Truth[2]. A new lamp was thus lighted in the world of ignorance and that lamp redeemed the whole Dark Age: *Kaliyug* with the Religion of Truth, the *Dharma* of God's living presence: *nām—balio changu andhar meh sabh kali udhari ik nam dharam*[3]. The Sikh Gurus established the New Faith "not for confrontation with any religion, but to bring all religions in the spirit of more and more spiritual cooperation in the love of God. The Sikh Gurus established a religion which like all higher religions of the world had its own social, cultural and religious institutions. But in their scripture and their spiritual teachings, they preached Fatherhood of God and Brotherhood of Man. This calls for realization of Oneness of spirit in all the religions and in all the races and cultures formed the rock foundation of Sikhism."

Prof. Arnold Toynbee is much nearer the truth when he says: "The Sikh religion might be described, not inaccurately, as a vision of Hindu-Muslim common ground. To have discovered and embraced the deep harmony, underlying the historic Hindu-Muslim discord, has been a noble spiritual triumph, and Sikhs may well be proud of their religion's ethos and origin[4]". *Adi Guru Granth* is revealed wisdom of the Primal Lord: *Adi Nath*. It contains 3,384 hymns and 15,575 stanzas; more than three times the bulk of *Rig Veda*. The holy *Quran* is in Arabic, *Bible* is in Latin, and the sacred Indian scriptures are in Sanskrit. But *Adi Guru Granth* is the only scripture of the world, which contains within its sacred body, the inspired lyrics of mystical love of seven prophets[5], fifteen Mystics[6], eleven Dooms *(Bhatts)*[7] and four devoted disciples of the Sikh Gurus[8], transcending all barriers of caste, colour, province and language. The multiplicity of our language, cultures, castes and communities and their co-existence is widely and loudly proclaimed, but it is only in the *Adi Guru Granth* that we can feel the divine and perennial wisdom, revealed in different languages. *Sant Bhasha* (language of the Saints)[9], Persian, Arabic, Sanskrit, Prakrit, Appabharmsa, Avadhi, Sindhi, Braj, Marathi, Punjabi etc. all blended into Gurmukhi script. Since the contributors of *Adi Guru Granth* belonged to different provinces of the country, we can see the blend of 64 different languages and dialects in their compositions.

In spite of the diversity of authorship and language, all the hymns in *Adi Guru Granth* are so mingled with one another that if the names of the authors of the hymns were not there, it would have been difficult even for learned readers to distinguish between them. It is for this reason that over a hundred hymns of Guru Nanak and hundreds by other medieval saints have found their way into *Kabir Granthavali*. Even slokas of Guru Nanak in the Punjabi dialect of *Sandal Bar* region of the Punjab are found in *Kabir Granthavali*. All authorities on Kabir, Indian and western, have not been able to differentiate between the real hymns of Kabir and those that have been picked up from other sources. Such uniformity of thinking and mystical experiences is really remarkable when we reflect that mystics of different provinces like Sheikh Farid (1175-1265), Jaidev (1201-1245), Trilochan (1267-1335), Namdev (1270-1350) etc. were separated from other mystics and the Sikh Gurus by a time gap of 200-400 years. Inclusion of compositions of mystics (*Bhagtas*) and Bards (*Bhatts*) of different provinces, castes and cultures was to demonstrate to the caste-ridden society of India that salvation depends not upon caste, colour, creed and rituals, but upon intensity of devotion in contemplating the Name of God (*Nam japa*)[10]. God, without any discrimination, blessed Kabir, the weaver; Ravidas, the cobbler; Sadhna, the butcher; Sain, the barber; Namdev, the tailor and Dhanna, the farmer. Secondly, the idea was to establish the fundamental unity of all religions. To have, thus, inspired lyrics of mystical love of Hindu Bhagtas, Sufi Saints and the Bards to the condition of the Logos was to bow before the Power of Word: *Sabada*. We find in the *Adi Guru Granth* such terms as *sahaj, sunya, turiya, anhad, nirvana, samadhi, mukti, maya, karma, atman, oamkar,* which had their origin in early Vedic literature, and acquired the basic philosophic content in *Upanisads* and *Mahabharta*.

These very terms underwent a dramatic transvaluation of ideas under Jainism, Buddhism, Saivism and Nāth Panthi Yogic cults. Two thousands years after the death of Buddha, the creative genius of the Sikh Gurus redefined these terms in the light of their own mystical experiences. Not only were the terms and concepts, emerging from Hindu-Buddhist traditions redefined, but even such terms from Islamic tradition as *namaz, kalimā, mārifat, tariqat, haqiqat, sidak, hukam and dhikr (zikr)* were redefined and given new meaning and content. The Sikh Gurus did no quarrel with terms, but redefined them in the light of the Truth. With all the differences, which are purely doctrinal, the Sikh Gurus maintained profound respect for the enlightened sages and mystics of various religious traditions. This is how the Sikh Gurus introduced oecumenicalism in philosophy and religion. In the *Adi Guru Granth*, they brought closer to each other not only the religion and philosophies of vedic origin but also the religions of Semitic origin, Guru Nanak rightly puts it when he says that just as the philosophic stone (paras) transmutes by its touch eight metals into gold, so also his philosophy transmutes the four Vedic and four Semitic traditions into the gold of Truth.

Perennial Oriental Wisdom of Mulmantra

According to Ancient Indian historical traditions, the ages of world have been divided into four cycles: *Yugas*: (i) *Satya (Krta) Yuga* (the Golden Age, when there was unity; One God, One Veda, One Ritual, and in which the people of all castes (*varnas*) perform their roles without oppression or envy; (ii) *Treta-Yuga*, when righteousness *(dharma)* began to decline by a quarter and sacrifice begins (iii) *Dvapara-Yuga*, when righteousness again declined by a quarter; the Vedas split into four, and few study them; (iv) *Kali Yuga*, righteousness further declined by a quarter, and dharma stands on one foot only[11]. *Adi Guru Granth* is the scripture of the *Kaliyuga* to restore the pristine purity of religion as established by God. It is the Dispeller of Darkness: Guru of the world. Bhai Gurdas, the co-compiler of *Adi Guru Granth*, aptly sums up the mission of Guru Nanak as a world teacher and essence of *Adi Guru Granth* thus:

> *Parbrahm Puran Brahm kaliyuga andari ik dikhaia.*
> *chare pair dharm de char varan ik varanu karaia.*
>
> *Thus Guru Nanak gave to dharma, its lost legs;*
> *He blended four castes and creeds into one: The Sikhs.*
> *He gave the lowliest, social equality with kings.*
> *He taught humility to all the world.*
>
> *Bhai Gurdas, Var.* 1:24.

In a pluralistic society like India, *Adi Guru Granth* emerged as spiritual home for people of all castes, colours and creeds, who want to live in peace with honour. Proem (*Mulmantra*) of *Adi Guru Granth*, is based on Guru Nanak's experience and vision of the unmanifest. Absolute One and only One God and His Manifest Immanent, All-Pervading Light: Oamkar. The divine attributes of God are given in the *Mulmantra*. It embodies the divine attributes, the Luminosity of the Unmanifest Absolute God and His All-Pervading Light, which gives life and divine light to all living creatures. It unfolds a vision of the Ultimate Reality and the creative power behind the universe. The epithets, used in the *Mulmantra*, though give the essence of ancient Indian wisdom, yet it has the stamp of Guru Nanak's times and place.

Ik Oamkar: *Ik* = Absolute God, and *Oamkar* = Manifest, Immanent, All-Pervading Light of God *Om*, *Aum*, as it is spelt in the Sanskrit and Buddhist texts, is the highest of all the *nirguna* (without attribute) *mantras* in the ancient Indian historical and religious traditions. It is the one Word which is considered the essence of all Vedas, the sacred syllable held in esteem by the Hindus, Jains, Buddhists, Zoroastrians etc. It was the greatest discovery by the ancient *Rsis* in the science of meditation. First, taught in Vedic period it is not in Sanskrit or any other language. It bears no special meaning and recalls no mythological event, it does not stand for any particular deity. It is the highest possible symbol of the Infinite, a sacred-sound to feel the presence of the Absolute within the body and the soul, called *Brahman* in the Upanisads. It is an inarticulate exclamation when man is confronted with His Presence. Because of its university *Aum* can be used by all who cannot find a Guru to initiate them into a *mantra*. Unlike other names of God, it has no gender, no number, no caste. For these reasons the ancient *Rsis* popularized *Oam* as the real name of God. Even the word *Brahma* is in neuter gender. In the four

Samhitas of the Vedas we do not find the description of God as *Oam*. But in the Upanisads it is described in details.

> "Just as all the leaves of a sprig are held together by its stem, so all words (*sarva vak*) are held together by the sound *Om*[12]."
>
> "*Om* is indestructible. He should be glorified and He should be worshipped and meditated upon[13]."
>
> "*Om* (God) is Eternal (*aksaram*). The whole universe is his manifestation[14]."
>
> "*Om* is the most prominent among the symbols (*pratikas*) under which the meditation (*upasana*) of the supra-sensible *Brahman* is possible[15]". Aum is Brahman[16]. The word which all the Vedas declare, which all the austerities proclaim, desiring which (people) live the life of a religious student, that word..... is *Aum*[17].
>
> "This syllable is, verily, the everlasting spirit. This syllable, indeed, is the highest end; knowing this very syllable whatever anyone desires will, indeed, be his[18].
>
> "*Om* is the bow, the soul is the arrow, and *Brahman* is the target[19]."
>
> "All that is the past, the present and the future, all this is only the syllable *aum*. And whatever else there is beyond the threefold time, that too is only the syllable *aum*. The syllable *aum*, which is symbol of Brahman, stands for the manifested world, the past, the present and the future, as well as the Unmanifested Absolute[20]."

The great sage Patanjali in his *Yoga-Sutra* says: "*Pranavah Om* is the *vachak* name of God[21]."

In the ancient texts, the words *Om*, *Aum* and *Oamkar* have been used for God, and there is no truth in the assertion of some modern scholars that the word *Oamkar* is the extended form of the word *Om*[22]. Beside *Om*, the word *Oamkar* is also used for God in the Upanisadic and Puranic literature[23]. Guru Nanak, by adding the numeral figure (One) before *Oamkar*, has once more emphasised that God is One, and rejected the plurality of the gods, then a feature of Hinduism. Total number of such gods and goddesses, which brought in the idea of image-worship in Indian society, came to 33 crores. In the beginning Guru Nanak did not express the Oneness of God through alphabetical spellings (*Ek* or *Ik*), but through the numeral, though at other places, in *Adi Guru Granth* alphabetical spellings have also been used to express the same thought[24]. Grammatically, the word, *Ik* or *Ek* is pronoun or an adjective, qualifying the noun *Oamkar*, but as a figure or numeral it is independent, suggesting that there is only One Supreme Reality (God) in the world. Though God manifests himself under various forms, yet He is not many. He is One alone[25], the diversity is the result of his *maya*[26]. In mathematics, numeral (One) is the first numeral, and it assumes all forms and calculations. If the numeral (One) is removed, figure ten (10) become zero; so is the fate of even the biggest amounts and figures e.g. hundred, thousand, millions and so on. Hence, in Mathematics, all amounts are reduced to nugatory, when numeral (One) is removed. Just as the numeral (One) is all-pervasive and goes on increasing by ten without loosing its shape or value if a zero is added; similarly God is One and pervades the entire universe. Numeral (One) or *Ekam* is the sound symbol of the Transcendent Absolute, the Supreme Being, also called *Nirankar:* Formless. *Oamkar* or *Om* is the symbol of the *dhavni*, the Music, the primordial sound, the Logos, which becomes the creative force and the Immanent spirit of God[27]. Ontologically speaking, *Ekamkar* is the One Eternal, Self-Existent Being, while *Oamkar*[28] is Being and Becoming.

Secondly, truthfulness is predominant and common feature of Vedic gods. In the Rig Veda, Agni[29] and Indra[30] are addressed with the attribute *Satya*. In the Upanisdic literature the concept of God as Truth is advocated. But Guru Nanak instead of using Truth (*Satya*) for god as an attribute has used it as a name; "*Satinamu:* Eternal Truth is His Name", and further declares that Eternal Truth is the only Ultimate Reality for us all: *adi sachū, jugadi sachū, hai bhi sachū, Nanak hosi bhi sachū*: In the beginning, He was, the Truth; throughout the ages He has been the Truth[31]; even now He is, the Immanent Truth; forever in future He shall be, the Truth." In Sanskrit *Sati* or *Satya* means "existing" "eternal". And if we read *Ik Oamkar Satinamu* as one phrase it denotes Only Absolute god is Eternal Truth.

After describing God and his Name, *Mulmantra* gives us the glimpses of divine attributes. The first attribute, used for Primal Lord is *Karta*; the Creater; Vedic and Upanisdic literature gives innumerable expressions of God as the Creator of the universe. In *Rig Veda* it is stated: "Never may He harm us who is earth's Begetter, nor He whose laws are sure, the heaven's Creator[32]. In the *Atharva Veda* it is stated: "God is the Creator and sustainer[33]. This multitude of human beings is God's Creation[34]. In the Upanisadic literature *Brahman* is highlighted as the primary and only source of birth, life and death. He is the Omniscient, the Creator of the universe[35]. And again it is stated: "The One, controller (of all), the inner self of all things, who makes His One Form manifold, to the wise who perceive Him as abiding in the soul, to them is eternal bliss-to no others[36]."

Next attribute of God in the *Mulmantra* is *Purakhu* - in the classical Indian literature, *Purusa* stands for the individual soul as well as for the Supreme or Universal soul. In the *Mulmantra,* it stands for the Supreme Sovereign soul. *Purusa* was first mentioned as the cosmic principle in the *Rig Veda*[37]. In the *Atharva Veda,* it is the principle of creation[38]. In *Vajasaneyi Samhita,* it is described as a resplendent principle, pervading the universe[39]. In the *Katha Upanisad,* it is the highest entity[40]. In the *Mundaka Upanisad,* it is the primeval person, who is heavenly (*divya)*, formless (amurta), breathless (aprana), mindless (*amanas*) and pure (*subhr*). Patanjali's *Yoga-Sutra* also introduced the concept of *Purusa Visesa*, also called *Isvara*[41]. In the classical concept of *Purusa*, we can have a faint glimmer of *Akal Purakh*, introduced by Guru Nanak in the *Mulmantra*. *Karta Purakh* here collectively means the Creator of the Universe," but taken separately *Karta* denotes 'the Creator' and *Purakh* refers to One God, who acts as uninvolved observer of the *Jivatmas* in their entanglements in the cosmic drama of His creation; *maya,* which finds them to countless rebirths.

Next, Guru Nanak defines the unique and positive characteristics of God: *Nirbhau* - Fearless, *Niravairu* -without enmity, *Akal Murati* - Deathless in Form and Essence, *Ajuni* - Unborn, Non-placental. Most of these attributes of God have been frequently mentioned in the classical Indian literature. In the *Rig Veda,* Immortality and death are two shadows of God[42]. God, being the Creator; is a compassionate and loving Father of his creatures. He is not bound by the limits of time and space. He has no beginning and no end. God existed before time; before the birth of day and night, before the creation of sun and stars. God is immortal, and not bound by time, as He Himself represents Time *(kala)* and that is why He is called Timeless (*Akal*) in the *Mulmantra*. In the classical Indian literature also, God is referred to as *Kalo*. *Kalo* i.e. God is Time itself, and at the same time beyond the limits of time[43]. *Kala* is conceived as the First Principle in *Atharva Veda*[44], Svetasvatara Upanisad[45] and Susruta sārira[46]. In the Atharva Veda, *Kala* is referred to as God Supreme.

> *Yea, having conquered all the worlds by Brahman,*
> *Kala as God Supreme is supplicated.*[47]
> *He is the Creator of yonder heaven*[48]
> *Realms of earth*[49], *Lord of all*[50], *Father of Prajapati*[51]

We are further told in *Atharva Veda* that Time (*Kala)* is a horse with seven reins... Him the knowing poets ride... and all the worlds are His wheels.

Even in the leading dictionaries, the words *Kal, Akal* and *Mahakal* have been used as synonymous, and represent God. Kāla, Akāl, Mahākāl in the classical Indian literature and the Sikh Scriptures is the Supreme Power, which is the source of all creation, and which has the power to end to creation. It is the Eternal Spirit of Time (*Akal*) in which Deathless (*Kala*) has merged itself; the immutable principle of time. It is Omnipotent and Omniscient principle and power; God as Creator and Destroyer, God who is Sovereign over life and death.

Lastly, the epithet used for God's existence is *saibham* (Sk. *suavaymbu*), which means Self-Existent, Pure, Perfect and absolutely self-dependent, who has no Master or Creator. The word *saibham* is used only in the *Mulmantra*; elsewhere in the *Adi Guru Granth* the word used is *sambhau* (Sk. *sambhava*), which means He who created Himself. Guru Gobind Singh has used the word *suyambhav*. This concept of *saibham* is further explained in *Pauri* (stanza) 5 of Japuji:

> *thapia na jai kita na hoi,*
> *ape api niranjan soi.*
>
> (God cannot be installed like idols of deity,
> Nor can He be created and shaped.
> God, the Stainless and Perfect
> is Self-Created and Self-Existent.)

Adi Guru Granth, Guru Nanak, p. 2

The word *svayambhu* has been used for *Brahma*, *Vishnu* and *Shiva* in the Puranic literature, but in the Upanisadic literature, it has been used specifically to denote the Self-Existing God.

From the above comparative study of ancient and medieval Indian religious traditions, it is clear that though Guru Nanak has used the epithets of ancient Indian religious literature, but he did so with amended and extended connotations; and he gave them new content, meaning and continuity.

References

1. *Adi Guru Granth*, *Raga Gujari*, p. 505; *Raga Ramkali*, p. 904; *Raga maru*, pp. 1008-09; *Raga Basant* p. 1190; *Raga Sarang*, p. 1233
2. Guru Nank minted a new coin of his Faith by founding the religion of the Pure in this world, Bhai Gurdas, *Var*. 1, *Pauri* 45.
3. *Adi Guru Granth*, p. 1387.
4. Trilochan Singh et al., *Sacred Writings of the Sikh Foreword*, p. 10.
5. Guru Nanak, Guru Angad, Guru Amar Das, Guru Ram Das, Guru Arjan, Guru Tegh Bahadur and Guru Gobind Singh under the signature Name of Nanak.
6. Sheikh Farid, Jaidev, Trilochan, Namdeva, Sadhna, Beni, Ramananda, Kabir, Ravidas, Pipa, Sain, Dhanna, Bhikhan, Parmananda, Surdas, under Bhagat Bani.
7. Bhatt Kalshar, Jalap, Kirat, Bhikha, Salh, Bhal, Nalh, Gayand, Mathura, Balh, Haribans.
8. Bhat Mardana, Baba Sundar, Bhat Balwant and Bhat Satta.
9. Sant Bhasa, deriving religious diction from the ancient Indian Scriptures, imparting their thoughts in the language of the people, because the mystics travelled throughout India and they revealed the inspired wisdom in the mixed language, which became the *lingua franca* of the country.
10. *Nam japa* also knows as *simrinn*, *dhikr, zikr* and *yad* is what the French Mystic, Brother Lawrance calls Practicing the Presence of God, and the tools may be *mala*, *kirtan* (music), *swas-swas nam japna* (with breath awareness) and with the Word of God (*sabda*) only.
    (i) *Adi Guru Granth*, pp. 445-46.
    (ii) Bhai Gurdas, *Var*. 1:24.
11. *Chandogya Upanisad*, II, 23:3:4., 227.
12. Ibid., I.i. 182.
13. Ibid., I.i. 182.
14. Ibid., I.i.
15. *Taittirtya upanisad*, 1.1. 136.
16. *Katha Upanisad*, 1.2:15, 55.
17. Ibid., 1.2:16.55.
18. *Prsana Upanisad* 98.
19. *Mandukya Upanisad*. 1.1.133.
20. *Yoga-Sutras*, 1.23.
21. Prof. Teja Singh, *Satigur Nanak Dev di Bani Japuji Sahib da Tika*, p. 37.
    (i) *Mandukya Upnisad*. 1.1; (ii) *Chandogya Upanisad*. III. 12:1: (iii) *Ganeska Purana*. 1.11, 2:11.

22. *Adi Guru Granth*, pp. 29, 30, 153, 185, 189, 222, 296, 688, 782, 821, 838, 885 904, 916.
23. *Adi Guru Granth,* pp. 350, 420.
24. *Adi Guru Granth*, p. 1237; *Katha Upanisad*, II. 12-13.
25. Bhai Gurdas, *Var.* 26:2, 39:2; Adi Guru Granth, pp. 838, Guru Gobind Singh, *Akal Ustati*.1.
26. *Adi Guru Granth*, Guru Nanak, *Dakhni Oamkar*.
27. *Rg Veda*. I. 1-5.
28. Ibid., II. 12-15.
29. *Sloka* (Couplet) attached to the *Mulmantra*, *Adi Guru Granth*, p. 1.
30. Ralph T.H. Griffith, *The Hymns of the Rg Veda*, x.121.9, p. 629.
31. Devi Chand, *The Atharva Veda* xiii. 3, p. 599.
32. Ibid., xiii.9, p. 599.

    esa sarvesvarah, esa sarvajnahm eso ntryami, eso yonih sarvasya prabhavapyayau hi bhuuanam. Mandukya Upanisad. 6. 132.
33. *Katha Upanisa*, II. 2:12, Trs. Dr. Radhakrishnan. 72.
34. *Rg Veda*, x. 90.
35. *Atharva Veda*, x.2.
36. *Vajasaneyi Samhita*, xxxi.18, xxxii.2.
37. *Katha Upanisad*, III. 10-11.
38. *Mundaka Upanisad*. II 1-10.
39. *Yoga-Sutra*, 1.26.
40. *Rg*. *Veda*. x. 121:2.
41. *Svetahsvatara Upanisad*, vi: 16.
42. *Atharva Veda*, xix. 53:10, 54:1-6.
43. *Svetasvatara Upanisad*, 1:2, vi: 6.
44. *Susruta sarita*, I, II.
45. *Atharva Veda*, xix. 54:6.
46. Ibid., xix. 53:5.
47. Ibid., xix. 53:5.
48. Ibid., xix. 53:8.
49. Ibid., xix. 53:10.
50. Ibid., xix. 53:1-2, *kalo asvo vahati sapto-rasmih.....jam arohanti kavaya vipasatah....tasya cakra bhuuvanana visva.*
    (i) Mukand Lal Srivastva, (Ed.) *Gyan Sabad Kosh*, pp. 156-57.
    (ii) V.S. Apte, *Sanskrit Etymology*, p. 160.

(iii) Rajbali Pandey, *Hindu Dharma Kosh*, vol. iv., p. 315.

(iv) Ram Chandra Verma, *Manak Hindi Kosh*, vol. iv., p. 315.

(v) Shyam Sunder Das, *Hindi Sabad Sagar*, vol. iii, p. 3240.

(vi) Dr. S.S. Joshi et al., *Punjabi-Angreji Kosh*, p. 654.

51. *Adi Guru Granth*, pp. 99, 120, 916, 1042, 1082.

(i) *sarb bisva rachio syyambhava garan bhanjankar.*

(ii) *syyaninbava sumbh sarbda sarb jugte. Dasam Granth*, pp. 5-10.

(i) *M. Monier William, A. Sanskrit-English Dictionary*, p. 128.

(ii) *Banjaman Walker, Hindu World*, vol. ii. p. 467.

(i) *Brhad-aranyaka Upanisad*, 6:3; *Katha Upanisad* II 1:1; *Iso Upanisad*, 8; *Svetasvatara Upanisad,* vi:

(ii) In Islamic tradition the word used is *khudai* or *khuda* from *khud* — self and *ai* = coming. The Self-Existing god.

Communion: A Cardinal Message of Guru Granth Sahib

Dr Gurmeet Singh Maan

Guru Granth Sahib enjoys unquestionable exclusivity and supremacy among all the Holy Scriptures of the world in ways more than one. May it be ontology, epistemology, cosmology, monotheism, religious pluralism, spiritual materialism, messages of divine love, empathy, gratitude, unconditional surrender, existential and experiential vision regarding vices plaguing the human consciousness and the inbuilt solution to shrug them off, so on and so forth, it doesn't disappoint the seeker. The Divine Word, which constitutes its unique hallmark, is panacea to all kinds of ailments and sufferings afflicting the human body and mind (*sarb rog ka aukhad naam*). The only prerequisite nevertheless, to my mind, is the sense of urgency and exigency with which the seeker explores and rummages into locate the hidden and subtle meaning of The Word (*Jo prabh ko milbo chahe khoj shabd mein leh*!).

The quintessence of Guru Granth Sahib also lies in its constitution, raised in the backdrop of Divine Music and the concept of establishing direct dialogue with the Superconsciousness (*Parmatma*), blessed of course by the Grace of the Guru (*Gurparsad*). This dialogue is ultimately transformed into a monologue, so to say, because there is no other way to describe this state of connection or communication with the self or The Self. It is because the Supreme Soul *(Parmatma)* is no different than the human soul (*har jan har antar nahin Nanak sachi maan*). This state can only be reached when the communicator and the communicatee dissolve into one (*Har appe khelai appe dekhai appe rachan rachaaya.... Jaat mein jot/jot mein jata*).

This state of communication is called Communion, which is the supreme and the only form of communication for attaining the ultimate goal assigned to a human soul in its lifetime, called, self-realisation. Such recitations as *Mann tu jot sarup hain, apna mool pachhan (*Guru Amar Dass), *Realise your true nature* (Krishna's message to Arjuna), *See your original face* (Jesus Christ), *Appo Dippo Bhav* (Gautam Buddha) are a pointer towards this cardinal message of all the holy scriptures.

To understand Communion we have to start from behind. Let us begin with one of central messages contained in Guru Granth Sahib, that of collective human welfare or *sarbat da bhala*. In the couplet *Nanak, naam chardhi kala, tere bhane sarbat da bhala, naam* indicates communication with the self. It is dilution of *amness* into *naam-ness* as *amness* is the last hindrance on the way to Him (*tun karta karna main nahi jaun haun kari na hoe*). Mirza Ghalib puts it like this:

Na tha kuchh to khuda tha
Kuchh na hota to khuda hota
Duboya mujhko hone ne
Na hota main to kya hota

The next stage in Communion is witnessing along three dimensions, that is, *the scene*, *the seer* and *the witness* or the Super Seer, who is watching both the scene and the seer. Guru Gobind Singh's recitation, *main haan param purakh ka daasa, dekhan ayo jagat tamatsa;* quite vividly describes this three-dimensional relationship. Krishna's advice to Arjuna in Geeta to just be a witness and Gautam Buddha's most fundamental commandment of 'awareness' too are directed towards this principle of communion. This truth seems to have descended on Mirza Ghalib too when he recites: *bna ke faqiron ka ham bhes Ghalib/ tamasha-e-ahl-e-kram dekhte hain.* In fact, saint Dadu Dyal's pronouncement that *sabhai sayane ek mat* (all spiritual masters convey the same message) can undoubtedly be applied as far as talking about the eternal truth is concerned.

Communion proceeds further to the stage of duality or dialectical state of human consciousness where the two dimensions of scene and seer merge into each other, leaving the witness alone. To take an instance, through the technique of *tratak* or *shivnetra* meditation, which requires the meditator to looking at an object continuously without moving, the seer and the scene at one stage become one. The first four sutras of Patanjli that is *yam* (mustering of all energies, which otherwise remain dissipated in us, and moving rightfully and unidirectionally), *niyam* (discipline and regularity, sans suppression, becoming master of all your senses to come out victorious, what Mahavira calls as *jin*), *asan* (sitting silently and restfully in a single posture) and *pranayam* (looking at your breathing patterns, what Gautam Bhuddha calls as anapansati yog, till they get orderly regulated) are helpful in establishing deep relationship between the witness and the scene with seer dissolved into it.

From here onwards starts the journey of melting of the duality, what Patanjli calls as pratiyahar (the process of moving inwards). The sixth sutra of Patanjli that is *dhaarna,* gives one the willpower to consolidate what you have attained by following the first five sutras. This helps in moving towards achieving a state of 'no-mind', where thoughts stop ruling the mind and one can stop condemning mind as the distracter conforming to the shabad, *eh mann sundar apna har naam majithe rang.* The body, *prana* and consciousness start developing affinity among themselves. The next dimension of Communion is resolution of this duality into one, more aptly called oneness. It applies to the seventh sutra that of *dhyana* or meditation which practically takes the seeker towards oneness, where the object of concentration also gets dissolved. All the temples or places of worship can take the seeker only up to the stage of *dhaarna* as they help in providing him with an object or form. Dhyan leads the seeker to self-remembrance without any outside object interfering. This idea of "I am-ness" however is not ego"; it is just *'isness'* which we call as *"asmita"*. In the last sutra, that is *Samadhi* even that idea of oneness or *asmita* is also gone but one remains alive to the happenings around. And that is the difference between deep sleep (*sushupti*), death and *Samadhi*. There remains nothing except nothingness, the *shunya* with individuality expanding into the entirety or whole. The drop dissolving into the ocean, the ocean finding abode in the drop, all boundaries vanishing.

The concept can be better understood with the help of an anecdote. A Master gave one pigeon each to two of his disciples to kill them at a place where no one is watching them. One of the disciples went inside a room, locked it from inside, switched off the lights, saw around and finding that nobody was watching him killed the pigeon. The Master laughed away at the disclosure. The other disciple returned after many days but still carrying the pigeon alive in his hands.

The Master asked, "Why didn't you kill the pigeon?" The disciple then narrated the whole incident. "I tried my best to find a place where nobody was watching me before killing the bird. Ultimately, I went to a lonely cave where there was nobody around. When I was about to kill the pigeon, it occurred to me that at least I am watching it. Then I turned the pigeon towards my back and was about to twist his neck when the idea came to my mind that at least the pigeon was watching it. I did my best, Master, but I am sorry I couldn't abide by your orders as I couldn't find any place where there was nobody to watch me killing the pigeon. I could have even forgotten about everything but don't' you agree with me my Holy Master that in any case I couldn't have stopped God watching me doing this criminal act?"

One of the few women mystic saints, Rabia was once condemned to have committed blasphemy for having erased a line from Quran where it was ordained that one needs to love even one's enemy. To the query, Rabia replied I did so because I fail to find anyone as an enemy around me. A similar type of act was performed by Bhai Kanahyia by offering water to the injured enemies during a battle being fought by Guru Gobind Singh against Mughals. When asked by the Guru, Bhai Kanahyia replied, "Master, I don't find any difference between a wounded Sikh and a Muslim." Guru Gobind Singh then went a step further by asking Bhai Kanahyia to supplement his effort by applying medicine on the wounds of the injured enemies. One can't imagine any message of humanity excelling this compassionate gesture of the Guru. Says Gurubani to elucidate this state of mind as:

**Sab mein jot jot hai soi,*
Tis de chanan sab mein chanan hoi.

** Balehari qudrat waiseya,*
Tera ant na jai lakhya, Rahau
Jaat mein jot, jot mein jata,
Aql kala bharpur reha.

**Har apai khele ape dekhe ape rachan rachaya*
Jan Nanak gurmukh jo nar khelai
so jin bazi ghar aya.

Says Sufi faqir, Baba Bulle Shah: *"Bulle Shah rab tethon wakh nahin, appe waj mare ape bolda ae"*. This all is the upshot of Communion reaching it climax.

The concept of Butterfly Effect also states that the entire cosmos is a synthetic unit. It is said that the gigantic ship, *Titanic* was drowned as a consequence of a child throwing a small stone in anger in a rivulet after having been slapped by his father. The angry waves traveled across all the waters before striking against the ship which ultimately lost all its might and control before caving in to the annoyed waves caused by a small stone. The very fact is endorsed by Guru Tegh Bahadur when he says, *ghat ghat mein har ju basai santan kahyo pukar.* What is said, done or even thought of by anyone has the potential of affecting the entire cosmos in some way or the other. It is also said that our life is an echo point. Whatever is said, done or thought of comes back to us manifold. The scientific standpoint on this count also confirms this religious aspect according to which the whole game of life is just a playfield of energies, the Tao of Physics (Fritzof Capra).

One nevertheless needs to remember that the entire voyage from multi-split consciousness transforming into superconsciousness is possible only during the lifetime of a human being. And the major objective of Communion too is to attain to this state of superconsciousness, being one with the Existence.

**Jyoti sang jyot rali sampuran thia Ram*

Communion though starts with concerted and redoubtable effort of resorting to surrender, till a stage arrives when all efforts result into a complete surrender or "let go". That's what happened with Gautam Buddha before attaining to enlightenment. Gurubani also has a number of references corresponding to this truth where the condition of 'let go' or complete surrender is rated as the quintessence of attaining Him:

**Jo jo tera hukm tivai tiv hovna,*
Jeh jeh rakhai aap teh jaye khlovana

**Doe kar jor mangu ik dana Sahib tuthe pavan*
**Hukm rajai chalna Nanak likhya naal*

The ultimate attainment nveretheless is not possible without the Grace of the Guru. Says Kabir: *Lakh khushian patshayian je Satguru nadr kare. Khushian* and *patshayian* however are not to be linked with worldly pleasures and statuses here, as in the next line Nanak makes it clear what he means by it:

Nimakh ek hari naam de mera mann tann sital hoe.

Guru Granth Sahib is replete with many a divine statement conforming to the thought that He is revealed only to those who are blessed by the Guru as *Gurparsad*. Only a few blessed ones become able to listen to the voice of silence or the soundless sound, the *Anahad Naad, The Onkar*, which is the only Truth, *The Satnam (Jisnu nadr karein tun apni so gurmukh karai vichar jio)*.

It is in the light of this proposition that this piece of writing constitutes an effort, guided by all humility and deference to the Existence aimed at sharing some ideas about Communion. It needs an effortless effort (*sehaj*) to accomplish The Ultimate, The Supreme, The Truth. The importance of *sehaj* can be gauged from the very fact that recitation of *Anand Sahib*, which epitomizes the state of blissfulness, achieved *just by the way, as it is,* is a must in all the religious ceremonies of the Sikhs.

Anand bhaiya meri maen satguru main paya,
Satgur tan paya sehaj seti mann vajiyan vadhayian

Even Gautam Siddhartha attained enlightenment after leaving all efforts directed towards attaining it. In Zen also it is said:

Sitting silently,
Doing nothing,
The spring comes,
And the grass grows by itself.

Though it's a bit difficult to understand that how the highest state of consciousness can be achieved in *sehaj avastha* (equipoise) but a deeper insight would reveal the underlying truth that, *it actually happens like that only*...Truth simply is! It is just like walking without feet, flying without wings, tasting without tongue, smelling without nose and thinking without mind. You can not apply the principle of syllogism to The Truth. Among various levels of communication, that is intrapersonal, interpersonal, group and mass communication, intrapersonal communication is closest to Communion but it is not exactly Communion. Intrapersonal communication, that is talking to oneself, is a mind chattering exercise without being aware of it, and is a continuing aspect of psycholinguistic process, what William James describes as 'stream of consciousness'.

Communion has one more marked characteristic, and that is of illustrating and bringing home a point by using paradoxes. At one place we find Guru Granth Sahib saying: *Jag rachna sab jhooth hai, jaan leyo re meet* and at another place it is mentioned: *Eh jag sache ki hai kothri, sache ka vich vaas.* Now look, what Guru Granth Sahib has to say about prayer through paradoxical vision: *Bin bolyan sab kichh janda, kis age kije ardas,* coupled with: *Birthi kade na hovie jan ki ardas.* The paradoxical vision reaches its zenith when in a single line we find two versions or aspects of ego flowering at the same time:

**Haumain diragh rog hai daru bhi is mahein*

In Japuji Sahib, Nanak elaborates the concept of paradoxical, the Ultimate Truth, in a very subtle way by revealing:

Sochai soch na hovei je sochai lakh vaar
Chupyea chup na hovei je lae raha livtar,
Bhukhyean bhukh na utri je bannai purian bhaar
Sehas seyanpan lakh hoiae tan ik na chalai naal
Kiv sacheyara hoiae kiv koorraie tutai paal
Hukm rajai chalna
Nanak likhyea naal.

(We can not comprehend him
though we think a million times;
Nor quiet the mind by silence, however long we sit;
Nor loads of bread appease the hunger of the soul;
Nor one hundred thousand feats of the mind
achieve unity with Him;
(But then) How can The Truth be attained and
the veil of falsehood torn?
Says Nanak: By submission to the divine order
which is preordained).

Though sharing of the divine revelation in its purest form has been regarded as a task impossible, yet all the spiritual masters and gurus have partaken in to explain the quintessence of this virtue of virtues. Starting with Guru Nanak when he says: *Jei hon jana akha nahi kehana kathn na jai* (those who experienced Him could not say it Truthfully because it cannot be said) and that *aakhan aukha saacha naon* (the True Name is most difficult to describe), chips in Guru Gobind Singh, the tenth Sikh Master:

Kaam, krodh, hankaar, lobh, hath, moh na mann suon lavai
Tab hi atam sat ko darsai param purkah keh pavai

(What to talk about attaining Him, it is not an easy task to even utter His name. It is only possible when one goes beyond such vices as desires, anger, ego, greed and attachment)

Yet, still at another place says Gurubani: *Jab lag duniya rahiye, Nanak kichh suniyae kuchh kahiyae*. Even the founder of Taoism, Lao Tse, when 'ordered' by the Chinese emperor to share his divine wisdom with the seekers before he leaves his body, has said in the very beginning of his only book, *Tao Te King* that "Truth can't be said because the moment it is said it becomes a lie". Mirza Ghalib too endorses this fact by saying: *Jisko khabar thi teri wo be-khabr mila, kis se pata puchhen janan-e-jana?*

Now it all seems unfathomable by the ordinary human consciousness. But that is The Truth. What one can do about it? Millions of ways have been described to reach Him. But whenever a person attains Him, he finds that He could not be attained through any means, ways, techniques and strategies. The situation can perhaps be better understood with the help of an example: Sometimes it happens that you are not able to recollect the name of a person despite hardest efforts. You try a million ways to recollect, get worked up inside, yet all your efforts prove futile. Then you give up the effort in desperation. You forget all about it when suddenly while doing something in a relaxed state of mind, the name comes to you like a flash and that too when you have least expected it. The great effort in itself sometimes becomes the hindrance. But the irony is that nothing happens without the initial effort, strongest on that when you give your hundred per cent to it. In fact all your efforts, when given up travel down into your subconscious mind and keep on working there. And when you are in a relaxed state of mind (*sehaj avastha*), the thought reveals itself on its own. Kabir categorically rejects the idea of Attainment with undue effort by saying: *Sadho sehaj samadhi bhali.*

Theses paradoxes are meant to encourage or instill a sense of query, curiosity or inquisitiveness among the seekers to find the hidden celestial or divine meaning by themselves and not to simply repeat the *shabd* without understanding its meaning before making it a part of their lifestyles. Such an act of repetition apparently can be better performed by a tape recorder than a human being. Blind followers simply get stuck or are exploited by the self-styled gurus or spiritual leaders even as they don't reach anywhere.

The whole conversation that we have received in shape of Gurubani started with Communion of Guru Nanak with *Parmatma* (The Supreme Soul). It then took the shape of interpersonal communication between him and his accompanist musician, Bhai Mardana. This was followed by Guru Nanak's conversation with many of his contemporary spiritual leaders, saints, siddhas and bhagatas in the form of group communication. With advancement of technology, Gurubani has now attained the status of mass communication available to everyone, through various means of mass communication with least possible effort.

But to understand Nanak one has to rise to that highest pedestal where the first Sikh Master had reached starting with Communion: *evad ucha hovai koi, tis uche ko janai soi*. Starting with communion and ending with it! That is the paradox; and that is the Reality!

Appendix-I

Hymns of Gurus

Guru Granth Sahib contains hymns of six Gurus:

1. Guru Nanak Dev
2. Guru Angad Dev
3. Guru Amar Das
4. Guru Ram Das
5. Guru Arjan Dev
6. Guru Tegh Bahadur

Hymns of Bhaktas

Out of the total 31 Ragas, 22 Ragas contain hymns of the following fifteen Bhaktas:

1. Bhagat Kabir
2. Bhagat Namdev
3. Bhagat Ravidas
4. Bhagat Trilochan
5. Baba Sheikh Farid
6. Bhagat Beni
7. Bhagat Dhanna
8. Bhagat Jai Dev
9. Bhagat Bhikhan
10. Bhagat Sur Das
11. Bhagat Parmanand
12. Bhagat Sain
13. Bhagat Pipa
14. Bhagat Sadna
15. Bhagat Ramanand

Appendix-II

Bhatt Bani

Eleven Bhatts have contributed their compositions *sivayyas* to Guru Granth Sahib:

1. Kalsahar
2. Jalap
3. Kirat
4. Bhikha
5. Sal
6. Bhal
7. Nal
8. Bal
9. Gayand
10. Mathura
11. Harbans

In addition to the above mentioned bards (Bhatts), Guru Granth Sahib also contains the compositions of Satta and Balwand, Baba Sundar and Bhai Mardana making the total number of contributors 36.

Appendix-III

The order of 31 Ragas in Guru Granth Sahib is as follows:

1. Srī Raga
2. Majh
3. Gaurī
4. Āsā
5. Gujrī
6. Devgandhari
7. Bihāgrā
8. Vadhans
9. Sorathh
10. Dhanāsarī
11. Jaitsrī
12. Todī
13. Bairari
14. Tilang
15. Sūhī
16. Bilāwal
17. Gaund
18. Ramkalī
19. Nat Narain
20. Mali Gaurā
21. Mārū
22. Tukharī
23. Kedārā
24. Bhairo
25. Basant
26. Sarang
27. Malār
28. Kānarā
29. Kalyān
30. Prabhātī
31. Jaijāvantī

Appendix-IV

There are twenty-two Vars in Guru Granth Sahib:

1. Vār Srī Raga of Guru Ram Das, the fourth Guru
2. Vār Mājh of Guru Nanak Dev, The first Guru
3. Vār Gaurī of Guru Ram Das, the fourth Guru
4. Vār Gaurī of Guru Arjan Dev, the fifth Guru
5. Vār Āsā of Guru Nanak Dev, the first Guru
6. Vār Gūjrī of Guru Amar Das, the third Guru
7. Vār Gūjrī of Guru Arjan Dev, the fifth Guru
8. Vār Bihāgrā of Guru Ram Das, the fourth Guru
9. Vār Vadhans of Guru Ram Das, the fourth Guru
10. Vār Sorath of Guru Ram Das, the fourth Guru
11. Vār Jaitsrī of Guru Arjan Dev, the fifth Guru
12. Vār Sūhi of Guru Amar Das, the third Guru
13. Vār Bilāwal of Guru Ram Das, the fourth Guru
14. Vār Rāmkalī of Guru Amar Das, the third Guru
15. Vār Rāmkalī of Guru Arjan Dev, the fifth Guru
16. Vār Rāmkalī of Satta and Balwand
17. Vār Mārū of Guru Amar Das, the third Guru
18. Vār Mārū of Guru Arjan Dev, the fifth Guru
19. Vār Basant of Guru Arjan Dev, the fifth Guru
20. Vār Sārang of Guru Ram Das, the fourth Guru
21. Vār Malār of Guru Nanak Dev, the first Guru
22. Vār Kanra of Guru Ram Das, the fourth Guru